Table of Contents

Introduction

by Susan Gano-Phillips *and* Robert W. Barnett

General education reform has dominated the higher education landscape for at least the past two decades. Whether large or small, research- or teaching-focused, community college or major university, higher education has been the target of widespread calls for curricular reform from across many sectors of society, from government, to business, to accreditation agencies, as well as recognition from within academia that new approaches to liberal education must be given our serious attention. In fact, a vast majority of U.S. institutions have recently been (or currently are) engaging in general education reform. A nationally representative large scale survey reported that 80% of institutions are engaged in significant revisions to their general education programs (Ratcliff, Johnson, and Gaff 2004). A majority of scholarship devoted to general education reform has focused almost exclusively on the *content* of the curriculum, seeking to increase its relevance and integration for twenty-first century learners (e.g., Association of American Colleges and Universities 2002; 2005; Ratcliff et al. 2004). However, despite tremendous effort and energy, significant reform has often not materialized (Gaston and Gaff 2009).

This book examines general education reform from a different lens. Rather than focusing on the content or outcomes of reform efforts, this book examines the *processes* or mechanisms by which campuses are seeking to achieve such curricular reforms. In doing so, we attempt to highlight the critical importance of reform processes on curricular outcomes/content. In examining the processes used to reform the general education curriculum, this volume recognizes that individual campus cultures must be assessed and examined in defining an institutionally-specific process for curricular reform. A one-size-fits-all approach has not proven successful historically. Rather, as campus culture and reform processes are examined in synchrony, we contend that sustainable and substantive curricular reform is more likely to occur.

Substantive and sustainable change is an elusive construct in higher education. Forces within institutions that value "tradition" propel even the most innovative of curricular plans back toward the status quo. Academia has long been known for its contemplative style and its slow and gradual pace of change. An inability to explore innovative curricular designs, political compromise in decision-making, and difficulties in implementation of new curricular approaches often perplex planners and result in new curricula that differ relatively little from those they are designed to replace. Because of this tendency to maintain equilibrium and status quo, the institutional processes for change and institutional cultures and histories must be directly assessed and examined, challenged, and sometimes changed, in order to allow for substantive and sustainable curricular change to emerge.

While the focus of this book involves the *processes* that lead to sustainable curricular change, the content of today's curricular reform is important in its own right. Societal expectations of the content and outcomes of general education curricula are rapidly changing in the twenty-first century as well. The latter half of the twentieth century saw models of general education focused on "breadth" experiences, while "depth" was considered to occur through intensive study within a major discipline. This approach to general education is intended to expose students to as wide a view of liberal arts as possible. An inherent problem, however, helps to explain its diminishing usefulness in educating our students: a lack of intentional integration of ideas across the curriculum. In contrast, a twenty-first century model of general education, one focused on the increasing expectations of an ever-evolving knowledge based economy, must do more. As institutions take up the challenge of reforming general education programs to meet the rising expectations of society—for disciplinary exposure *and* integration of learning, the development of critical thinking *and* applied problem-solving, understanding of Western *and* global cultures and issues, breadth of knowledge *and* more intensive depth of understandings—they often meet with resistance, failure, or little ability to move the institution away from the status quo.

The slow pace of meaningful reform can be attributed, in large part, to the fact that general education programs have long been focused more on their discreet component parts—areas of study, distribution of courses, credit requirements—and less on the sum of those component parts—the vision and mission of general education. Such a focus on the individual

A Process Approach *to* General Education Reform

TRANSFORMING INSTITUTIONAL CULTURE in HIGHER EDUCATION

edited by
Susan Gano-Phillips *and* Robert W. Barnett

Atwood Publishing
Madison, WI

A Process Approach to General Education Reform:
Transforming Institutional Culture in Higher Education
Edited by Susan Gano-Phillips and Robert W. Barnett

ISBN: 978-1-891859-81-6

Cover design by TLC Graphics, www.tlcgraphics.com
Cover illustration ©iStockphoto.com/Kamaga

Library of Congress Cataloging-in-Publication Data

A process approach to general education reform : transforming institutional culture in higher education / edited by Susan Gano-Phillips and Robert W. Barnett.
    p. cm.
  ISBN 978-1-891859-81-6 (pb)
  1. General education—United States. 2. Education (Higher)—United States. 3. Educational change—United States. I. Gano-Phillips, Susan, 1966- II. Barnett, Robert W., 1964-
  LC985.P76 2010
  378'.01—dc22

                      2010029318

Acknowledgements

SUSAN GANO-PHILLIPS would like to thank Gary, Allison, and Tyler Phillips, and Bill and Shirley Gano, for their unwavering and unconditional support of her work and this project. She would also like to thank her co-editor, Bob Barnett, for the dedication, creative energy, and humor he has shown over the 5 year collaboration that culminated with this book. Finally, Susan would like to thank the faculty, staff, and administration of the University of Michigan-Flint who enthusiastically undertook the challenging process of general education curriculum reform, providing the impetus for this work.

BOB BARNETT would like to thank all of his colleagues who contributed to the robust conversations that helped make this project a reality. He would also like to thank his partner, Philip T. Greenfield, for his expertise in line editing and for his willingness to listen to the ideas that made their way into the book. And finally, Bob would like to thank his co-editor, Susan Gano-Phillips for challenging him to push ideas to the very limit and for reminding him of the intellectual satisfaction of collaborative work.

components that make up the content of our general education programs has left little time or attention to focus on how we actually facilitate and manage the creation of meaningful programs. But as new philosophies and new approaches to general education reform continue to emerge, and as more colleges and universities attempt to align reform efforts to their core institutional missions and visions, a new conversation is also emerging.

This new conversation is being defined by a process-focused reform and is beginning to replace the traditional content-focused model. It may help to think of the process-focused approach as the "how" of reform, while the content-focused approach may be considered the "what" of reform. A process-focused agenda suggests that a clear, realistic, and shared process must be established *prior* to engaging in broad conversations of changes in program content. Process-focused reform begins with defining the problem to be solved *before* any attempts are begun to actually solve the problem. Separating the management of the initiative from the creation of the curriculum, the learning outcomes, and the assessments is one way in which process-focused reform differs from traditional content-focused models. Process-focused reform is further distinguished from a content-focused reform approach in that it includes advocating for a redistribution of authority in decision-making so that the voices of all constituents are included in the conversation. It attempts to minimize the tensions between competing bases of power by bringing everyone to the table for discussion, debate, and negotiation (Rice 2006).

Moving from a traditional general education reform approach to one that looks completely new and distinct from what we have struggled with for so long is no easy task. Stephen Trainor, a pioneer in process-focused general education reform, acknowledges that even the best-intentioned efforts to reform general education curricula "prove frustrating for the participants, and they often end in failure," and that the end goal of creating the best possible program tends to remain "elusive, sacrificed to the exigencies of political compromise or financial constraints" (Trainor 2004, 16). Writing of a reform effort at Salve Regina University, Trainor engaged in some institutional soul searching, and he discovered why his institution had failed at reform efforts for so long. The answer for him was quite simple. With all of the attention on what the program should look like, there had been no focus on how to get from point A to point B. In other words, by starting with the content of reform as the focus, and by ignoring the process by which the content is developed, successful reform would always remain out of reach.

Trainor's approach to reform represents a significant paradigm shift in that it rejects the old conventional wisdom that institutional change is best accomplished by charging a committee to create a plan and then bringing it back to the rest of the community for discussions and votes. Granted, this old way of doing business has a process attached to it. The problem is that the process is always secondary and does not allow constituents to capitalize on the best ways to solve a problem. When we start with a focus on the product, when we engage in conversations of substance, and when we do this without a well-established plan that frames and guides those discussions, then we may well know what we want, but it does little good if we do not know how we are going to get there. Hence our first principle of general education curriculum reform: *Define a reform process before engaging in curricular content discussion.*

The second key to creating substantive and sustainable curricular change relates to institutional culture. We contend that any effective reform process must identify and address institutionally-specific cultural issues that could impede or facilitate successful reform efforts (Gano-Phillips and Barnett 2008). Institutional culture is difficult to define, despite its rather colloquial use. In this book, institutional culture refers to the set of shared attitudes, values, goals, and practices that characterize an institution—the unwritten rules of business that determine who contributes to what decisions, when, where, why, and how (Trice and Beyer 1984). An institution's culture is typically viewed as extremely stable and relatively immoveable. The erosion of an institution's shared cultural identity, however, may well contribute to a level of instability that can severely hamper attempts at institutional change.

Until recently, any serious examination of institutional culture has largely been ignored by higher education. Academia has taken a peripheral approach to culture issues, acknowledging that culture provides a backdrop for institutional functioning, but never actively assessing its characteristics or challenging the need to alter it. There are, however, a wide variety of cultural problems present on many university or college campuses. These problems vary, of course, from institution to institution, but include such things as tendencies to operate in secret or with little sharing of information, feelings of powerlessness by faculty relative to administrative decision-making, tendencies toward suspiciousness of others' motives, poor communication, and a host of other issues. Because most cultural factors remain unacknowledged, unnamed, and unaddressed, we have not expressly tied institutional culture or cultural problems to our curricular reforms—we have set about curricular change processes blind to the cultural factors that inevitably affect the curricular product.

The interaction of campus curricular reform processes and institutional cultures is exceedingly complex. For example, consider how curricular decision-making processes interact with aspects of campus culture involving communication and trust among constituents. On many campuses, general education curricular decision-making looks like this: a charge is handed down by the provost, president, or chancellor; a campuswide committee is selected; this committee is sequestered for the better part of an academic year; they come up with a plan, present it to the faculty, suffer the slings and arrows of criticism and opposition, and the plan comes up for a final vote. On some campuses, this process-culture interaction may be extremely problematic, while on other campuses, extremely effective—the difference being each campus's unique culture. On campuses characterized by limited communication and a sense of mistrust among various factions, this approach to general education reform is doomed to failure from the outset, because the various constituents do not feel they have a voice in the decision-making process and their only option for input is to reject the plan that is eventually put forward by a committee. In these cases, cultural factors, so long ignored, contribute directly to the failure of the curricular reform project.

In short, higher education has failed to account for underlying cultural problems that have long stood in the way of significant institutional change and curricular reform. Reform processes must be selected and implemented in light of each institution's unique campus culture. When we are willing to identify, embrace, and address our cultural shortcomings through a process-focused reform, we lay the essential groundwork for creating substantive and sustainable curricular change. Hence our second principle of general education curriculum reform: *Assess, challenge, and change institutional culture while simultaneously selecting and implementing process-focused reform.*

The two primary principles of general education curricular reform therefore, together, provide a synthesis of approaches that is likely to lead to more substantive and sustainable institutional change and curricular reform than either approach independently. By separating process from content and defining a process-first approach, *and* by recognizing and addressing cultural issues within the process, institutions are beginning to address the long standing impasses that have stymied well-meaning efforts at substantive and sustainable programmatic change.

This book presents multiple examples of general education reform in which both process and institutional culture are an explicit focus. This approach is built upon a set of process-culture variables, which allows institutions to work toward the kind of curricular change that is substantive and sustainable. The foundation of process-centered general education reform then, is built on the premise that efforts toward meaningful institutional change should consider the following seven process variables within the context of each campus's culture:

1. Leadership
2. Time frames
3. Use of Data
4. Communication
5. Engagement of Constituents
6. Faculty Governance
7. Institutional Politics

These variables are relevant to all institutions engaged in process-focused curricular reform. Collectively, they create the framework by which reform might be approached, and they do so by intentionally incorporating universal cultural factors that influence the success or failure of institutional change. The book opens with an extensive examination in chapter one of the cultural considerations that can help a process-centered reform initiative get started. The authors tie issues of engagement, leadership, politics, and national trends to the early stages of reform and illustrate how one institution was able to move beyond the status quo and lay the groundwork for sustainable change in its general education program.

Certainly, institutions may identify additional process-culture variables beyond those presented here, but the seven variables provide a firm foundation from which to assess institutional culture while embarking on process-focused reform. Each of the process-culture variables that frame the book is defined more fully below, providing a new approach to consider all of the process variables within a cultural context.

Establishing Effective Leadership for the Reform

Creating and sustaining an institution's change initiatives is directly related to the depth of self examination that occurs within its own culture (Awbrey 2005). Nowhere is self-examination more critical to general education reform than in the area of leadership. By acknowledging strengths and challenges in their leadership structures, institutions can begin to identify and establish the strong, visible leadership—at the faculty and administrative levels—necessary for achieving success in the reform efforts. The true test of leadership, no matter who leads a reform initiative, is how well and how completely the voices of all constituents are incorporated into the process. When the burden of creating the content of the initiative is separated from the management of the process, leadership efforts can focus on diplomacy and consensus building efforts among the constituents who will create the new program.

The authors of chapter two examine how a group of faculty charged with general education reform worked within the culture of their institution to create gradual sustainable change by building coalitions, identifying common rallying points, and demonstrating a willingness to compromise on issues, while adhering to agreed-upon standards and principles. Faculty leaders from the university's five colleges initiated an institution-wide conversation about the reform initiative that led, in just one year, to significant and meaningful changes. The reform leaders succeeded because they identified and managed a process that allowed their constituents to create, vote on, and approve the changes.

Strong leadership, though, needs to extend beyond those charged with creating and managing the process. Close coordination with the top leaders of the institution is necessary to provide support for the reform work and to signal a firm sense of commitment to the whole institution. Most colleges and universities have operated historically from a top-down approach to leadership, where initiatives and decisions are controlled by administration and handed down to the faculty. A process approach to reform challenges this leadership structure in that it empowers everyone —faculty, staff, students, and administrators—to "own" the initiative and the decision-making process. Chapter three explores some of the challenges to process-centered reform when changes in leadership occur at the very top levels. Juxtaposing the leadership styles of their previous and current presidents, the authors describe how their reform efforts were impacted and altered under different leaders.

A process approach to leadership is intended to create a shared responsibility for decision-making among all members of the community at every step of the initiative. Developing visible direction from leaders at all levels will positively impact the success of the other process variables.

Establishing a Timeframe for the Process

The decision to engage in general education curricular reform is not one that is entered into lightly or without great care. Nevertheless, most institutions do eventually undertake this challenge. At the start of the reform process, it is helpful for institutions to carefully consider their cultural identities and the internal and external pressures to produce a new curriculum in deciding what type of timeline, if any, may be useful to the reform process. The cultural context of the institution must help to define the need for and nature of a timeline to be undertaken in general education reform.

The importance of timelines and timeframes is examined throughout chapter four in the context of both institutional reform and culture. The authors recount examples of resistance to and eventual acceptance of a timeline, but they make a compelling argument that engaging in general education reform with a clear timeline in place can help shorten the curricular reform process.

Many, although certainly not all institutions, find that having a well-structured timeline and clear definition of the task is desirable. In those cases, there is a strong and persistent need to communicate the timeline and definition of the task to all constituents, helping to clarify the process and to dispel suspicion or mistrust in the process. Further, it may be useful to seek approval of the timeline itself from the relevant constituents so that, later, as the process unfolds, the reform leadership or committee can simply refer to an approved process as the foundation for its timing and actions.

Using Data (National and Local) to Inform the Process

Too often, institutions of higher education become insular in their activities. For example, in times of tight budgets, faculty and even administrators' travel budgets become tighter — the restrictions on travel make pedagogically-focused or systems-level-focused conferences out of the reach of most faculty members who instead prefer their disciplinary-based research conferences. Over time, the failure to look outside of one's institution can lead institutions to fall out of touch with major trends in higher education, despite the enormous resources that are available on a whole host of pedagogical and systemic issues. With organizations like the Association of American Colleges and Universities (AAC&U), the American Council on Education (ACE), the Higher Learning Commission, the National Survey of Student Engagement (NSSE), the University of California at Los Angeles's Higher Education Research Council, and so forth producing theoretical papers, policy reports, and empirically-derived research, it is incumbent upon institutions to tap into the relevant resources when undertaking major institutional change. As institutions evaluate the degree to which external resources have been or are currently being used to inform reform processes and curricular decisions, many find a significant void in need of filling.

National data and information can be accessed in many ways: sending representatives off-campus to conferences, bringing nationally known speakers to a campus, or through personal reading and study of relevant literatures. Regardless of the mechanisms taken, when the leadership of the reform efforts turns to data to inform decision-making, they achieve added credibility among campus constituents.

Another trend in higher education regarding the use of data is affecting the cultures of institutions over the past decade. That trend relates to accountability in higher education, particularly in the area of student outcomes assessment, whereby institutions are demonstrating the "value-added benefits" of their educational programs. Like all reform efforts, some institutions have been front runners in outcomes based teaching, learning, and assessments while others have been reluctant to comply with external accreditors' demands for accountability. In institutions where there is a deep value in assessment to improve performance on an ongoing basis, it is only logical that local data produced for institutional self-study purposes and for student outcomes assessment be used to inform decision-making regarding curricular reform.

More surprising, perhaps, are the institutions who decide to begin a search for local data as the starting point of their institutional reform. These institutions are doubly challenged to make a cultural shift, one regarding the practice of assessment on campus while simultaneously making a shift in the general education curriculum. Chapter five examines how the use of local data and national trends contributed to campus-wide engagement in the reform process at their institution, which in turn, led to a greater collective commitment to change.

Establishing Effective Communication Structures

Every campus has its own established channels of communication, both formal and informal. The systemic problem that so many institutions face is that little, if any, attention is given to the enormous impact communication has on the success or failure of any given initiative. Even the most well-planned projects can be undermined by a lack of communication. The problem is compounded by the fact that most communication systems operate in only one direction—from the top down. This approach is inadequate, because when information flows in only one direction, it creates a barrier to the robust and meaningful conversation in which the community should be engaged. It also creates the perception that information is being controlled by one person or group, and thus works against an environment of transparency and inclusion. Community members who feel disenfranchised by a communication structure that does not value their voices will disengage and further complicate attempts at collective forward movement.

The authors of chapter six argue for a communication structure that involves all constituents by creating transparency and openness throughout the reform process. The deliberate and participatory nature of the reform work, created through a broad communications system, allowed the movement to maintain momentum, especially during critical discussions and decision-making moments.

A plan that encourages input, feedback, and participation from every person at every stage of the process will work toward reversing historical trends by creating an atmosphere of transparency and inclusion. By challenging past practices, a well-defined communication plan can help influence the success of the other process variables as curriculum reform efforts unfold.

Engaging Constituents

Process-centered reform takes a significant departure from the traditional approach in the way it attempts to engage the campus community. From an historical–cultural perspective, faculty and staff have felt disenfranchised by an approach to institutional change that made little effort to include their voices in the conversation. Even with a representative committee structure, faculty perceive their role in curricular initiatives as limited and their ownership of curricular decision-making as marginal. Consequently, such perceptions have fostered a sense of suspicion and mistrust between and among constituents that, left unchecked, has contributed significantly to the failure of reform efforts.

Engaging all constituents, then, in a process-first initiative—one that sets aside the old top-down structure—will allow an institution to directly address long-standing cultural problems by adding inclusion and transparency to the process. Chapter seven presents an example of a wholesale engagement campaign launched as part of the general education curriculum reform to address a culture where faculty disengagement from the curriculum had predominated. Drawing on what we already know from the literature on general education about collective engagement, the author explores the necessity of engaging others and considers what successful engagement of constituents can bring to a reform process.

When members of the community are invited to help solve a problem, when their opinions matter and their voices are heard, they are much more likely to contribute to successful institutional change. A process approach to reform attempts to reinstate curricular autonomy by challenging constituents to engage fully in shaping and defining the initiative, and thus reestablishes a sense of ownership. As members of the community begin seeing themselves drawn into the process, and as they begin seeing the impact of their collective involvement, the cultural ground will shift away from suspicion and distrust, giving way to a new sense of cooperation and increased levels of transparency as the reform effort unfolds.

Governance Structures

Governance processes on campuses are extremely diverse, from elected and appointed governing boards, administratively powerful and providing centralized governance, to campus advisory committees who work in collaboration with administrators (various models of shared governance), to decentralized governance processes on small and large campuses whereby individuals, schools, or faculties operate quite autonomously, to fully demoralized and disengaged faculty governance situations creating dysfunction and an inability to accomplish basic operations of an institution due to low engagement.

The quickest way to stall an initiative is to deviate from traditional governance processes or structures in the midst of the approval process for that initiative. Efforts to change the way decisions are made in the midst of controversial decisions are almost always seen as mechanisms to gather support for one side or the other as the governance process becomes tangled with the issue under consideration for decision-making. Trying to add voting members or to disqualify others from voting at the time a controversial vote is being held almost always results in a loss of trust in the results of the vote. Similarly, efforts to change governance rules such as the need to circulate a document in writing for a specified period of time prior to a vote, are often met with resistance and anger.

Regardless of the structure of governance on a particular campus, it is important for the general education reform leadership to carefully understand the approved governance processes on their respective campuses and to be intimately familiar with the mechanisms of discussion, debate, and decision-making on the campus. Chapter eight demonstrates how change can be implemented by analyzing the process from the perspective of meeting challenges at the institutional, college, and department levels at a university with a strong decentralized system of governance. More specifically, the authors explain the efforts to develop an outcomes-based Achievement-Centered Education (ACE), designed to reflect the values of constituents at all levels of governance.

Transparency in governance processes will serve to reduce distrust and suspicions throughout the campus, so part of managing the reform process may be specifying in clear and uncertain terms the particulars of the governance procedures that will be used during the reform process. If there is good reason for alterations in governance processes (and sometimes there is), those issues need to be taken up separately from and in advance of decisions on the general education curriculum itself. Further, it is important that reform committees or leaders, while following governance processes, are sure to provide opportunities to air the concerns of all constituents in open and fair ways.

Negotiating the Political Structures of the Institution

The work of curricular reform is inherently a political process. In higher education, political realities play out in a manner as diverse as the number of campuses themselves. However, some common themes that impact institutional politics include: "siloing" and distrust among separate units, schools, or colleges; territoriality over various aspects of the curriculum and who is "qualified" to deliver them; fear of change among segments of the population; and "old guard" versus "new guard" approaches to pedagogy and curricular design. Sometimes issues break down along administrative versus faculty lines, sometimes among groups within the faculty, and sometimes between the campus and other constituents more removed from day to day campus functioning (e.g., governing boards, state educational commissions).

Political realities have the potential to derail a reform process, even in situations when good judgment and reason should prevail. Regardless of the exact nature of the power/authority struggles on campus, they are an important component of a campus's culture which often are best addressed directly and proactively. General education reform leaders often find it necessary to engage in various forms of diplomacy while shepherding the reform process toward its conclusion. The foundation for that diplomacy is the development of as thorough and complete a knowledge of campus politics as possible. Armed with this knowledge and a keen ability and desire to listen, general education reform leaders put their "ear to the ground" to assure that they are not surprised by political upheaval. It means expressing an openness to listen to any one at any time about any issue related to the reform process, and being willing to act upon some information that is obtained, as deemed necessary to move the reform process forward.

The author of chapter nine contends that the most successful initiatives are achieved through a political process that seeks to find common positions and that builds consensus among constituencies. The chapter explores one institution's attempt to address key political assumptions and agreements that ultimately facilitated significant changes in their general education program.

Awareness of the power struggles on campus and knowing something of the origins of those power struggles can help reform leaders to manage other aspects of the reform process that have already been discussed, such as communication or timelines.

Beyond the Seven Process Variables

This book concludes with three chapters that broaden the conversation about process-centered general education curricular reform beyond the seven specific variables. In chapter ten, we consider how general education reform efforts can be sustained and serve to revitalize campuses on an ongoing basis. Alverno College reports on its over-30-year history of creating a culture focused on students' successful achievement of the college's collectively agreed-upon general education outcomes. By simultaneously considering both the campus's cultural contexts and process variables, Alverno College demonstrates how the reform of a general education curriculum can become an ongoing process, rather than one in which cycles of reform are followed by periods of stagnation.

We broaden further our conversation in chapter eleven where the authors provide a theoretical foundation for our thinking about curricular and other institutional change. By recognizing and relying upon organizational change theories, institutions can develop awareness and engage in careful planning that increases their chances for successful curricular reform. The authors contend that application of change theories does not guarantee the success of a reform effort, but it does increase the likelihood of success.

Finally, in chapter twelve, we explore emerging trends in general education reform processes, both nationally and internationally. Two of the most compelling trends that institutions around the globe are coming to grips with are the changing nature and diversity of the student body and the increasing calls for accountability and measurement of student learning as a result of our general education programs.

Ultimately, these three chapters affirm the importance of both the process variables and the assessment, challenging, and changing of our institutional cultures in defining substantive and sustainable general education curricular reform.

A Road Map for Readers

In addition to providing a range of theoretical foundations for meaningful general education reform, this volume illustrates the influence of groundbreaking work done by institutions of higher education at virtually every level, from community colleges to Research I universities. Each chapter presents a model for other institutions to consider, while examining the philosophical and practical implications associated with the national and international conversation on general education reform.

Because the process variables are so interconnected and interdependent, the chapters that make up this collection reflect that interdependency. While each chapter addresses at least one of the primary process variables, they also give secondary coverage to one or more of the other variables. Contributors have shared drafts of their articles with each other to further capitalize on this interconnectedness. Seen this way, the volume creates a set of conversations that transcends the telling of individual stories and offers a new collective approach to institutional reform and cultural change.

The "Road Map for Readers" (see Table 1) illustrates the richly complex interaction of cultures and processes that are critically examined throughout the volume. It also presents multiple approaches to reading the book. For example, readers who take a chapter by chapter approach will

Primary Variable	Primary Chapter	Secondary Coverage in Chapter	Other Chapters Addressing
Leadership (administration, faculty, & committees)	2, 3	9	4, 5, 8
Time frames	4	3	2, 7
Using data (national resources & local outcomes assessment)	5	6, 9	4, 8
Communication	6	7, 8	3, 5, 9
Engaging constituents	7	3	4, 5, 6, 8
Governance	8	3, 6	2, 9
Politics	9	8	2

TABLE 1. Road Map for Readers:
Key variables in process-centered reform and cultural change

see each of the process variables contextualized in a way that explores in-stitution-specific reform practices and examines those practices in relation to underlying cultural challenges. Readers can also focus on one or more particular process variables by reading a cluster of chapters around that is-sue, an approach that invites them to participate in a deeper conversation and apply what they have learned to their own institutional attempts at general education reform. However the book is approached, readers will find an emerging conversation that challenges long standing cultural tradi-tions and encourages new ways of thinking about curricular change pro-cesses that will finally bring about the successes we have all worked so hard to achieve.

References

Association of American Colleges and Universities (AAC&U). 2002. *Greater expectations: A new vision for learning as a nation goes to college*. Washington, DC: AAC&U.

Association of American Colleges and Universities. 2005. *Liberal education outcomes: A prelim-inary report on student achievement in college*. Washington, DC: AAC&U.

Awbrey, S. M. 2005. General education reform as organizational change: Integrating cultural and structural change. *Journal of General Education 54*(1): 1–21.

Gano-Phillips, S., and R. W. Barnett. 2008. Against all odds: Transforming institutional culture. *Liberal Education 94*(2): 36–41.

Gaston, P., and J. G. Gaff. 2009. *Revising general education —And avoiding the potholes*. Washington, DC: AAC&U.

Ratcliff, J. L., K. Johnson, and J. G. Gaff, eds. 2004. Changing general education curriculum. *New Directions for Higher Education, No. 125*. San Francisco: Jossey-Bass.

Rice, R. E. 2006. From Athens and Berlin to LA: Faculty work and the new academy. *Liberal Education* 92(4): 6–13.

Trainor, S. L. 2004. Designing a signature general education program. *Peer Review 7*(1): 16–19.

Trice, H. M., and M. M. Beyer. 1984. Studying organizational cultures through rites and ceremonials. *Academy of Management Review* 9: 653–669

CHAPTER 1

Culture *as* Process

USING CULTURAL FACTORS
to PROMOTE GENERAL EDUCATION REFORM

by Kathleen Rountree, Lisa Tolbert,
and Stephen C. Zerwas

In reviewing reform in general education, one is struck by the fact that meaningful reform has not been widespread, despite demands from parents, students' future employers, educational leaders, and politicians. One reason for this phenomenon may be higher education's long tradition and broad experience in resisting change. This reticence has served it well, but may have also inhibited needed innovation and the ability to respond to demands for reform. Increasingly, resistance to reform may imperil the autonomy of higher education as calls for reform go unheeded in a culture demanding accountability.

The complexity of higher education creates significant challenges for general education reform efforts. Higher education embodies many different cultural elements simultaneously, including political, bureaucratic, collegial, traditional, and chaotic elements. Each of these cultures has its own entrenched norms, as well as sanctions for violating them. In order to implement a reform agenda, it is necessary to respond not only to a single culture or group, but a multitude of cultures simultaneously. Even institutions that are committed to innovation have well-established norms and behaviors that impede change. Change efforts must exist within the prevalent institutional culture and cultural norms. This requires a substantial repertoire of innovative approaches, short-term tactics, long-term strategies, and creative solutions. The more that it is possible to align the reform effort with the history, culture, and purposes of an institution, the more likely the reform will proceed.

In initiating any reform effort, it should be recognized that any current, unreformed general education program came to exist through some past process of intensive study, deliberative thought, and considerable faculty effort. It was crafted by the institution to meet perceived needs, and may continue to do so. The status quo exists because, in some way, it meets institutional, departmental, and personal needs. It is also the product and the source of existing political and cultural realities. Any change in general education may be threatening to departments or individual faculty members who have vested interests in the current system. Accepting the need for reform places all previous agreements open for review and reconsideration, which may be perceived as a source of significant risk. It is critical to honor the time and effort invested in the current general education program, while at the same time examining it against new best practices or educational goals, and moving to reform or adapt it.

Whether the change process is driven from the top down or initiated as a grassroots movement, faculty support is essential for any meaningful general education reform to succeed. It is important to understand that faculty responses are complex and may be driven at different times by seemingly contradictory roles. While being genuinely committed to student learning, individual faculty members may have differing views on how general education fits into the learning paradigm. Some may view general education as an unwanted and perhaps even unnecessary intrusion into the important work pursued in the major. Others may have difficulty defining the distinctions and the overlap between the goals of their own discipline-based curriculum and those of general education. The coherent delivery of a general education reform may be perceived as a challenge to academic freedom and faculty autonomy. To be successful, general education reform requires the development of consensus across many of these competing agendas.

Because of the complexity and diversity of higher education, each institution is a product of its own history and traditions. The diversity of each institution will often mean that an approach that was successful at one institution may not be successful at another. It is imperative to adapt the reform process to each institutional culture. In this chapter we use our experiences in creating momentum to initiate general education reform to illustrate the application of a particular reform process. The chronology and analysis that follows describes the use of both internal and external pressure to create a call and willingness for change that is of sufficient strength to compel a faculty-led revision. Such a process approach to change has proven, and is continuing to be, slow, laborious, and gradual, as opposed to a top-down administrative mandate, which may move more quickly. It is certainly the hope of all involved in this reform at the University of North Carolina at Greensboro (UNCG) that the approach used may accomplish the desired reforms while creating a culture of continuous improvement marked by widespread faculty involvement and ownership, thus leading to more effective implementation. When applying these principles, we encourage you to adapt our reform strategies to your distinct institutional environment.

Background: The University of North Carolina at Greensboro

Cited as a model of a "faculty-friendly campus," the University of North Carolina at Greensboro is a public, research-intensive university of approximately 17,000 students. Harmony is highly valued, and the campus enjoys an uncommon level of cooperation and respect between faculty and administration. Both administration and faculty work hard to preserve this culture, and some on campus feel that this may create a reticence to engage in initiatives that may cause dissension or dissatisfaction.

Unlike many campuses where reform of general education is initiated by a mandate from a provost or president, UNCG's reform stems from faculty and faculty committees. Thus, the "story" of the ongoing reform of general education is one of an inclusive, organic process that is largely focused on the continuing goal of increasing faculty understanding, awareness, and willingness to create a system of governance around general education that can and will ensure ongoing evaluation, review, and revision of the general education goals, curriculum, and student performance.

The reform process that began in 2004 occurred within the context of a general education curriculum and governance structure that had been implemented only four years prior (2001) during a period in which the campus was preparing for a regional accreditation visit. The 36-credit program focused on a set of student learning goals and skills that were to be achieved through a distribution of courses in various subject disciplines (such as history, fine arts, etc.) and an additional set of skill-based "markers" (writing, speaking, global understanding). A set of ten subject-based faculty committees was formed to provide governance to the process. More than 400 different courses were approved as general education courses.

Upon implementation of the program in 2001, general education was viewed as "finished" by faculty. A system of ongoing student learning assessment was called for in the program, but was never put into place. Faculty engaged with general education almost totally through the lens of a specific discipline or subject. The ten-committee governance group focused on each subject, and very little oversight of the broad spectrum of general education existed, causing the program to begin to lose direction almost immediately. However, the stage for change had already been set by the requirement for a campus-wide program review in 2006. That review became the focal point of the activity that is described in this chronology and outline, activity that became as much about the goal to create a culture of continuous improvement as it was about specific content of the general education program itself. Much of the next reform, starting in 2008, focused on reestablishing a workable system of faculty oversight, and encouraging general education reform to be viewed as a continually-ongoing process rather than a one-time outcome.

Even before the 2006 review began, dissatisfaction with the plan began to be noted in various constituencies. Faculty dissatisfaction with the general education program focused largely on the confusing general education course approval process. Students viewed the distribution requirements as a disconnected list of difficult-to-negotiate hurdles. Failure to provide an engaged system of student learning assessment resulted in criticism from the regional accreditors. Despite pockets of dissatisfaction, however, there was no campus-wide consensus that further reform was required and no shared understanding of what reform, if any, might be needed. The ten discipline-based faculty oversight committees did not provide a workable structure for coordinating reform efforts or monitoring the delivery of the general education goals. This administrative process, focused on subject-based committees reinforced by enrollment-driven budgetary pressures, encouraged a political context that privileged the status quo. In such an environment, one must question how an institution could mobilize internal and external pressures to shift the balance between forces encouraging status quo and pressures for reform.

Even before the review of general education began, a requirement from the Southern Association of Colleges and Schools played a critical role. Responding to a requirement for increased assessment, the university held an assessment summit in 2005, which raised faculty awareness of the need for reform. Pulling together an array of faculty who were members of the ten discipline-based committees and the Undergraduate Curriculum Council, the day-long assessment summit featured the presentation and discussion of available data on student performance. Although the focus of the day was assessment, the results set the stage for all the future activities and changes to general education, and provided the impetus for building a culture of continuous evaluation and improvement.

At the end of the day-long summit, faculty reached three major conclusions: (1) the course distribution requirements did not cover all the stated general education goals, (2) several requirements (such as critical thinking) were not covered by any of the ten subject-based oversight committees, and (3) student performance on some goals was not at the level desired by the faculty, with the most notable areas of concern being math and writing skills. By identifying these conclusions in a public session, the faculty themselves established the need for change. The summit provided a mechanism for documenting faculty recommendations regarding general education. That data served as a benchmark foundation for ongoing reform efforts.

Despite the fact that the assessment summit had exposed substantial faculty concerns about the general education program, it had not created a substantive energy to ensure a reform movement, and the planned review of general education in 2006 was generally expected to produce only minimal recommendations. The review involved a faculty taskforce and two external consultants, and included focus groups of constituencies (students, faculty), open forums, and review of best practices and national writings, including *Liberal Education and America's Promise* (Association of American Colleges and Universities 2007). This document cogently articulated the purposes of general education, described the need for reform, promoted greater discussion of the purposes and intents of general education, and highlighted the discrepancies between UNCG's existing program and national best-practices. This provided greater clarity about general education and helped to shape the reform agenda.

The General Education Review Taskforce (GERTA), a faculty and student group that carried out the program review, reaffirmed the findings of Assessment Summit I, concluding that (1) general education goals were not expressed in the catalog in a clear manner that could be easily understood by students or effectively implemented by faculty, (2) the alignment between the general education goals and the required course distribution was unclear, and (3) the inability to operationalize the learning goals made it difficult to assess student learning.

The internal review emphasized continued strong faculty commitment to the "distributive approach," an approach not considered to exemplify current best practices. External reviewers recommended that the reform efforts start by building a shared faculty understanding of the purposes of general education for UNCG students before revision of the curriculum. Both internal and external reviewers agreed that the administrative structure of the ten discipline-based committees should be replaced by a single oversight committee. The resulting report, published widely on campus and reviewed by senior administration, began to create a significant call for reform, although it did not offer a definitive blueprint for the process or the outcome.

Based on the recommendations of the GERTA taskforce, the Faculty Senate formed a General Education Council (spring 2007), and charged it with ongoing course approval and assessment of the existing general education program. The council was not charged to revise the curriculum or create a new general education program. Nevertheless, the creation of a single oversight committee provided a more responsive administrative structure that would, for the first time, focus on the broad general education goals from a campus-wide perspective, rather than the discipline-based viewpoint of the ten faculty subject committees. The council brought together faculty representatives from all academic units, providing the potential for a new political context that could enable faculty members to transcend compartmentalized ways of thinking and focus on the interests of the institution as a whole. All members of the council received the *Liberal Education and America's Promise* (LEAP) report published by AAC&U and, in addition to reviewing proposals for new general education courses, council meetings during the first year of activity focused on study of best practices in general education. Charged by the Faculty Senate with ongoing course approval, the council continued to review new general education course proposals despite the fact that more than 500 courses were already approved as general education courses. The council considered recommendations to declare a moratorium on new course approvals, but felt that declaring a moratorium as a first step would create unnecessary tension about the role of the new oversight committee in administering the general education program. The ongoing review of new course proposals turned out to provide a valuable practical tool for developing a shared consensus among council members about the definition and purposes of general education.

Defining the Purposes of General Education

Defining general education and characterizing reform is a critical element of any change process. Before it is possible to begin any reform effort, it is first of all essential to answer the question, "Is reform necessary?" As simple as this sounds, there are several prerequisites that must be accomplished before this question can be answered. As an initial step, it may be necessary to develop a consensus about the definition of general education and liberal education. The UNCG experience illustrates that common understanding of these terms cannot be assumed. Although institutional decision-makers are themselves likely to have completed a general education program in their undergraduate degrees, those programs were likely widely diverse both in content and in when they occurred. Thus, the fact that all faculty are the products of a general education process does not guarantee that there is a clear, shared understanding of the intents and purposes of general education. Many faculty may have limited understanding of general education and of their institution's general education program, often focused on those areas in which they are directly responsible for delivery.

The council's examination of the existing general education program, within the context of best practices in liberal education, created a new recognition that the distribution requirements served as a delivery system for the general education goals. A greater understanding of liberal education centered on programmatic learning outcomes was instrumental in developing a shared understanding of the purposes of general education and the need for reform. The level of need for general education reform is determined by the degree of incongruence between the existing program and the reforms demanded. It must be recognized that this process requires a great deal of honesty and integrity. It is not easy to admit that something is missing, because that admission requires that something be done about it. Knowing that something needs to be done and actually doing it are two different issues; however, knowing is still a prerequisite to doing.

Using national data has been essential to creating a shared understanding of the need for general education reform and a recognition of broad national patterns of reform. The council also considered local data in targeting reform efforts. A second assessment summit, held in 2007, once again supported the fact that it was very difficult to operationalize the general education learning goals, thus developing a stronger call for reform. In an initial attempt to better understand goal delivery, the General Education Council sponsored a web-based faculty survey in which general education instructors were asked to identify which general education goals were addressed in individual general education courses. The purpose of the survey was to determine the relationship between the general education student learning goals and the general education categories. Survey results indicated that goal delivery could not be ensured—that is, a substantial proportion of faculty reported that they were not covering the specific goal for which the course had been approved. Results of the survey indicated that, without faculty commitment to covering the learning goals in the courses approved for those goals, it was quite possible for students to complete their undergraduate careers without adequately covering all of the learning goals envisioned by the UNCG general education program.

The evidence from the general education review begun in 2004, Assessment Summits I and II, and the faculty survey, created a multi-year history of similar issues brought to the surface. Each of these events or documents reinforced similar conclusions about the need for reform. Although the publication, *Liberal Education and America's Promise*, introduced council members to new understandings of the definition and purposes of general education, it did not in itself provide a template for reform at UNCG. Multiple strategies were required. However, it was at this point that the call for reform reached a tipping point, moving from an option to a necessity, and gaining support from the central administration. The provost reinforced the reform effort through purchasing books and sending teams to participate in important national conferences, such as AAC&U and other assessment conferences. Interaction with faculty and administrators from other institutions that were also struggling with general education reform introduced the developing leadership team to creative problem-solving strategies that might be successfully adapted at UNCG. The chair of the General Education Council, an attendee at the annual meeting of AAC&U, with the support of the provost, submitted a proposal for the AAC&U Institute on General Education in the spring of 2007.

Defining the Reform Agenda

UNCG was accepted for participation at the AAC&U institute where curriculum, change strategy, and best practices in assessment were topics of discussion, thus creating an informed leadership team. The team project at the institute was designing an on-campus summer workshop as a strategy for implementing reform. The team made a conscious decision to examine model practices in general education reform but not to attempt to adopt them wholesale. It was felt that faculty needed an opportunity to examine the extent to which their current general education program was already achieving elements of general education reform. Simply presenting or adopting a general education reform without first engaging the faculty might have encouraged apathy and disengagement with the reform process. The workshop was designed to expand the reform process beyond the council by engaging important constituents in the delivery of general education across the campus community.

The workshop, organized as a series of large group presentations and small group working sessions, created an informed and greatly expanded leadership cohort, much larger than the General Education Council itself. Participants in the workshop represented every academic unit and important co-curricular programs, and two undergraduates provided a critical student perspective. The provost provided funding for faculty stipends and administrative support for the two-week workshop. He charged the participants with assisting the General Education Council in the following ways: (1) defining the purpose of general education at UNCG, (2) clarifying the overall general education learning goals, (3) articulating the relationship between the General Education Council distribution and the general education program as a whole, and (4) outlining a plan for operationalizing the learning goals. Four external consultants offered hands-on guidance for articulating measurable student learning goals, assessment planning, change strategy, and model practices. The workshop achieved two of the provost's four charges, producing a revised philosophy of general education and a revised set of learning goals. The drafts produced by the workshop were submitted to the General Education Council in the fall of 2008 and the workshop participants agreed to advocate for their adoption.

Many of the activities of the General Education Council have been directed towards expanding the dialog about general education. It became clear as the summer workshop evolved that the participants would be unable to complete the provost's charge for articulating the alignment between the goals and the general education core distribution requirements and creating a plan for operationalizing the goals. Successful achievement of those essential reforms would require broader consultation with the faculty responsible for delivering those courses. It is a challenge to create systems of communication that can be transparent, responsive, and elicit broad perspectives. For meaningful implementation, it is important that faculty feel ownership of the general education goals. Rather than spend an extended period of time editing the drafts, the council has set operationalizing the learning goals as its priority. The process-driven reform agenda sets a higher priority on clarifying the relationship between the general education core distribution and the goals and ensuring goal delivery (old or new) than on producing a perfect new set of goals.

With that in mind, the General Education Council revised and simplified the drafts produced in the summer workshop and forwarded a revised

General Education Mission and Learning Goals report to the Faculty Senate for campus-wide review. A faculty senate forum provided the first opportunity for the wider campus community to comment on the draft goals. In order to broaden opportunities for faculty discussion of the goals, the council also created a moderated web-based discussion board. A series of faculty meetings organized around each of the general education core categories and markers was scheduled for spring 2009. It is hoped that the General Education Council faculty meetings will provide a systematic forum for identifying faculty consensus about goal delivery.

A number of significant changes by the General Education Council have begun to address the administrative procedures involved in general education delivery. For example, all current course approval requests are now required to clearly articulate which general education goals are delivered, as well as describe how the course "fits" the general education category approval that is being requested.

The matter of ensuring a sufficient number of courses to address each goal has proven to be a highly contentious issue. Rather than addressing this unilaterally or administratively, the General Education Council has begun a process for goal delivery discovery. Faculty will be consulted through open forums organized to focus on particular general education categories and markers. The forums will be designed to identify which general education goals must be mandated in certain general education courses. The goal delivery commitments made by the general education categories will be used by the General Education Council in the course certification process. Courses will also be required to be periodically recertified for a category, thus assuring that the course content has not "drifted" from the required general education content.

Again working within the institutional context, the General Education Council has begun to consider what action they will take if (as expected), it is discovered that some general education goals are not being addressed in the course list. And, once again, the faculty will be involved in a substantive way, as the General Education Council plans to seek direction from the Faculty Senate to provide resolution and implementation. The reform process is carefully designed to promote communication. The need to maintain open, transparent communication about the reform process and content is critical for creating broad faculty support. Many different avenues must be followed simultaneously to ensure shared participation at all levels and address misunderstandings of the reform effort that might undermine support for the process.

Addressing the Emotional Component
of the Change Process

It is obvious from the chapter content thus far that the energy required to set a reform movement into motion at UNCG was enormous, due to the campus's culture and the lack of a single mandate to inspire campus commitment to the initiative. So far, the story of initiating change at UNCG has focused on approaches to define the purposes of general education and build an administrative structure and leadership team to initiate the reform. In addition to developing rational, educational approaches to general education reform it is also essential to address the sometimes strong emotions generated by the change process.

Any general education reform effort represents a fundamental cultural change in an institution. Some people are by nature uncomfortable with change, because change creates uncertainty and uncertainty creates anxiety. The specific emotional responses are multiple, varied and unique to each individual. Apprehension has been observed, including the concern of wasting time, fear of making things worse or doing the wrong things, discomfort about criticism, qualms about violating tradition and norms, uneasiness about being overwhelmed, worry that reform cannot be accomplished, and suspicions about assessment practices, to name a few. These concerns may be expressed or may remain unexpressed, but in either case they have an impact on any reform process, sometimes even paralyzing it.

Although we do need to recognize the emotional aspects of reform, it is also possible to work with these emotions productively. Taking a process approach to reform makes managing emotional responses simpler, because it allows many of these concerns to be addressed over time. This allows stakeholders the opportunity to become familiar with the issues and to become involved and engaged in problem solving, rather than simply responding at an emotional level.

Rather than dwelling exclusively on the potential negative aspects of a reform effort, it is necessary to replace negative emotional expectations with potentially positive outcomes. For example, an important positive outcome of general education reform might be the production of students who are better prepared to perform at higher levels in the major. Communication is critical to creating the sense that the benefits of change outweigh the costs. Clearly articulating stages in the reform process and identifying specific deadlines for different stages helps reinforce a sense of progress and closure. By focusing on the vision of the ways in which reform will make the educational process more meaningful and achieve defined objectives, it is possible to create more excitement and investment in the potential benefits, enabling faculty to accept that this process is faculty driven and faculty controlled.

Important Sources of Support
for the Reform Process

Colleges and universities are currently being buffeted about by demands that come from outside the academy, thus automatically viewed as suspect. These include increased pressure for greater efficiency and effectiveness, and a shift in focus from a teacher-centered to a student-centered learning paradigm. Many faculty view these demands for reform as unwarranted and unwelcome intrusions into academic freedom. The more that it is possible to align the reform effort with the history, culture, and purposes of an institution, the more likely it is that the reform will proceed.

Support for the reform process at UNCG has been provided from both internal and external sources. Though the local administration did not mandate the creation of a new general education program, strong administrative support from the provost and the chancellor has made general education reform an explicit institutional priority. General education has been identified as one of five strategic directions of a campus-wide planning process to identify goals for the next five years. The chair of the General Education Council has also been appointed to chair the work group charged with articulating goals for general education in the strategic plan. The fact that general education will be an important strategic direction for the next five years will provide sustained momentum for a process-driven approach to reform. Despite the pressures of budget cuts in a lean economic year, the provost has also approved funding for faculty redevelopment grants to assist faculty in retooling their syllabi to address the revised learning goals and to achieve a successful course recertification.

The local campus planning process is proceeding in the context of a University of North Carolina statewide initiative entitled "UNC Tomorrow." After consultation with faculty, students, parents, business leaders, and community constituencies across the state, UNC Tomorrow has identified a specific set of transferable skills and abilities that graduates of all UNC institutions should possess, thus emphasizing the importance of general education and enhancing reform efforts at UNCG. System-wide assessment initiatives also include a mandate that all campuses administer the Collegiate Learning Assessment (CLA; Council for Aid to Education 2006) to measure critical thinking skills. The UNC system has committed to participate in the Voluntary System of Accountability (VSA; AASCU/ NASULGC 2007), which includes measures of critical thinking such as the CLA, the Collegiate Assessment of Academic Proficiency (CAAP; American College Testing Service 1991), and the Measure of Academic Proficiency and Progress (MAPP; Educational Testing Service 2007). This heightens awareness on the part of the local community that the delivery of general education goals is not only a source of interest, but also that there is an intent to assess student achievement and use that achievement as a basis for comparing institutions across the state. The Southern Association of Colleges and Schools (SACS) will return to UNCG in 2012 for its ten-year reaccreditation visit. The requirement by SACS that general education be assessed and the results used to improve student learning will once again place external pressure on the process of general education reform at UNCG.

The Role of Assessment in the Reform Process

Assessment activities can drive the reform process in a variety of ways, including: (1) identifying both the strengths and weaknesses of the current general education system; (2) highlighting discrepancies between the stated outcomes of general education and the achievement of those outcomes; (3) identifying the same sources of concern over a period of time; (4) assessing the delivery system for general education; and (5) evaluating faculty and student perceptions of competency and satisfaction with general education goal delivery. Through assessment it is possible to identify ongoing areas of concern. In addition to measuring student learning, assessment can also measure the success of the general education delivery system itself, an element found to be critically important at UNCG. For example, the faculty survey mentioned previously highlighted the gaps in student access to courses adequately covering some general education goals. Surveys, not usually a good measure of student learning, do provide an important measurement of perceptions of both faculty and students in areas such as critical thinking, problem solving, and communication. A survey of students provided a valuable student perspective on general education goal delivery. The surveys also gave important indications of awareness, indicating whether faculty were adequately aware of the general education goals of their courses, and whether students were aware of the expected learning to take place in those courses. At UNCG, assessment findings indicated that some goals were not being consistently delivered by faculty nor consistently achieved by students.

Campus Culture and Process-Centered Reform

Transforming the UNCG culture from one in which General Education is perceived as "finished" to one in which it receives ongoing quality improvement and changes are made based on assessment is a critical element that will determine the success of this reform initiative. If the reform process has been truly successful, it will never be possible to view general education as a finished product again. Rather, the campus will have created an active process for maintaining the coherence and intentionality of the general education program both now and in the future. The ultimate goal of the UNCG reform is nothing less than a cultural transformation—creating a culture of continuous improvement marked by widespread faculty involvement and ownership, thus leading to more effective implementation. The processes of highlighting the need for improvement of the curriculum, of bringing the various constituencies to the discussion, of providing a system of organization for decision-making, must themselves be ongoing. Similarly, the processes of defining and redefining General Education goals, and ensuring that students achieve those goals, must be an ongoing and engaged process, one that continues despite changes in faculty and administration.

The UNCG case has presented some of the practical strategies we have developed for initiating a faculty-driven reform process within an institutional culture that highly values harmony. One of the first steps to reform was creating a new administrative structure for general education. The General Education Council offered a new political and administrative context for defining the purposes of general education and the need for reform. The council also generated a leadership team for organizing reform efforts. Engaging constituents beyond the council has been essential to expanding the reform effort. Various communication strategies, from open meetings to web-based discussion boards, have been critical to both broadening the discussion about general education and developing an understanding of broad perspectives about the purposes of general education at UNCG. The ongoing reform effort is influenced by both internal and external pressures. It has been important for UNCG to consider a changing culture of system-wide planning, as well as the larger national culture of accountability. Culture is itself a process, not a fixed condition. It is important to begin any reform initiative by identifying the cultural factors that support and inhibit reform. These may be specific to the local institution or connected to a larger system or community context.

Though reform strategies at UNCG have been tailored to our own institutional culture, they nevertheless involve careful consideration of the seven process variables addressed in this book. Creating a leadership team has been an integral part of the process of initiating reform. UNCG has taken an incremental approach to reform, while defining stages in the reform process with specific deadlines. National data and local outcomes assessment have provided important focal points in the reform process. Developing effective communication strategies to inform and involve the broad campus community, identifying and engaging key constituents in support of the reform effort, and addressing issues of politics and governance have been central factors in designing change strategies that can work within the institutional culture. The chronological approach to presenting the UNCG case study shows how these factors must be considered repeatedly as the reform process unfolds. While the specific change strategies employed at UNCG may not be successful at every institution, the reform process has elements that can be transferable in a variety of institutional contexts. We invite readers to consider the seven key variables for process-centered reform and cultural change in the specific cultural context of their own institutions.

References

Association of American Colleges and Universities (AAC&U). 2007. *Liberal education and America's promise*. Washington, DC: AAC&U.

American Association of State Colleges and Universities (AASCU) and the National Association of State Universities and Land-Grant Colleges (NASULGC). 2007. *The voluntary system of accountability* [database]. Washington, DC: AASUC/NASULGC.

American College Testing Service (ACT). 1991. *Collegiate assessment of academic proficiency* [survey]. Iowa City, IA: ACT.

Council for Aid to Education (CAE). 2006. *The collegiate learning assessment* [survey]. New York, NY: CAE.

Educational Testing Service, Inc. (ETS). 2007. *The measure of academic proficiency and progress* [survey]. Lawrenceville, NJ: ETS.

CHAPTER 2

Distributed Leadership

A TOOL for CREATING LEARNING OUTCOMES and TRANSFORMING CURRICULUM

by Nona M. Burney *and* Priscilla Perkins

Mid-level administrators and faculty frequently complain (or, more rarely, boast) about the quality of support they receive from their institutions' central administration: "We could make big curricular improvements if we just had real leadership at the top." While recognizing the symbolic and material impacts that engaged upper administrators can have on reform efforts, our chapter argues that sustainable, transformative headway requires academic workers at every level to see ourselves as leaders with the power to organize and implement curricular change. As bioethicist Howard Brody (1992) writes about members of the "expert class," "power that is unrecognized is hard to channel into responsible uses" (114). Like the medical doctors he studies, we faculty and mid-level administrators need to "own," "aim," and "share" the power we do have. Academics who admit that even provosts and presidents rarely have as much power as we (or they) think they do are better-positioned to transform their own units and the larger institution.

The insights we explore in this chapter grow from our experiences guiding general education transformation at Roosevelt University between 2006 and 2009. In our thinking about this process, which so far has resulted in a university-wide undergraduate learning outcomes statement and college-wide curriculum mapping in two of five units, we have identified three conditions for the effective and ethical exercise of distributed academic leadership:

- First, we must positively value our institution as a political site, peopled by political actors. Instead of seeing politics as "the activity of seeking and exercising influence, control, power, and coercion," we choose to see politics as "all the activities of cooperation, negotiation, and conflict, within and between societies, whereby people go about organizing the use, production, or distribution of human, natural, and other resources in the course of the production and reproduction of their ... social life" (Donahue 2008).

- As political actors, we vigorously pursue the best interests of our own programs, but we are also willing to compromise narrower goals in order to further our university's larger mission. We recognize that, as members of a medium-size, tuition-driven private institution, we often experience our common life as a quasi-familial dynamic of intimacy and conflict, within which we must work together in order for the institution—and our students—to thrive.

- Finally, as individuals, we embrace fluid roles as provocateurs, role models, translators, and horse traders—whether we are administrators or regular faculty. The more we identify with a single role, the less equipped we are to redefine dysfunctional working relationships and curricular structures. We understand that, in the words of Burns:

> Planning must recognize many faces of power; ultimately the authority and credibility of planning leadership will depend less on formal position than on the capacity to recognize basic needs, to mobilize masses of persons holding sets of values and seeking general goals. (1978, 421)

In the Beginning . . .
Creation of the General Education Task Force

As with any reform process, campus culture and history matter. Between 1990 and 2006, general education curricular design at Roosevelt University was piecemeal and content-driven, sometimes motivated by troubling assessment data, at other times by new administrators' desires to put their own "stamp" on Roosevelt undergraduate learning. The strategic planning process completed in 2002, shortly after the arrival of a new president, addressed curriculum only tangentially, a sign that while the faculty "owns" the curriculum, we were not then galvanized to examine it systematically and globally. Over the years, the five colleges (Arts and Sciences [by far the largest], Education, Business, Performing Arts, and Professional Studies) occasionally cooperated, frequently chose to opt into or out of specific requirements, and the other four sometimes even developed curriculum intended to parallel Arts and Science offerings (but in a time-shortened format). Structural impediments to comprehensive reform have included articulation agreements with area community colleges, state requirements for teacher certification, over-reliance on contingent faculty, and pressure from market competitors to keep the "fast-track" programs as short as possible. In other words, faculty and administrators responsible for curriculum in Roosevelt's five colleges have felt ourselves pulled and pushed in perhaps twenty-five directions. Likewise, depending on which college a faculty member belonged to, a university-wide general education program has been something to strive for—or to avoid at all costs. Competition for scarce institutional resources has consistently undermined attempts at cross-college collaboration.

Even midway into the reform process we examine here, centrifugal structural forces sometimes make it hard for outsiders to see what we have accomplished. Because distributed leadership—in other words, collaboration among colleagues who thoughtfully exert the multiple forms of power they possess as administrators, members of a discipline, and/or university citizens—blurs the lines between "top-down" and "bottom-up" reform, the change it enables does not always show up as bullet-points in an annual report to trustees. Indeed, more than once, we have been told that we are not generating enough dramatic changes to satisfy our top leaders. National trends and our own recent history, though, confirm that provosts and faculty do not necessarily work on the same timetable: on average, a provost serves less than four years at one institution before moving on, while tenured, nonadministrative faculty tend to take a much longer-term perspective (while still, in most cases, recognizing the importance of consistent responsiveness to changing student needs). The clash of perspectives can be startling: In early 2008, during an on-campus interview for the chief academic officer position at Roosevelt University, a candidate was asked how he could help the university strengthen its general education curriculum. "What Gen Ed curriculum?" the candidate responded. "You don't have one." When the questioner tried to explain the challenges of devising a common core curriculum acceptable to five disparate colleges, the candidate broke in: "That's just politics—nothing but politics and turf." *Just* politics: the petty game-playing of people who seek power for their own posse, rather than progress for the whole community. At first, the comment stung. Looking back, though, on almost three years of building coalitions, identifying common rallying points, compromising on negotiables, and sticking with principles, we now grant that we have been practicing politics — *just* politics, in keeping with our commitment to *justice* for our students and the communities we share. And we have made progress.

An earlier provost supplied the first impetus to systematic change — being brand-new, however, she did not know the institution's culture well enough to nurture the process she put into motion. In June 2006, she dispatched a team of faculty members — academic leaders — to the Association of American Colleges and Universities (AAC&U) Institute on General Education in Washington, DC, with only the following instructions: "Go and see." We were a microcosm of the larger university dynamic — an associate provost, four associate deans, and a nonadministrator/associate professor — representatives of our respective colleges but selected by the provost for distinguishable, strategic attributes. Each was a tenured, respected member of the faculty, known for her or his integrity (in other words, mission-focused, "walking the talk"), and, therefore, de facto leaders in our units. We later discovered that we also possessed a sense of humor, tenacity, and love of food (and a good bottle of wine), valuable personal resources to weather the challenges that awaited our return from the institute.

The first hint of what "go and see" really meant came from a pre-institute reading, Jerry Gaff's (1980) *Avoiding the Potholes: Strategies for Reforming General Education*. In it, Gaff notes, "Task forces usually bring much talent and enthusiasm to the task of reforming general education, but few have experience in providing leadership for institutional change" (50). "Reforming general education"?! "Leadership for institutional change"?! These phrases activated our internal alarms: Ambiguity! Suspicion! Conflict! Why would anyone spend so much money for this set of faculty members *just* to "go and see"? Were we about to be pawns for some "hidden agenda" because of our personal reputations among our peers? Were we being set up to usurp the existing General Education Committee, housed in the College of Arts and Sciences, chaired by one of us, and clearly not looking for top-down reformation?

Although the university had completed a major strategic planning process during the previous five years, the focus and impact were primarily administrative, not curricular. For example, goal number 3 of the strategic plan proposed to "Express the University's Historic Commitment to Social Justice through Academic Program Development and Civic Engagement." The first objective under this goal, "Coordinate and implement curricular changes and graduation requirement to make social justice integral to the Roosevelt experience in and out of the classroom" (Roosevelt University 2006), is the most direct reference to curriculum in the entire document. What we began to see, through the institute presentations and the mentoring of AAC&U consultants, was an unprecedented opportunity to spark the faculty's desire to strategically transform the curriculum. At the institute, phrases like "collective commitment to outcomes" and "collective efficacy of our practices" replaced "ambiguity." "Student-centered," "integration," "deep learning," and "the process of making meaning" became our buzzwords in the face of "conflict." Finally, "suspicion" was suspended when, during one team caucus at a picnic table, we read the back of one of our university-issued business cards: *Roosevelt University is a national leader in educating socially conscious citizens for active and dedicated lives as leaders in their professions and their communities.* An epiphanic moment: Instead of arguing with each other about who "owned" general education and who was guilty of thwarting reform, what if we focused our colleagues on making this mission transparent and explicit throughout the curriculum, as well as in the co-curricular and extra-curricular experiences of our students? With unanimous agreement, our university's mission for its students became the group's mission for the faculty, and "Transitioning Our GenEd Aspirations through Engaging Academic Members" (Toga Team) was born.

"Working the Crowds":
The Politics of Community Transformation

The General Education Task Force (a.k.a. Toga Team) began "working the crowds" before we even left D.C. As lofty as "making the curriculum transparent and explicit to the mission" sounded, we knew we had colleagues who would not be buying that line without a fight — a potential return to ambiguity, suspicion, and conflict. At the same picnic table, we began listing, by college, those most likely to oppose this new way of thinking about general education. We then considered strategies to win them over, or at the very least, neutralize (not eliminate) their impact. The examples of trial and error were rife in Gaff's "Potholes" and even among the teams attending the institute with us. For some, it was their third, fourth, or even seventh visit, still counting *and* persisting. Resurrecting Saul Alinsky (1971), the Chicago community organizer whose ideas shaped a young Barack Obama, we resolved to mobilize ten percent of our colleagues in order to get the process moving, rather than concentrate too much energy on the potential opposition.

Toga Team decided to use the provost's annual faculty forum, held in August, to launch our campaign. Wanting to "disengage," "disidentify," and "disenchant" (Tichy and Devanna 1986, 64–65) the faculty from its historical way of thinking about general education as the responsibility of the College of Arts and Sciences, we chose to be intentionally irreverent. We would parody Zero Mostel's *A Funny Thing Happened on the Way to the Forum* (Sondheim 1962), inserting "Faculty" before "Forum." Though not unanimously enamored with this approach—the College of Arts and Sciences, we would later learn, was officially "not amused"—we engendered our own *esprit de corps* as we plotted this "roll-out." We outlined an agenda that would replicate our own institute experience, engaging the forum attendees in similar collaborative, conversational, and creative activities —the beginnings of a paradigm shift. For the rest of the academic year, we anticipated holding regular dialogues with all of the power bases—the provost's monthly leadership forum, bi-semesterly college councils, and our monthly university senate.

We were not so intoxicated by the rarefied air of this six-day retreat to forget that, back in Chicago, two key people must be convinced of our intentions and given language that they would consistently use in reference to our "mission impossible"—the provost and the president. Late in June 2006, we debriefed with the provost, describing how we came, what we saw, and what we intended to conquer. Toga Team's face-to-face meeting with the provost provided visual evidence of our commitment to pursue this process. Members took turns talking during this presentation, clarifying what we needed from the provost's office to sustain our work to completion: access to and restructuring of monthly leadership forums, differential time and assignments in order for the team to focus on this initiative, and clerical and financial support.

The provost liked our institute report, in which we outlined the following goals:

- Achieving a university-wide consensus about what skills, areas of knowledge, and ethical dispositions all Roosevelt graduates should attain.
- Recognizing the degree to which these elements are addressed in current course offerings in all colleges and departments.
- Moving from a two-year to a four-year general education paradigm—to include not just foundational courses, but most

courses in the majors—that would create multiple paths toward the same outcomes.

- Developing a continuous review cycle to determine the effectiveness of the general education model and to ensure sustained success over time.

Our presentation and message at the subsequent meeting with the president were more conceptual: we were continuing the strategic planning process, from the curriculum side up. We made it very clear to both of these chief administrative officers that our reputations among our peers were at stake, and that we would not persist if this process was not really a priority for both of them.

The entire Roosevelt faculty received a "Save the Date" postcard: August 21, 2006—A Funny Thing Happened on the Way to the *Faculty* Forum! The subtitle read "A Holistic Approach to General Education," an accurate description, though by no means one that fully revealed the challenges that would follow its implementation. In planning this four-hour meeting, which in previous years had emphasized top-down pronouncements about enrollment and retention trends, we chose to create a carnivalesque environment: music, comedy, and presenters who spoke from both the physical center and the edges of the crowd would increase participation by inverting traditional academic hierarchies (administrators over faculty, Arts and Sciences over Business, Education, and Performing Arts). We hoped that our de-centered, inverted approach to this symbolic (and almost universally dreaded) annual meeting would help faculty embrace the distributed leadership model we were developing. To make it clear that we expected involvement from everyone attending, we asked faculty members to bring copies of their current syllabi to study and share. On the big day, attendees were greeted by laurel-wreathed Toga Team members while the Broadway musical version of "A Funny Thing Happened . . ." played in the background. The PowerPoint presentation of our general education institute experience was punctuated with the appropriate Stephen Sondheim lyrics: "something familiar, something peculiar . . . something convulsive, something repulsive . . . something aesthetic, something frenetic . . . nothing that's formal, nothing that's normal . . . something for everyone!" (Sondheim 1992).

Moving from the introduction to the participatory focus of this forum, we gave each attendee a picture of a cap-and-gowned student, and instructed them to (1) think of a graduate from your program who makes you really proud; (2) try to distinguish the personal qualities the student arrived with from those he or she acquired through his/her studies at Roosevelt; and (3) share your insights about this graduate with colleagues at your table. We had assigned seating to ensure that there were at least two different colleges represented at each table, recognizing that Arts and Sciences would probably predominate. As we debriefed the table discussions, three team members used large newsprint pads to create lists of faculty responses under the headings of "Skills," "Content Knowledge," and "Dispositions," while another rapidly typed, printed, and then photocopied a one-page table encapsulating the discussion. At the end of the forum, attendees were presented with this first, very rough draft of what we then termed "core concepts": the expected learning outcomes for a Roosevelt graduate. We were convinced that we had won the first "referendum" on this process when a perceived nemesis captured our intent in her standing summation at the closing of the event: she announced that "we, the faculty, have the responsibility to be explicit and transparent with our students about our expectations, and our curriculum should be reflective of the same." If a colleague we had expected to oppose our efforts could articulate them so clearly and positively, maybe our work would not require as much lobbying as we had anticipated.

In the days after our apparent triumph, we ambitiously mapped out the next steps to full faculty engagement in this process of re-visioning general education and transforming our curriculum. The provost's monthly leadership forum, composed of associate deans and department chairs, those closest to the development and implementation of curriculum, would be the next venue through which we would fine-tune the draft of the "core concepts." We were so bold as to set this goal at our September 15, 2006 team meeting: *Completed curriculum maps for all programs with supporting syllabi by the end of the academic year.* A blitz of college council meetings would sufficiently expose our "core concepts" to those who had missed the faculty forum, so we thought. We would then "work" our respective colleges to shepherd this mapping phase to completion.

This first leadership forum in mid-September 2006 revealed how naïve we had been. Not controlling the meeting agenda as we had been promised, our presentation followed an hour of thorny topics introduced by the provost. All Toga Team members present, we gamely tried to resume the dialogical approach of the faculty forum, seeking the input of these academic leaders to refine the forum draft of "core concepts." In this testy all-administrative environment, in which the task force was too closely identified with the provost's office, our audience was unwilling to set hierarchical and partisan assumptions aside, even for a little while. We learned that our goal of distributed leadership was unrealistic in a setting that (perhaps unintentionally) discouraged cooperation among the colleges' administrators and members of the provost's staff.

For example, some of the leaders—especially, perhaps, those who had been part of earlier, less global curricular reform efforts at Roosevelt —wanted to cut to the chase by borrowing lists of learning outcomes from other institutions (which we had supplied for illustrative purposes only) and adding the Roosevelt University "flavor." We immediately recognized this urge as Gaff's "Pothole #1: Find a program to import" (1980, 50). At one point, there were dueling lists being drafted on the chalkboard, a Toga Team member versus the provost's former assessment coordinator, who had not been assigned any explicit role in the reform process. The conflict represented these leaders' legitimate anxieties about their specific spheres of authority, juxtaposed with the team's desire to be inclusive and build consensus that could cut across disciplinary units and levels of administration. Finally, taking the initiative to "own" and "aim" the team's leadership power, the associate provost on the team noted the suggestions that were common to the two lists and agreed to post them on an interactive website for future input from all of the constituents, so that they, in turn, could "own" and "aim" their power, and, with some more work, we could "share" the responsibility for reform. To this end, we scheduled a follow-up meeting with this group of leaders, explaining:

> The most important thing is that whatever happens is faculty-generated through a process that includes all faculty from all programs. This kind of an inclusive process takes time and can be ambiguous, and we know that can be uncomfortable. We ask your patience and indulgence. (Personal communication September 16, 2006)

The team resolved to continue to make regular presentations at our respective college councils and, most importantly, the Faculty Senate. Through October and November, 2006, we conducted a series of work sessions on each of our campuses, the first titled "Forum Reprise," to give more details about the entire curriculum transformation process to interested faculty. Still aiming for Saul Alinsky's "ten percent," we facilitated dialogue on what the faculty wanted students to know and be able to do, and how we might map our curriculum to determine whether and where these "wants" were addressed. Attendance at our workshops was spotty, though faculty who came showed enthusiasm and created some word-of-mouth publicity for the process.

By the end of the first semester, we were ready to call in a "big gun" consultant from AAC&U, because we were at a loss on how to proceed. Our scheduled meetings with the provost were frequently being postponed or canceled. Scattered faculty complaints about the process, channeled through the deans, seemed to sway the provost away from the plan we had so carefully outlined and for which we had been promised support. We began to see the limits of provostial power: though our chief academic officer could inaugurate a controversial project, she did not see herself as able to sustain it, especially given its potential to drain her store of political capital.

This waffling led the team to use institutionally established deliberative processes to move a majority of the faculty—not just ten percent—to consensus on the "core concepts" and general education reform. Instead of trying to get faculty to identify with us as representatives of the provost, we re-clothed ourselves as university citizens, collaboratively-minded representatives of our individual colleges, to bring closure to this initial process through the elected representatives of the faculty, the senate. In February, we presented the current, best draft, announcing our intention to bring the core concepts to a senate vote. Offhand comments from the provost and president revealed their alarm with the new plan—a fact that, given the university's quasi-familial dynamic, actually increased faculty engagement in the process. The imminence of a vote increased the volume and ferocity of feedback on a rapid succession of "core concepts" drafts. There was a flurry of emails across the Arts and Sciences departments of Computer Science, Mathematics, and Biology, who argued that "Quantitative Reasoning" (the term introduced when representatives of the fast-track programs announced that any document with the word "mathematical" in it would not receive their votes) was an inadequate descriptor of the intended outcome. A face-to-face encounter with the leadership forum prior to the last senate meeting of the academic year, where the proponents of numeracy were the most vocal, was a serious test of the team's adherence to a nondefensive posture in order to promote this dialogical, transparent process for consensus. At the end of that session, for that moment, there appeared to be agreement.

In April 2007, the Faculty Senate considered for a vote the resolution presented by the team. The resolution was under "old business," one of the last items on the agenda. Five minutes before the scheduled time for adjournment, Senator Nona Burney successfully motioned for approval of the following:

RESOLUTION FOR THE ADOPTION OF THE CORE CONCEPTS OF ROOSEVELT UNIVERSITY

Whereas, decisions regarding curriculum rest with the Faculty of Roosevelt University; and

Whereas, strategic planning for the University has not yet directly addressed curriculum; and

Whereas, a process of strategic planning about the curriculum has begun through the facilitation of faculty and leadership forums, workshops, college council meetings, and a dialogical website by the General Education Task Force; and

Whereas, these various modes of dialogue among Faculty have generated a working draft of Core Concepts, identifying content, skills, and dispositions we expect to engender in Roosevelt University graduates;

Therefore Be It Resolved that the Senate hereby adopts the working draft of Core Concepts as the benchmark for further strategic planning of the curriculum by the Faculty.

Copies of the most current draft of the "core concepts" had been sent electronically to all members of the Senate. At the meeting, an alternate version was distributed, creating confusion about which was to be adopted. This led to a momentary resurrection of the "quantitative reasoning" issue, resolved because team members used parliamentary procedure to contain and focus debate on the resolution. With two minutes remaining, the university-wide set of goals was unanimously approved, and we looked forward to addressing the curriculum itself.

Beginning Again: [Re]Distributing the Leadership of Transformation

The team's early commitment to distributed leadership was a political strategy that took us through the difficult (but invigorating) academic year following our pilgrimage to the AAC&U Institute on General Education. In the months after Roosevelt's senate approved the "core concepts"—now called the Undergraduate Learning Outcomes statement—an earthquake's worth of change hit our institution: the provost who initiated the reform process became president at another institution, two of the five team members left the university, and a third member went on a one-year leave. New administrative duties, all arising out of the institution's sudden leadership vacuum at the highest levels and the shuffling of several deans' positions, meant that the remaining task force members could not maintain the momentum (or camaraderie) of the previous academic year. On the rare occasions when we came up for breath, though, we saw that, even without the team's explicit leadership, the Undergraduate Learning Outcomes statement had already created a foundation for reform in the College of Professional Studies (which quickly mapped curricula for their fast-track programs) and, most promisingly, among the library's information literacy specialists. With personnel attached to every college, librarians were using the Undergraduate Learning Outcomes to improve the services they provided to students across the university.

Seeing reform move ahead, even on a small scale, was a relief, as the previous academic year—from the trip to the general education institute to the approval of the Undergraduate Learning Outcomes—had exhausted us. Hints of buyer's remorse could be heard around the university, especially among a few Arts and Sciences faculty, who complained that having a university-wide set of Undergraduate Learning Outcomes undermined the college's academic sovereignty. What was left of the team needed time outside of the institutional spotlight, but we also needed to keep renewal alive, especially in the College of Arts and Sciences, which houses most of Roosevelt's general education courses. Consequently, though our larger transformative strategy (open political advocacy, informed by a spirit of compromise and a commitment to flexible roles) continues, we have revised our tactics (or the local, day-to-day practices that enable us to carry out strategic goals) to make them work in the unit that has most frequently resisted a systematic, outcomes-based approach to reform.

Our experiences doing general education reform as a cross-college team taught us that "translating" vocabulary across areas of expertise helps academic constituencies co-create the thinking tools we need for curricular problem solving. In the semesters since our reform team has dissolved, we have carried forward this leadership tactic into our work within the College of Arts and Sciences, where disciplinary differences sometimes threaten collaboration. As Reese writes, "Although academics belong to several communities (discipline, academic profession, university enterprise, and national academic system), the culture of the discipline, especially in the United States, generally has the strongest bonding power because it is often easier to leave the institution than the discipline" (1995, 544). While the majority of faculty members at Roosevelt understand the "university enterprise" of preparing students for success in their majors and beyond, we have learned that colleagues who get stuck at the level of defending their discipline can sometimes be moved to participate in (or at least not undermine) conversations about general education.

One especially effective tactic is to adopt (however imperfectly) the disciplinary language and methods of the resister when stressing how important the resister's participation is to the success of the reform effort. Natural science faculty, for instance, respond less positively to narrative accounts of assessment data than they do to graphic presentations; therefore, when administrators trained in the humanities use the language of hypotheses and inferences or ask whether their conclusions are statistically significant, quantitatively-oriented faculty are sometimes more willing to contribute their expertise to discussions of general education reform. Such "code-switching" (to use a term from linguistics and composition studies) helps academic workers, both administrators and faculty on standing committees, model for their colleagues the breadth of preparation we say we want our students to show when they graduate. Even if we sometimes use their terminology incorrectly, they can tell that we have been listening to them and valuing their perspectives. In a couple of cases, our very mistakes have turned an intransigent foe into a (temporary) collaborator: the impulse to correct can, if met with a gracious response, morph into a cross-disciplinary exchange of ideas about student learning. Disciplinary code-switching works, of course, only when the "switcher" operates in good faith—and, again, when she or he is not afraid to look dumb and accept some schooling.

Flexible administrators, we have learned, "own" and "aim" their power so that they can share it with the non-administrative faculty who have the most direct responsibility for carrying out general education learning goals. Before this can happen, though, all parties need opportunities to examine their own motives and insecurities. At Roosevelt, associate deans (who are also tenured teaching faculty) may believe that "pure" faculty cannot be bothered with big-picture questions about transfer credit articulation or enrollment management. Associate deans are used to students' complaints that the college's math prerequisites, for example, slow their time-to-degree; such unhappy students (who also typically email the president with their complaints) regularly threaten to switch to universities without math prerequisites. The mandate to keep students happy, common to so many tuition-driven institutions, is felt intensely by these mid-level administrators. In addition to the top-down pressure experienced by mid-level administrators (and then passed along to faculty), social pressure (say, to keep relationships between college deans smooth by avoiding mandates that might negatively affect another college's fragile en-rollments) tempts mid-level administrators to write off the concerns of non-administrative faculty. These administrators need safe spaces to dis-cuss with peers the pressure they feel, and to imagine, perhaps through in-formal role-playing, what their problems look like to colleagues above and below their own spot in the institutional food chain. At Roosevelt, such dis-cussions take place at confidential, bi-weekly strategic meetings between each college's dean and her or his staff of associate deans.

On what initially looks like the opposite side of the wall, nonad-ministrative faculty often respond to administrators' programming sugges-tions as though the administrators have no stake in academic quality. The college's economists, for instance, frequently work with mathematically underprepared students in their statistics courses, so they have practical reasons to resist administrative models of higher education that treat stu-dents as customers needing to be pleased: in their experience, students with inadequate math preparation typically fail statistics. Because they be-lieve that some administrators place a relatively low priority on student learning, though, they sometimes use their power passively, by digging in their heels and ignoring student complaints about math prerequisites. Leaders who practice seeing their roles as fluid, and who focus, as Burns suggests, on "recogniz[ing] basic needs" (1978, 421), can help disparate in-terest groups move beyond impasse without coercion. Picturing the con-flict from the faculty's side and assuming that they care as intensely about student success as administrators do are tactics that create the conditions for shared power.

When it came to the math prerequisite, the dean's staff in the College of Arts and Sciences had to accept some schooling from the economists, so that we could place their careful interpretations of assessment and reten-tion data within the context of the Undergraduate Learning Outcomes. The dean's staff in the College of Arts and Sciences convinced the provost and peers in the other deans' offices that students from economically disad-vantaged groups often need extra math instruction to succeed in quantita-tively-oriented fields. Therefore, because the prerequisite could be argued to contribute directly to student retention in colleges other than Arts and Sciences, the economists' insistence on math prerequisites for everyone en-rolled in their courses, including fast-track students from the College of Professional Studies, amounted to what we have called *"just* politics." Ev-ery time we respond openly to the re-visionary potential of faculty's disci-pline-specific input, our ability to share power becomes more effective, which can lead to better outcomes for students in all of our institution's colleges.

Sometimes the same standing committees that wield deliberative power over curriculum can, through the power of distributed leadership, become sites for what Paolo Freire (1970) called "co-learning" about curricular change. The College of Arts and Sciences General Education committee, chaired by an associate dean, determines which courses fulfill writing, math, and distribution requirements, and articulates courses transferred from the university's "feeder" colleges—potentially boring work. But because the committee includes faculty and administrative representatives from all five colleges, plus librarians and student services personnel, it is also a prime site for examining theories and practices of general education, both at Roosevelt and at other schools around the world. With the Undergraduate Learning Outcomes statement as its touchstone, representatives have presented rationales for foreign language study, and evaluated the usefulness of traditional Western Civilization requirements for students from ethnically and academically diverse backgrounds. Not everybody loves the bureaucracy-plus-study circle model, to be sure, but most committee members appreciate this ongoing opportunity for faculty development and incubator for new thinking about general education.

The ideas developed by the General Education Committee, of course, need channels to circulate back into the larger faculty and then up through the decision-making bodies that represent the faculty. Just as the Undergraduate Learning Outcomes probably would not have become university-wide policy if the Toga Team had not switched from a person-to-person approach to an all-out legislative campaign, the new general education courses that will create students' most concentrated, intentional exposure to the Undergraduate Learning Outcomes require booster rockets, as it were, to get into orbit. One effective tool for "boosting" discussion from the committee to the college level has been online surveys that simultaneously measure attitudes toward curriculum and propose new courses. Such surveys—created on sites like Survey Monkey or Zoomerang, both of which also offer basic data analysis—turn hallway grumbling into information that can then be presented to college councils as justification for the creation of the new courses we need.

Our tactics in situations like this have been influenced by our awareness of two facts about Roosevelt's culture: First, as a group, our colleagues generally rebuff new ideas when they do not have ample opportunity to shape proposals through questioning and debate within college council or senate, contexts set aside for official deliberation. Second, because curricular matters are only one of many agenda items at such meetings, discussions of a single curricular change can drag out over a semester or more, a pace that satisfies some colleagues' need for dialogue but impedes the progress we need to make in improving students' experiences at Roosevelt. A proposal that is tabled (again) for further discussion is one that misses the deadline for inclusion in the upcoming semester's course schedule. In order to compress the timetable for the process without losing the dialogue, online surveys combine background (explaining the ancient and recent history of current general education requirements for newer faculty, whose support for innovation is crucial), market research (finding out what colleagues would like to see in a new requirement), and a pedagogical invitation (presenting a proposed global studies course as a partly-developed framework and encouraging respondents to invent course themes that could flesh it out). In this way, mid-level administrators as well as non-administrative "regular faculty" collaborate to "own," "aim," and "share" their respective powers via a distributive leadership model.

Leadership in Issues of Territoriality and Academic Freedom

As we write, coordinators from each Arts and Sciences department are helping their colleagues map the undergraduate curriculum—an initiative strongly recommended by consultants at the AAC&U Institute on General Education, and made do-able by the informed cooperation of the College of Arts and Sciences chairs council, whose bi-weekly meetings are attended by the dean's staff. The College of Arts and Sciences could not begin this process until the university senate had approved the undergraduate learning outcomes statement shepherded by the Toga Team through the faculty governance structure. College of Arts and Science faculty familiar with the goals of curriculum mapping (most of whom also appreciated the value of the Undergraduate Learning Outcomes) have expressed quiet support for the process. However, their voices are sometimes drowned out by a few colleagues who complain that curriculum mapping is a waste of time, an unwelcome incursion into "our" territory by what they see as K–12 style bureaucracy, or even, in a few cases, as a violation of their academic freedom. These responses cast college administrators as bureaucratic functionaries who do not respect faculty time or expertise; distributing responsibility among departmental coordinators (who, in most cases, do not have official administrative duties in their programs) creates a buffer between faculty and the dean's office. Faculty vent their annoyance to their departmental coordinators, who then vent to the associate dean; both complaints and suggestions for improving the process find their way to the dean's office, and the work gets done.

Convinced that curriculum mapping is a worthwhile tool for curricular reflection and planning—one that addresses the legitimate concerns of students, parents, accreditors, and public policymakers—we consistently display our enthusiasm for the process, an expedient that, in spite of the buffer provided by the departmental coordinators, still draws on our social and political capital. Three tactics have so far proven useful. First, we emphasize the concrete, short-term benefits of curriculum mapping: the process will show individual teachers how their courses fit into the overall education of our undergraduates, and will help departments generate assessment activities that respond directly to what faculty learn from their programs' curriculum maps. Department chairs, in particular, appreciate these benefits. Second, as a way of supporting the efforts of departmental mapping coordinators to educate and lead their colleagues, we supplement face-to-face explanations of curriculum mapping with short, upbeat, carefully written handouts that reiterate both the "whys" and the "hows" of the process. We circulate these talking points at every meeting where curriculum mapping might come up, and attach them to our responses to faculty or administrator emails. Every handout includes a small graphic—in one case, a map of the world drawn by Korean sailors in the 1700s—intended to generate creative, curious responses to the process we are asking colleagues to join. Conversations with colleagues in marketing have taught us the value of "brand management": participants who notice such images, intentionally or not, may be more likely to identify positively with the process when they see the images again.

Because almost every Q&A session about curriculum mapping elicits unhappiness from a few colleagues, however, we sometimes invoke the "bad cops" in the provost's office, who, responsible for satisfying the mandates of our accreditation agency, will take control of curriculum mapping if we are too slow. This tactic, number three, momentarily disarms critics within Arts and Sciences, but we prefer to avoid it. "Bad cop" rhetoric works only where, as Gano-Phillips and Barnett write about the prereform environment at the University of Michigan–Flint, "disengagement and apathy ha[ve] . . . embedded themselves in our cultural identity" (2008, 38). Our belief in our colleagues' abilities to lead and co-create change makes optimistic, transformative rhetorics much more attractive. (One other reason to avoid "bad cop" rhetoric: our earliest experiences with general education reform taught us that, even where the stakes are high, top administrators may not wish—or may not know how—to appropriately "own" and to "aim" their power. As we have shown, though, we can use ours.)

Lessons Learned
in Transforming General Education

At the University of Michigan–Flint, Gano-Phillips and Barnett's team decided to "guide the *how* of reform and leave the *what* to the rest of the campus" (2008, 38). Before we ever attended the AAC&U Institute on General Education, we watched Roosevelt faculty subtly sabotage peremptory curricular changes (like January-term courses and one-credit sophomore seminars) because the provost did not "go through channels"—in other words, because top administrators never formally conferred with faculty or polled students about the feasibility of their initiatives. After initially accepting the support of our administrative sponsors, the Toga Team quickly learned, over the period of a pothole-filled semester, not to bypass collegial mechanisms already in place for creating curricular change. Since the dissolution of the team, we have come to appreciate how a university's constitutionally-based processes can work very well—*if* change is urgently desired, and the organizers leading transformation know how to "work" institutional governance structures and parliamentary procedure. Both within the College of Arts and Sciences and in the university more generally, Roosevelt's reform process has been discursive and dialogic, in keeping with our identity as a (relatively) democratic, deliberative, and, yes, proudly political faculty body. The culture of Roosevelt includes high esteem for and engagement with our students, an historic social justice mission that is increasingly tangible in the Chicago community, and a sometimes rough-and-tumble tradition of shared governance. In the presence of flexible, imaginative leadership, our academic subcultures reveal themselves to be more cooperative than conflictual.

Franklin Roosevelt is widely quoted as having said that "There are many ways of going forward, but only one way of standing still," while Eleanor Roosevelt once advised other progress-minded people to "have convictions. Be friendly. Stick to your beliefs as they stick to theirs. Work as hard as they do." At a school that derives strength from the Roosevelts' political legacies, we now know that (with all respect to FDR), there are actually many ways of standing still. We have practiced most of them. Through our ongoing experiences with general education reform, we have also learned how to be friendly, principled, hardworking leaders and politicians: the kinds of advocates our students—and our colleagues—deserve.

References

Alinsky, S. 1971. *Rules for radicals*. New York: Vintage.

Brody, H. 1992. The social power of expert healers. In *Literacies: Reading, writing, interpretation*, edited by T. Brunk, S. Diamond, P. Perkins, and K. Smith (2nd ed., 107–125). New York: W.W. Norton.

Burns, J. M. 1978. *Leadership*. New York. Harper & Row.

Donahue, T. J. 2008, December 10. *Research note: 43 ½ conceptions of politics*. Available at SSRN (Social Science Research Network): http://ssrn.com/abstract= 1151265.

Freire, P. 1970. *Pedagogy of the oppressed*. New York: Continuum.

Gaff, J. G. 1980. Avoiding the potholes: Strategies for reforming general education. *Educational Record* 61(4): 50–59.

Gano Phillips, S., and R. W. Barnett. 2008. Against all odds: Transforming institutional culture. *Liberal Education*, 94(2): 36–41.

Reese, T. R. 1995. Mapping interdisciplinarity. *Art Bulletin* 77(4): 544–549.

Roosevelt University. 2006. *Strategic plan*. Retrieved December 15, 2008, from http://www.roosevelt.edu/strategicplan/goalsandobjectives.htm.

Sondheim, S. 1962. *A funny thing happened on the way to the forum*. Retrieved February 14, 2009, from http://www.sondheimguide.com/forum.html#BWP.

Sondheim, S. 1992. Comedy tonight. In *All Sondheim, Vol. 1*. New York: Revelation Music/ Rilting Music.

Tichy, N. M., and M. A. Devanna. 1986. *The transformational leader*. New York: John Wiley & Sons.

CHAPTER 3

Change *and* Curricular Physics

LEADERSHIP in the PROCESS
of REFORMING GENERAL EDUCATION

by Christopher Dennis, Terry Halbert,
and Julie Phillips

Accomplishing well-designed, curricular change on a wide scale is fa-
mously fraught, and among the most difficult kinds of institutional change
colleges and universities may attempt. General education reform may be
the most difficult of all curricular change; in so many ways, general education defines an institution's decisions about what its students most need to
know, how introductions to the most important fields of knowledge should
be shaped, and how much curricular time should be devoted to fostering
key competencies. The attempt to develop or change these crucial institutional decisions activates powerful forces of faculty, departmental, disciplinary, and administrative prerogatives. Little wonder that starting—
overcoming these intense inertial forces—can be so challenging, or that
finishing can seem a kind of institutional fantasy.

In mapping the currents of curricular change, few factors are more
telling than the styles of leadership—at all levels—how they engage dynamics of faculty and collegial governance, and define or reshape the processes of planning and decision-making. When leaders change, not only at
the presidential or provostial level, but at the committee level, there is both
risk of loss of momentum, perhaps as radical as an abandoning, rethinking,
or restarting of the curricular reform effort itself—and, perhaps surprisingly to those most involved, opportunities for significant breakthroughs
to the existing process that enable or hasten forward progress. In this
chapter, we describe how the process of general education reform at a
large, urban public institution began as a formally negotiated, even

scripted, process—and was significantly modified when several years into the effort, a new president, provost, and several new general education committee members modified the ongoing approach to reform.

In the previous chapter, Burney and Perkins describe a model of curricular change that, from the faculty committee point of view, reflects an increasingly decentralized, distributed pattern of leadership, ad hoc and tactically committed to extensive dialogue and full faculty engagement. By contrast, the evolving institutional process described here traces an arc from an almost legislative, statutory beginning, including a formal Faculty Senate resolution slightly modifying and adopting a presidential document, codifying and defining general education curricular parameters and governance, very much top down, to a more flexible and collaborative set of decision-making practices, adapted from the former model.

Over six years in the making, the creation, evolution, and sheer scope of implementation of Temple University's general education program also offers a story of institutional dynamics, of leadership challenges and setbacks, and of object lessons in creating a program, a governance structure, and a set of courses reflecting twenty-first century knowledge and pedagogy in the university's national and international urban settings. The play and interplay of divergent leadership styles and the evolution of implementation strategies as they encounter and negotiate curricular and other dynamics are crucial factors in the account. No leadership or leadership style operates in a vacuum. Leaders encounter existing university cultural habits and dynamics, and some key terms from physics (inertia, entropy, supernova, and enthalpy), which we use in our exposition, offer analogies and terms for helping define institutional motion and change—and the forces and processes that shape efforts to reform a general education curriculum.

Entropy: A Brief History
of the Former Core Curriculum

Temple's predecessor to the new general education program was the "core curriculum." The core, in use since the late 1980s and reformed in the early 1990s, included a signature "intellectual heritage" course, a required two-semester humanities sequence for all undergraduates. What were the dynamics that shaped the old core and necessitated a new general education program? As is typical of an older general education program, the gravitational pull of the majors resulted in a core that over the years evolved from a more focused set of distributional courses, introducing general categories of knowledge (such as American culture, the individual and society, quantitative reasoning, studies in race, and intellectual heritage) with specific intellectual and pedagogical criteria, to a less focused set of courses that proliferated and became largely introductions to the major. At its height, a student could fulfill core requirements by selecting from among over four hundred courses and could double count core courses for their requirements in the major:

> The breadth requirements are also attractive because their stated purpose is to examine broad areas of knowledge rather than academic specialties. Despite this purpose, it does appear that over time many of the courses in core areas have come to be introductory courses or survey courses in specific disciplines, rather than courses designed to provide a broad introductions to knowledge, concepts, and epistemology in fields of knowledge. All these tendencies are common in core and general education programs as they age. Renewal and revision of these programs, therefore, are essential. (Adamany 2001)

By 2002, there was general agreement across the university that Temple's core curriculum had become overgrown and incoherent. Faculty had difficulty reaching agreement, however, on how the core might be changed. While many recognized emerging interdisciplinary trends in research and teaching, and there was a growing interest in experiential and collaborative pedagogies, entrenched turf interests played themselves out in lengthy, unwieldy discussions—and attempts at creating a broadly accepted, comprehensive plan foundered. Recognizing the slowness of the process, Temple's then-president, David Adamany, assumed a major role in defining what became Temple's general education program. He announced that he would still welcome a faculty plan, if one could be agreed upon, but would be presenting a general education plan, in any event, to the board of trustees at the end of 2004.

Under the pressure of that deadline, the first general education plan, slightly modified and endorsed at the eleventh hour by the Faculty Senate, was passed by the board of trustees in December, 2004 (Temple University 2004). The plan, understood to be largely written by the president, was a "top-down" model, highly centralized and standardized. It outlined program objectives and defined nine program areas. It specified limits to the number of courses that could exist within each of those areas (five recommended; eight maximum). Given the size of the undergraduate population at Temple University, this meant that general education courses would have to be offered in multiple sections; for multiple sections the founding document mandated common syllabi with common readings, and common final exams.

Supernova: The Development and Evolution of General Education Planning During Significant Change in University Leadership

The 2004 document took pains to create a general education program that was set against the gravitational pull of the majors that had captured the core, repeatedly describing general education as a "separate program of courses within the university," mandating repeatedly that "general education courses may not be introductory courses to specific majors," and specifying more than once that general education courses were to be listed in a separate section of the university bulletin. Additionally, the document required students to complete all of their general education courses within their first 62 credit hours, further emphasizing a separation between the program and the rest of the undergraduate experience within the majors. In these and other ways, the initial general education document was rich with specific instructions.

The document established a single governing body, the General Education Executive Committee (with the now affectionately accepted acronym, "GEEC") chaired by the vice provost for undergraduate studies, composed of nine faculty from across the university and three students. GEEC would have broad oversight responsibility, and would evaluate new courses, review approved courses after five years, and nominate to the provost "area coordinators." Faculty area coordinators would carry multiple responsibilities, working to develop appropriate courses and to "monitor and evaluate" them once they were being taught.

The original document stated that the university should endeavor to provide "substantial resources" for general education, specifying that they be targeted for course development, for release time or stipends for faculty serving as directors, area coordinators, or course developers, for "the evaluation of the effectiveness of courses and the program," and for "innovative course materials that may be necessary from time to time" (Temple University 2004).

The founding document was primarily concerned with creating a set of coherent, consistent learning experiences for students. It prioritized basic skills development: " (1) analytical reading and interpretation of texts, well organized and analytical writing, and identification and evaluation of information, and (2) quantitative thinking and reasoning"; and emphasized an approach that would "introduce students to the intellectual paradigms and ways of discovering and affirming knowledge in the broad fields of contemporary life" (Temple University 2004). The original vision embraced interdisciplinary approaches, to the extent possible, and called for general education courses to be taught, again, to the extent possible, by tenured professors.

The president and provost asked the vice provost for undergraduate studies to chair the duly constituted GEEC and lead the implementation effort. That effort was largely shaped by the general education document, which itself became an instrument of authority, because it had been (barely) approved by the Faculty Senate, the president, and the board of trustees, and outlined much like a constitution, the governance structure, parameters and limits, and even the time frame for implementing the new program. The administrative staff would keep the implementation plan on schedule, and the faculty members of the university-wide GEEC were to make the curricular decisions, applying and interpreting the rules of the document—and approving new general education courses on behalf of their collegial constituents, along the model of a college curriculum committee.

In May 2005, at the direction of the vice provost for undergraduate studies, a Temple team of faculty and staff, constituting the vanguard of the GEEC implementation team, a team in need of a crash course on getting a new general education program up and running, attended the AAC&U Institute on General Education. While most participating institutional teams faced the daunting task of how to begin or how to accelerate progress, the Temple team was faced with the opposite dilemma: crafting a detailed implementation plan based on a fixed, board-approved document that would need to deliver a new general education program for 4,000 students by fall 2007. Dozens of new general education courses would need to be created and loaded into the university's registration system in the fall 2006, little more than a year away. An AAC&U consultant understatedly characterized the plan as "somewhat over-determined" and predicted (accurately) that the main challenge would be securing faculty buy-in and engaging constituents on a broad scale. For better and for worse, the university had overcome the inertia of beginning general education reform by being shot out of a cannon.

GEEC members faced the difficult task of distilling a "Request for Course Proposals" from the founding document. The mission statement they produced encapsulates much of what Temple faculty had expressed in their earlier efforts to revise the core:

> In the 1980's, when the core was under construction, our debate was primarily about content—what belonged in the "common body of knowledge" that every Temple student should be exposed to; how exactly to define the "cultural capital" which every Temple student would need. Since then, much has changed. Technology has vastly accelerated the rate at which information is created and accessed. What there is to know is increasingly complex and beyond any person's capacity to contain it all. Our students need the ability to make sense of the blizzard of information that confronts them. They need the ability to see how information is linked, how pieces of seemingly disparate information are interrelated. Where the Core was focused on content, general education is focused on making connections.
>
> We can do this in a variety of ways. We can draw connections across disciplinary boundaries. We can draw connections between disciplinary knowledge and current controversies. We can draw connections from theory to experience. These and other modes of stretching and contextualizing traditional disciplinary content will prepare our students to deal with a rapidly globalizing world, in which the resolution of complicated issues increasingly calls upon the ability to see a problem from many angles, and to synthesize divergent perspectives.
>
> Ultimately, general education is about equipping our students to make connections between what they learn, their lives, and their communities. It aims to produce engaged citizens, capable of participating fully in a richly diverse world. (Temple University, 2005; revised 2007; Request for Proposal)

The administration faced a simple imperative: general education had been passed by Temple's board of trustees, and with an aggressive timetable—the official start date was fall 2007. The president and central administrators made the rounds of the schools and colleges with the message that general education was imminent and that the flow of resources—from credit hours generated to budget lines for Teaching Assistants (TAs)—would depend to a large extent on participation in the new program. Word went out that, although the general education program would not become a separate college, it would behave as one, with control not only over general education course approval, but over staffing, scheduling, and all the administrative details that were normally handled within departments and colleges. Credit hours would flow first, it was initially understood, to general education as a virtual entity—known as "College 65" (so named from the coding the new entity would have in the Student Information System)—and from there to the appropriate academic units. This new structure was intended to produce definitive change. In the curricular physics of the old core course system, enrollments tended to be driven by requirements in the major, rather than by (or chiefly by) consistently compelling instruction and content. Now with students able to choose courses independent of their connection with an intended major, it was thought that enrollments would move in a free market manner to schools and colleges creating attractive general education courses. College 65 would facilitate this.

Resistance and Reaction

In the fall of 2005, a sense of foreboding hung over the general education enterprise. Many faculty and second and third tier administrators had profound concerns. It was felt in some quarters that the president had manipulated the faculty in the first place, claiming they had timed out their chance to rethink the core, and had imposed a document with (no doubt) admirably stated goals that were impossible to implement without straitjacketing faculty and students. Since the founding document limited the total number of possible general education courses, each general education course would have to serve hundreds of students in multiple sections. It was thought that faculty—particularly tenured faculty—would not want to teach in the program, or would quickly lose enthusiasm for doing so. Course categories or areas as described in the document were often confusing. For example, humanists and scholars of global studies felt excluded by a document they felt was overly "Americanized"; studio artists and teachers felt excluded by a document that called for skills development, but also appeared *de facto* to require large lecture courses. General education's pronounced pushback against departmental and collegiate gravitational pull would end course "ownership" as it had been known. Departments and colleges would seemingly no longer be responsible for approving, staffing, and monitoring general education courses that might emanate from their own faculty. Indeed, for nearly two years the route to general education course approval— from faculty in any school or college to area coordinator to GEEC— could entirely circumvent chairs, associate deans, and deans.

Courses were approved for general education without necessarily having been vetted or supported by the schools and colleges. According to many observers, this absence of control over general education courses by those who would be called upon, in the end, to make them work did not bode well for quality of instruction. Some grumbled suspiciously that the underlying motivation for general education reform was to create a few highly standardized, large lecture classes that could be more easily assessed and less expensive to deliver.

There were logistical concerns as well. Many worried that Temple did not have the infrastructure (enough large lecture halls and breakout rooms) to accommodate the initial general education design, which limited the total number of courses in any particular general education topical area. They wondered how the processes associated with Temple's undergraduate programming—course registration procedures, section merging, instructor assignments, adding or dropping courses, handling course evaluations, and so on—could be managed from a relatively small central office. There were concerns that fall 2007 was an unrealistic start-date given the complex implementation issues to be worked out, including policies to be set for transfer students, who make up about 45 percent of Temple's student population. Some used words like "stillborn," or "train wreck" to describe prospects for the new general education program. Faculty and administrative constituencies were engaged, to be sure, but in a resistant way—and there was growing suspicion about the leadership's motives.

Overall, there was confusion regarding resources. While no specific information was proffered, the administration adopted a carrot and stick approach, assuring departments and faculty that resources would be made available to achieve the transition from core to general education, while stating that TAs would be pulled back and re-allocated in response to the new curricular "landscape," a message that sounded threatening to many.

The founding document called for the appointment of a director for general education, a faculty member who, although not a voting member of the GEEC, would somehow lead the program. Understandably, the vice provost had some difficulty finding a faculty member to take this position. In late 2005, however, a professor in the business college agreed to serve. She had little "administrative experience" (and thus little political "baggage"), but with 25 years of experience on the faculty, she was open to experimenting with different teaching models and had developed several interdisciplinary courses.

Accepting the new job with some trepidation, the new director soon felt herself to be "monkey in the middle," between the president's administration, which was moving forward gamely with implementation, and the rest of the university, which was confused at best and more often quite hostile towards general education. It quickly became clear to her that her most important function would be to listen and learn—from both the administration and the faculty. If these were two warring camps, her role might be to simply understand why general education was a battlefield and to try to reengage the constituencies more productively.

In a sense, then, general education leadership was happening on two planes. As the administrator most responsible for the implementation of the program, the vice provost chaired the General Education Executive Committee, where a mission statement was being drafted, policies debated, and course proposals vetted. While she observed all of this hard work, the director was also going about gathering information from a variety of sources outside of the official process. Given her longevity at the university and her "soft" people skills, her networks were wide and deep, and given the fact that general education had been presented in such a way as to up-end the traditional distribution of power and resources at the university, there were very few people who did not want to talk to her. For weeks, the director sounded out deans, chairs, tenured and untenured faculty, adjuncts, the faculty senate president, as well as administrators and staff from a range of functions, including advising, registration, computer systems, student affairs, the teaching and learning center, and the library.

The director felt herself to be the embodiment of the cognitive dissonance that was general education at Temple. She was in both worlds: On the one hand, interdisciplinary course proposals from teams of faculty were being painstakingly reviewed by the GEEC. Meetings could last three hours and took place weekly, with the vice provost leading discussions that were consistently respectful and grounded in a commitment to student learning. On the other hand, the rest of the university was roiling. The director was being told, for instance, that the faculty names on general education course proposals represented a "polite fiction"—that they were listed to lend an interdisciplinary flavor to proposals that were being proffered in order to hold on to or produce supplies of TAs. The director knew that the GEEC members were perceived as well-paid (each received a $10,000 stipend in that first year) shills for an increasingly unpopular president and his increasingly unpopular program. It was a delicate task to lead general education at this stage. While she felt she could not be an outright "cheerleader" for the program under the fraught circumstances, the director tried to cultivate her networks, communicating a willingness to listen and a style of openness. Her instinct was that, for general education reform to have any chance of success, the mass of the faculty who were now so opposed to the program would somehow have to reverse direction, buy in, and re-engage.

In the midst of this difficult situation, a serendipitous event occurred that changed the contours and implementation of general education at Temple University: in January 2006, the president resigned. On July 1, 2006, a new president, Ann Weaver Hart, assumed the leadership of the university.

By January 2007, the president announced her very different approach to general education moving forward: there would be overriding principles of flexibility and partnership across the university; implementation would be collaboratively determined; the time frame and launch of general education would be delayed one year, until fall 2008. Under the new president's leadership, Temple's board of trustees passed an amended general education document which, while cleaving to the interdisciplinary philosophy of the original, allowed all aspects of "implementation" to be crafted by the president, her administration, and by the faculty. That is, the founding document would have a less substantially constitutional status —and changes to the program's parameters and processes could be made in a less constrained way. There were twin leadership signals clearly emanating from this eventuality. The first was that general education would go forward. (For the many who resisted the original plan, there was always hope that general education would simply fall of its own weight; during the months of interregnum this hope gained momentum: would the new president want to continue general education reform?) The second was that the general education program was to be a joint venture, with all the various Temple constituencies involved and invested:

> The success of a university-wide general education program depends on a partnership of faculty, administrators, and students at the department, school/college, and university levels. This partnership includes a balance between trust in the professional judgment of the participants and a willingness to challenge each other to meet the emerging needs of students, disciplines, and the greater society. (Temple University 2007)

Interestingly, President Hart holds a Ph.D. in Educational Leadership, and has published on the topic of organizational change in higher education. The language of her addendum to the new board-approved general education document not only reset the balance of power, calling for a partnership of professionals, but identified students, too, as partners. Casting the entire process in a fresh light, with mention of "the greater society," she placed general education reform in a broader and potentially more meaningful context.

This turn-around in communication from the central administration on general education can be traced to the new president herself, but it did not occur in a vacuum. In large part it occurred because of dozens of informal conversations over several months. The general education director and the faculty senate president had been voted by the faculty to be on the search committee for the new president. As the sole faculty representatives, they participated in intense discussions with a small group of trustees through a search process that went on for several weeks. Their comments about how the faculty felt about leadership style and the need for the university to transition to a president with a more open, consultative approach may have been influential in the search committee's ultimate choice.

President Hart was keenly interested in the general education initiative. The general education director, the faculty senate president, key deans, and other administrators were asked to and did share their thoughts on general education with President Hart even before she arrived at the university in mid-2006. Soon after she arrived, the president had her academic chief of staff, the acting provost, the vice provost, and the general education director revisit the founding general education document and recommend changes. In spite of whatever differences these individuals had over the implementation and organization of general education, they reached consensus relatively quickly, aware of the new president's overall philosophy and of her wish that they produce a revised document that would sit comfortably with her priorities. It was this document that, with slight revisions, became the official presidential addendum.

One important feature of the presidential addendum was language explicitly reasserting the traditional authority of departments, schools, and colleges: "School/college leadership is essential for the success of the general education program. The schools and colleges are in a critical position to address the unique character of the academic programs, while challenging them to strive for higher levels of excellence . . ." and "Under enrollment-based budgeting, credits are distributed to the School and Colleges responsible for the course sections. . . ." Not long after this document became public, the committee members and those working within and outside the general education program came up with a set of recommendations that were put into effect over the summer of 2007. "College 65," as the general education virtual, administrative entity was known, was dissolved, and the schools and colleges resumed responsibility for course and section management and many aspects of implementation planning. Resources in the form of "credit hours generated" would continue to flow directly to the schools and colleges responsible for mounting general education courses, in the traditional way. "In the best tradition of academe, curricular innovation is a prime responsibility of faculty," reads the second guiding principle in the presidential addendum to general education (Temple University 2007; policy 02.10.03, 1). This document—along with the general education program's new, comprehensive communications plan—emphasizing the new spirit of collaboration in meeting after meeting—began to turn the tide of faculty resistance.

President Hart further extended the collaborative and shared responsibility for general education to university administrators and personnel by establishing several new committees, including a Dean's Liaison Committee and the General Education Implementation Group (GIG), consisting of associate deans and advisors from across the university. The General Education Executive Committee and the general education staff were faculty members with little to no knowledge of the university's day-to-day administrative tasks. Now GIG membership, with deep experience of the inner workings of the university, would become a critical, complementary body for GEEC. These new governance structures embodied a broader, more collaborative process to implementing the new program, and improved communications about many practical matters involved in transitioning to the new curriculum.

By the end of the summer of 2007, the GEEC had officially rewritten its Request for Proposals (RFP) for new courses. The document was made more concise. Goal statements were altered to emphasize goals that were prominent in GEEC's discussion of course proposals and consonant with faculty objectives as evidenced by their course proposals to that point; and three key thematic approaches were added to the list of "desirable" course goals. "Thematic courses make it easier to make connections across general education courses," the Presidential addendum stated (Temple University 2007, 3), citing the three themes that GEEC was already considering: sustainability, globalization, and community based learning. From where did the leadership for the emerging focus on thematic connections come? Before the presidential transition, while the GEEC had to concern itself with drafting an RFP and reviewing courses against a (then) tight deadline, and while the faculty director of general education was setting about trying to read the mood of the university at large, in particular the faculty mood, with the goal of developing a modicum of faculty buy-in, she learned through the grapevine that there was an ontological problem: There was little understanding of the underlying reasons for the change from the old core curriculum. Questions that kept popping up were along the lines, "What makes general education distinct from the core? What is the *vision* of general education?"

There were various ways to respond to these questions. One would have been to communicate the new emphasis on innovative pedagogy, and on the development of skills and habits of mind, in contrast to the core, with its strong emphasis on disciplinary-based content. While the director did offer open seminars and visited the schools and colleges with this message, she realized that it was falling flat. People still focused on general education as "an unfunded mandate," and seemed resistant to being told that they might need to learn new ways of doing what they felt themselves quite expert at doing—teaching. What did seem to perk up the faculty ears was mention of specific course ideas. Even some of the new general education course titles (e.g., *Sustainable Design*; *The Jazz Century*; *Food and Eating*; *Disasters: Geology vs. Hollywood*) would spark curiosity. It became clear that the best way to alter perceptions would be to engage faculty over their own creativity in teaching and course design.

Drawing from several informal conversations along these lines in the early months of 2006, the director sensed that the best way to articulate the fundamental difference between the core and general education would be to look at the teaching innovations that had already surfaced and try to express what they might have in common. What they appeared to share was an emphasis on *making connections*. Where the core was a plethora of seemingly unrelated courses, most of them tethered to a discipline, the contextualized, integrative learning of general education might be described as an effort to break out of the disciplinary silos, and even over the wall of the ivory tower itself:

> In a world where no one can hope to know it all, the best way to prepare for the future is to learn how information is linked and interrelated. GenEd is about making connections—connections between academic knowledge and current controversies, connections across different areas of study, and connections between the classroom and the dynamic city of Philadelphia. (Temple University General Education web site: http://www.temple.edu/provost/gened/)

So the vision was connection, and the different ways to make it happen. As the new administration arrived and began to signal opportunities for altering the original document, including adding more courses than were first permitted, the GEEC began to discuss how general education could communicate its vision to both faculty and students. The idea came forward to create themes that would span the entire program, enabling students to make connections by taking thematically-related courses in each area of general education, building their own connective pathways the way faculty do when choosing to attend events along certain tracks at conferences. Based on what GEEC had been noticing in the course review process, and on what the director had been hearing around the university, three themes were identified: Sustainability, Community-Based Learning, and Globalization; along with one special "linking" context—the "Philadelphia Experience."

The Philadelphia context came to mind because so many faculty course proposers had checked the box indicating their courses would make links with "Temple's urban setting." By the summer of 2008, a review of the approved courses revealed that between one third and one half included assignments that would bring students into direct contact with the city or metropolitan region. "The Philadelphia Experience," which seemed to have developed almost organically as a matter of Temple's DNA, caught the attention of the media too. In late 2008, articles highlighting Temple's general education Philadelphia Experience appeared locally (*Philadelphia Inquirer, Philadelphia Metro*) and nationally (*Inside Higher Ed, The Chronicle*).

Leadership through the process of thematic development—and through the many other processes that were being changed at this time—was accomplished in stages, in several different settings, with a light touch, and with more than a modicum of luck. Underlying all of it was a significant shift in the power dynamics of the entire general education effort. Initially, power had been highly centralized. Decisions were understood to be top-down, with a drive towards standardization, codified in the particularities of a board-approved governing document. As the shift occurred, power became diffused, pushed downwards, and spread laterally outwards through all the "capillaries" of the university. More individuals were welcomed to bring their expertise and creativity to the table. Individual talents were brought to bear on problem-solving; specific accomplishments and fresh ideas were highlighted. In this instance, as general education began to develop thematically, this shift was accomplished as a result of convergences. There had been a change at the top, with a new presidential leadership style and understanding. Faculty felt—and were encouraged to feel—that their creativity in course design mattered, and these contributions were highlighted publicly. The absolute cap on the number of new general education courses was first slightly moderated and then relaxed altogether, allowing as a matter of process, more varied course proposals to be considered. At the same time, the director suggested to the GEEC that thematic connections among courses and across the areas of the program would assist students in seeing the connective tissue of their own educational experiences. Over time, all these elements aligned, and a change seemed to come organically, almost as a matter of a Gladwellian "tipping point."

Like the original document, the new president's addendum indicated that a variety of delivery models were acceptable ("General education courses may be taught in large lectures, in small sections, or in large lectures supported by small sections," but unlike the original, the addendum urged deans and GEEC to support a "diversity of modes of instruction . . . to take maximum advantage of the breadth of strengths of Temple's faculty . . . including participation intensive methods," pointing to a need to welcome faculty creativity to general education course development and pedagogy (Temple University 2007; policy 02.10.03, 1). This and other changes —the elimination of the requirement for common exams and of strict quotas on number of courses per area, for example—had the effect of stimulating faculty interest and involvement. The changes in leadership, in the status of the governing document, in the creation of supplementary advisory structures, changes in the timeline, and a persistent communication strategy engendering positive faculty engagement all combined to transform resistance by more carefully balancing change with some deference to existing campus cultural dynamics governing curricular change.

Moreover, a significant culture change was taking place within the GEEC. The group for two years had functioned as the gatekeeper, approving a short list of courses supported by faculty teams, in compliance with the limitations of the original founding document. GEEC realized simultaneously that it would be able to approve many more courses, and that it would need many more course proposals—a range of different types across the entire program. As the months went by, and GEEC looked hard at the numbers, it became clear that the program had approved only about 40 percent of the courses that would have to be on the books for the first entering general education cohort of fall 2008.

Enthalpy: New Structures for Implementing the General Education Program

Physics defines the dissolution of energy in a system as entropy. Entropy's antonym is enthalpy, a measure of energy released to a system, the opposite of dissolution. So by analogy the process of curricular change at Temple accumulated energy. Temple's new provost, Lisa Staiano-Coico, who arrived on campus in July 2007, was quick to signal both her interest in moving forward in the spirit of the new general education, and her concern that the university had plenty of work to do in order to officially launch general education within one short year. She took a number of steps to support the program. In February 2007, general education had hired a part time administrative coordinator, but besides the director—a faculty member on reduced course load—there was no other general education staff. The provost made the director a full time administrator, moved an additional faculty member into position as full time administrator (co-director), and authorized the hire of a full time assistant director. The provost also decided to move the general education program out of the vice provost for undergraduate studies' portfolio, where it had been associated among some faculty with the earlier implementation strategies, and provided the program with its own office space. This enhancement of general education program staffing and the provision of separate space were communicated broadly and became part of the new president's strategy to depict the program as revitalized with the necessary resources to succeed.

In January 2008, the deputy provost and head of the general education Dean's Liaison Committee met with the area coordinators and the GEEC to discuss course review and implementation. The group reached a consensus to expedite the course approval process in response to new factors, including logistical necessity and the need to take advantage of the faculty enthusiasm that was beginning to build. Many new course proposals were beginning to arrive, and area coordinators and the GEEC found themselves hurrying to keep pace. Working hard in subcommittee and plenary, the GEEC approved many more excellent courses.

The new administration provided a revised timeline for implementing general education, and with the fall 2008 deadline approaching, the momentum changed dramatically. The new administrative approach and energy encouraged a flurry of course development activities, but the general education program also needed, increasingly, to work in the pragmatic realm of policy and procedures to assure a successful implementation. Key leadership decisions, made at a high level, enabled the necessary flexibility to approach implementation issues in the transition from the old core to the new general education curriculum, but decision-making necessarily devolved to the committee level as complex questions of policy, procedures, and interpretation required decisions of a finer granularity. Under the pressure of the looming start date, the committee governance structures and functions themselves evolved to create guidelines and enable logistical tasks to be accomplished.

As of 2008, Temple's general education program operated with the support of several of these committees, each with its distinct orientation and its amusing acronym.

- The General Education Executive Committee (GEEC) is composed of nine faculty members from around the university—no more than two from any one school or college—plus three students. GEEC continues to deal with course approvals and policy issues, although this kind of work, so absorbing in the supernova stage, has lightened as assessment has taken center stage. Recently, the GEEC was asked to form subcommittees, one focused on developing a process for peer observation of teaching, one focused on the building of rubrics for the basic general education competencies, and one focused on the selection of winners of the various prizes and opportunities that have been made possible by funding for academic year 2008–2009.

- The General Education Implementation Group (GIG), composed of administrative and advising staff from the various schools and colleges, has also found its work has shifted. During supernova, GIG was grappling with several problems combining policy and logistics in an iterative process with GEEC, recommending rules, systems, and communication mechanisms for the transition from core. At this point the GIG must concentrate more on planning related to the rapid scaling up of the program. General education offered 20,000 seats in fall 2008, half of them to continuing students and half to new students. In fall of 2009, the seat capacity for general education courses needed to expand to accommodate the new incoming class of first-year students. The need for "old" core seats was reduced, and GIG, working closely with the general education office, had to determine how to best estimate and meet anticipated demand, providing general education an appropriate mix of class size—small, medium, and large classes with breakout sections, while keeping a sharp eye on efficiency.

- General Education [Subject] Area Coordinators (GAC) are faculty members. They have been responsible for building the general education course inventory—for bringing innovative, interdisciplinary courses in for GEEC review. They explain to faculty colleagues the philosophy behind general education, encouraging creativity in response to that philosophy, and coaxing (and/or "torturing," as one area coordinator has put it) them into writing proposals linking specific assignments and the learning goals of the new program. At this point, while GAC continues to identify new courses, it is also charged with managing the problem we have euphemistically dubbed "proliferation." During academic year 2007–2008 some fifty general education courses were piloted in small sections. General education had to expand rapidly to provide for its first incoming class in the fall of 2008, and so schools and colleges began offering courses in multiple sections, with untenured or part-time faculty slotted in as instructors of record at the last minute. As we have noted, the core suffered from this kind of proliferation, one result of which was that fewer tenured or tenure track faculty taught core classes. In the general education organizational structure, by contrast, the area coordinators are positioned to provide early warning to GEEC and the general education leadership of potential problems. Tasked with calling meetings for everyone teaching a particular general education course, and with helping the group agree upon the central questions, issues, or themes that define it, they have been privy to some disturbing tales—about heavy teaching loads and increasing class size. The job of the GAC is becoming a matter of providing intelligence to the general education staff. Knowing what is going on "on the ground" is essential, and the starting point for conversations with other stakeholders, as well as for budgetary planning.

The three groups mentioned above, then (GEEC, GIG, and GAC) have three separate and separately valuable functions: roughly speaking, GEEC creates policy, GIG deals with logistical nuts and bolts, and GAC interfaces with the teaching faculty. All three functions are tremendously useful, and through the general education staff, the work of the three groups continues to inform and influence one another.

The president's addendum to the general education founding document created another entity: the Dean's Liaison Committee (DLC). Composed of the deans of the four biggest contributing schools and colleges (liberal arts, science and technology, communication and theater, and business), the DLC has been critically important not so much as a working group, but as a sounding board, an essential check at major developmental points. When the general education committee has needed to request funding, or to agree upon a process for spending funds, the Dean's Liaison Committee has been invaluable. Consensus reached from the grassroots that then receives the imprimatur of this group is more likely to receive favor from upper administration and the board. Indeed, the very existence of the DLC is an important political statement, as general education curricular physics continues to play itself out. In its original form, general education would apparently exist without reference to the traditional power structure of the schools and colleges; general education's regular consultation with the committee of deans sends an entirely different signal.

The leadership and governance style of the general education program office, identified as the directorate of the implementation effort, itself evolved. The GEEC and the general education central staff primarily consisted of former faculty members with little or no knowledge of the university's day-to-day administrative tasks and deadlines. A series of deadlines well known to associate deans and other administrative personnel increasingly set the agenda for general education staff, and the GIG provided critical counsel as deadlines approached for university publications, registration, and admissions.

Balancing Consensus, Collaboration, and Directive Leadership in the Decision-Making Process

Initially, the general education staff attempted to create contexts in the several committees for decision-making in which consensus or democratic process reigned. These conversations often presented GEEC members, for example, with a topic such as the transition from the core to the general education curriculum, where policies and procedures were discussed in sweeping terms. However, the discussion often deteriorated into tangents and side conversations where individual participants sometimes approached the discussion with disciplinary blinders. Indeed, the devil was in the details.

Students were required to complete the new general education courses "successfully." The way success—in the currency of grades and grading standards—came to be defined illustrates the complexity of governance and decision-making and the dynamics between and among various stakeholders as specific policy details were addressed. Some GEEC faculty made decisions based on the grounds of abstract principle. For example, in debating the minimum grade necessary for successful completion of general education requirements, some faculty suggested students achieve a cumulative grade of "C" (2.0) in general education courses. The ensuing debate over the minimum grade for "successful" completion of the general education curriculum serves as a representative example of the convergence of forces confronting the general education program.

To be sure, curricular reform represented a renewed commitment to a common undergraduate experience in the best tradition of liberal education, broadly introducing students to areas of knowledge. General education courses should also provide students sound academic footing for departments to build subject area expertise for their undergraduate majors. When GEEC favored a cumulative "C" average in all 11 general education courses, the council of deans, representing the several schools and colleges, responded negatively. The decision would result in a case whereby a student theoretically could graduate from the university with an "F" in quantitative literacy, an "A" in general education arts, and "C"s in all other general education courses.

Under general education rules, most majors outside of the Colleges of Business, Engineering, Health Professions, and Science and Technology would be required to complete only one quantitative literacy (QL) course. The council of deans understood the QL to be these undergraduates' only exposure to quantitative subject matter, and the majority viewed the possibility of students graduating without a minimum level of proficiency in quantitative literacy with alarm. Likewise, the Boyer College of Music and the Tyler School of Arts found the chance that a student required to complete just one arts course, which the student could theoretically fail and graduate, equally problematic. The deliberations shifted to the renewed commitment to providing a comprehensive common undergraduate experience, and GEEC agreed to require a minimum acceptable grade (C-) in each general education class—rather than a cumulative acceptable grade.

GEEC's reconsideration and accommodation resolved the possibility of mixed messages and inconsistencies around the issue of minimum grading standards. As advising directors made clear to GEEC, three distinct undergraduate populations would be taking classes together—continuing students under old core requirements, incoming transfer students, and incoming first-year students under general education requirements. Absent GEEC's reconsideration, each of these populations would have been covered by different policies. If GEEC's initial recommendation of a C average across all of general education had been adopted, two standards would be in existence for students at Temple: Those students admitted prior to fall 2008 would still be required to earn a C- or better in each course for "successful" completion of individual core courses, while those admitted for fall 2008 and after would not be held to a minimum grade per course — but to a minimum cumulative average. The new policy would have caused confusion among students and university staff, particularly advisors who would be largely responsible for communicating requirements to the various student populations.

The academic concerns expressed by the deans and the pragmatic concerns raised by advising directors also found common ground with a third force acting upon the governing policies and procedures — the limitations of the information systems. When GEEC investigated the technological implications for adopting a cumulative C average across general education, the committee discovered that the policy would be next to impossible to implement in an automated way. The university's degree audit report system (DARS) could not segment and calculate the student's grades on a selection of her or his undergraduate courses. Such calculations would have to be completed manually by an already understaffed advising cadre.

Other personnel intimately knowledgeable about the university's student data, registration, space and scheduling, and course inventory systems also proved critical in establishing or shaping other general education implementation policies, including a student deadline for completing general education courses, limits on the number of courses a student could take from any one department, general education course waivers (particularly for existing science course sequences), and a course-repeat policy. Both the general education program staff and GEEC, with its policy making mandate, made a crucial discovery regarding leadership and governance of the program, namely, the focus on a purely democratic process had to be revisited — and decisions regarding crucial implementation policies and procedures could not be made in the vacuum of a single committee.

The iterative process involved multiple parties and perspectives, but the collaborative leadership model inevitably slowed progress in what was a time-sensitive, increasingly deadline-driven environment. Propelled by looming deadlines, general education administrative staff shifted away from the more democratic or consensus leadership styles to a more consultative role. Thus, a decision-making process emerged where the general education program staff identified knowledge specialists or leaders among the key offices and units affected by the transition from core to general education. In small group discussions, the general education staff queried the specialists who were asked about specific issues related to the implementation of the new general education curriculum. Based on these discussions, the general education program office created written policy recommendations and presented the documents to the GEEC for consideration. With faculty notions of policy (GEEC) engaging administrative knowledge of practicalities (GIG), general education began to make headway on the range of new policies and procedures that would govern general education's implementation.

GEEC might raise concerns about course delivery modes or space needs that would be placed before GIG; GIG might pose questions related to the repeat or minimum grade policies which would be directed to GEEC. Separately, the groups would provide input on the policy recommendations developed by the general education staff. The general education administrative team would then introduce the revised recommendations in successive meetings. With each set of questions that arose, new individuals were consulted (from the registrar's office, computer services, measurement and research, or space management, for example) and asked to join GIG or to serve as advisors on an as-needed basis. GEEC and GIG reviewed the recommendations prior to a GEEC vote. If the vote failed to pass, the iterative process began anew; if the vote succeeded, the recommendations went before the existing Educational Policy and Planning Committee (EPPC) of the Faculty Senate and then to the provost for a final approval.

General education administration mediated the various conversations with GEEC, GIG, and the consultants and developed a useful policies and procedures manual, which attempted to codify the decisions. The work of communicating the decisions about new policies and procedures then took precedence, and the general education office began another round of intensive discussions with the deans, advising units, and key faculty and administrators, hosting an informative briefing for all academic advisors and meeting with stakeholders across the university.

Each of the policy or procedural decisions was predicated upon the mantra "do no harm" to students. Stakeholders analyzed with due concern each policy option's likely impact on students. Many stakeholders were involved in developing the communication strategy for informing students, and that plan involved the multiple university publications (hard copy and electronic), the on-line registration system, the Office of the Registrar, advising offices, targeted emails to students, and multiple university web pages. During the piloting year of general education (academic year 2007–2008), when a subset of general education courses was offered and tested, the *Guide to Registration* contained information about the general education curriculum and invited on-going students to register for general education courses to satisfy the old core requirements. In spring 2008 (the semester prior to the full scale launch of general education), a special guide was created that provided a table of eliminated core courses and those new general education courses that continuing students could use as "core substitutions."

The effective and collaborative communication strategy illustrated the unprecedented support provided to the new program. The general education office, for example, missed the stated deadline for university publications, which was extended an additional 48 to 72 hours to accommodate late-breaking changes and additions necessary to explain the transition from one curriculum to another. The gatekeepers and editors had become valued collaborators and were able to provide critical feedback and valuable suggestions about the crucial effort to inform students in various categories about the curricular and policy changes that were unfolding.

The transition from a singular, committee model of leadership, with up or down votes, to a more broad-ranging, consultative, and iterative mode of decision-making and implementation contributed positively to the general education program's momentum. Groups previously outside of traditional decision-making channels suddenly found themselves at the center of defining and contributing directly to the process of change, which necessarily had to occur at ground level. No doubt, Samuel Johnson's famous maxim, reported by Boswell (1965, 352), that "when a man knows he is to be hanged . . . it concentrates his mind wonderfully," applied in this context—as the implementation date approached. However, the collaborative and iterative decision-making environment allowed for a clear appreciation and understanding of the various stakeholders' knowledge and roles in making general education's timely implementation possible.

Leadership and Campus Culture

The events recounted here trace the development of two divergent leadership styles at the presidential or macro level, where initially a general education program and process was fashioned—in the main—in a top-down approach and evolved under new management to a more flexible and collaborative approach, one that allowed a change in the time frame for implementation. The change in leadership also allowed a rethinking of crucial decisions about, for example, the allowable number of new courses and re-situating general education courses in traditional school and college curricular and financial structures, rather than in a separate entity. Changes in leadership and practical governance tactics at the committee level (GEEC) and in the general education office enabled a sustained culture of engagement with faculty and administrative constituencies that accommodated existing cultural dynamics, especially by negotiating de facto power sharing between the central GEEC, which approves courses and policies, and the schools, colleges, and departments, whose concerns about class sizes, TAs, and resources initially impeded widespread support for the general education reform.

Students from some colleges were granted general education waivers (in math, sciences, and the arts, for example) that allowed traditional course sequences in those schools and colleges to be maintained. This accommodation, specifically restricted in the initial governing document, resulted from the strong gravitational pull of the majors in curricular matters, yet a balance was achieved in that new general education courses were created in a way that has largely refreshed the curriculum and enabled new thematic and interdisciplinary approaches to flourish. Unlike the old core curriculum, there are limits on how many courses from a particular department students may use in fulfilling general education requirements and on "double counting" courses for general education and for the major. This fact will inevitably give general education courses in the various areas a greater coherence and clearer focus on general education learning goals, which the old core, largely overwhelmed by the individual majors, lacked. The new leadership and the reengagement of many faculty and administrative constituencies afforded a more orderly transition from core to general education. That engagement was enabled by a move, incremental and painstaking, from a democratic or committee-based model of leadership, especially in GEEC—to a more consultative model of leadership over a period of time. The transition is not yet complete—and the implementation was neither effortless nor orderly. The evolution in leadership at the micro level developed with repeated attempts to move affected constituencies toward a consensus, and once it became clear that a consensus could not be achieved on every front, general education administration made informed, executive decisions. With the official launch of general education and despite the widening circle of people consulted in the decision-making process, some informed decisions which aroused little concern or ire at the time, have produced unintended consequences, and will have to be revisited.

The momentum that had been generated around gearing up for a successful launch of the general education program has been diffused somewhat as the real impact of general education on students, the colleges, and participating departments manifests itself. Key questions remain as the GEEC and general education staff turn increasingly to matters of assessment and gauging the success of the new courses. How best can we determine the effects of these significant curricular changes on student learning? Are the general education (and other institutional) governance structures flexible and nimble enough to adjust to changes in the development and organization of knowledge—and to evolving approaches to teaching? What structural solutions might be incorporated to ensure that the program is successful, sustainable, and renewable?

In facing the inevitable challenges that follow implementation of such a huge curricular change, the university can be guided by the current president's most important statement governing change in general education: "Success will depend on a degree of flexibility in the design and implementation of the program. We will adapt our general education policy and practices on the basis of new data. The focus on student needs and student success must be paramount in our considerations" (Temple University 2007, policy 02.10.03, 1). Such a strategic view of what is most important in changing campus culture and curriculum helps position the university for the leadership challenges ahead.

References

Adamany, D. 2001. *The president's self study and agenda.* Philadelphia, PA: Temple University.

Boswell, J. 1965. *The life of Samuel Johnson.* New York: Random House

Moran, C. 2008. At Temple University, the city is the classroom. *The Chronicle of Higher Education* 55(14): 1, A20.

Temple University. General Education Executive Committee. (n.d.). *Request for proposal: New GenEd course.* Retrieved December 1, 2008, from Temple University general education web site: http://www.temple.edu/provost/gened/

Temple University. Board of Trustees. 2004. *Board of trustees policies and procedure manual. General education curriculum* (policy no. 02.10.02; amended 6/22/06, 10/10/2006, 06/21/2007). Retrieved December 1, 2008, from http://policies.temple.edu/getdoc. asp?policy_no=02.10.02

Temple University. Board of Trustees. 2007. *Board of trustees policies and procedures manual. General education curriculum: Guidelines for implementation* (policy no. 02.10.03). Retrieved December 1, 2008, from http://policies.temple.edu/getdoc. asp?policy_no=02.10.03

CHAPTER 4

Using a Timeline

SHORTENING the CURRICULAR REFORM PROCESS

by David Brailow *and* Dedaimia S. Whitney

With 20/20 hindsight, almost anything can be made to look logical and well reasoned. . . . But there were countless times when this process felt anything but logical and reasonable. We produced some interesting changes, but not everyone is a fan of the new curriculum. How can I explain what happened in a way that does justice to the complexities of the process, but is also sufficiently understandable to guide others who want to build on our results? (Thomas Moore, quoted in Zolner 2007, 1)

Franklin College is now in the final phase of a five-year curriculum reform, a process that employed the efforts of several incarnations of its change committee (referred to as the "task force" in this document) and two different kinds of timelines. Franklin began its curriculum reform effort with an ambitious and optimistic timeline; two years into the process, however, we realized that the divisions in our community were going to prevent us from agreeing on a new curriculum. The leadership was wise enough to see that drastic measures—including a change in the timeline—were required if a new program was going to be adopted.

Written by the vice-president for academic affairs and the chair of the task force(s), this chapter explores the reasons—perhaps not yet fully known—why the first timeline led the campus off track while the second one led to success. We also explain why we think it is so important to use a timeline to guide a curricular reform process. We argue that the effectiveness of a timeline in a curriculum reform process depends on three factors:

(1) an understanding of the campus culture, particularly its readiness for change; (2) the willingness of the leadership to share important decision-making power; and (3) the ability to change direction if the process appears to be headed toward quicksand.

First, some definitions. We use the word "timeline" to refer to a set of clearly defined intermediate steps that must be accomplished to achieve a larger goal, accompanied by a (hopefully realistic) estimate of how much time it will take to be completed. "Completion" in this context means not only getting the paperwork done, but also gaining broad faculty approval. The two timelines we present in this chapter were informal in the sense that they set out major milestones in broad strokes; they functioned largely as guidelines for the task force and the dean, and in some sense were constructed after the fact. What we refer to as the "one-year timetable," on the other hand, represents only a single year out of the five-year process. This timetable was a one-year schedule for the actual writing and choosing of a new curriculum. In contrast to the broad timelines, which were never expressly endorsed by the faculty, the one-year timetable was carefully constructed, given a first and second reading, and formally approved by faculty vote.

Begin at the Beginning

How long the curricular reform process will take any particular campus depends on the starting point. Institutions behave much like individual students in this respect: A well-prepared math student can take calculus in the freshman year and do well. A poorly prepared student may need to take pre-calculus or even basic algebra before he or she can succeed in the course. Likewise, a faculty that is ready for change and knows where it stands on most of the important curricular matters can construct a timeline that will march everyone efficiently toward their final goal. A faculty that is not yet convinced that a change is necessary, or is seriously divided over basic curricular issues will, we believe, have to make space in the timeline for discussion and consensus-building. The first step in a successful curriculum reform process is to find out whether a change is really needed, usually by taking a critical look at the existing program.

First Step: Assess the Old Program

The reassessment that led to our reform was part of the "pre-process," that is, the time before we had decided to change the curriculum (see Figure 1).

2001–2002	• Franklin hires a new academic dean, experienced in curriculum change. • College is engaged in evaluating all of its academic programs for the ten-year reaccreditation visit by North Central Association. • First team goes to AAC&U conference on general education.
2002–2003	• Self-study documents assembled for external review team. • External reviewers recommend major reform. • Assessment of the general education program begins.

FIGURE 1. The "pre-process" timeline

In 2001, when the college hired its current dean, it was already engaged in writing a self-study for its 10-year reaccreditation by the North Central Association (NCA). As part of the reaccreditation process, the college had conducted a cycle of program reviews to get assessment data for the self-study document. By the time the self-study was due, however, the review of the general education program had not been done.

Franklin's 25-year-old general education program, generally agreed to be solid and well developed, had become departmentalized and no longer belonged to the faculty as a whole. Adjunct faculty were teaching many of the first-year general education courses, a factor some suspected might be contributing to the college's relatively weak retention of first-year students. Most students and faculty regarded the general education program as a set of hurdles to jump, rather than a program essential to the learning process. There was no coordinator of general education and no independent budget. A faculty committee made up of representatives from the various departments that delivered individual courses made a few centralized decisions for the program, but individual departments were forced to provide staffing and budget for the program, a system that resulted in long-standing inequities in time, energy, and money—and resentment among various factions of the faculty.

Several years before coming to Franklin, the dean had chaired a faculty committee that developed a pilot program for a new general education curriculum, one that ultimately had not been successful. The experience had value for Franklin because, through that process the dean had become acquainted with national trends in general education, and was introduced to Professor Jerry Gaff and his work for the Association of American Colleges and Universities (AAC&U), (Gaff 1980). To prepare the college for the general education program review, the dean sent a team of faculty members to the AAC&U Institute on General Education in the summer of 2002, hoping that through their exposure to national trends they would bring a larger context to the review. The Franklin team included several faculty members from the General Education Council, the group charged with writing the program review statement. When it returned, the team reported that while Franklin's existing program was no longer cutting-edge, it had attracted a lot of attention from other participating institutions because of its long history and the intentionality behind the "student learning plan," a document that articulated how each general education course helped the program achieve its goals (see Appendix A).

Franklin's first AAC&U team created the preconditions for a change timeline in the sense that a small cohort of faculty returned with ideas about what a new program might look like. At the same time, however, it also created the preconditions for resistance to change: The Franklin team, representing a general education program nearly 25-years-old, had been thrown together with teams from institutions that were just beginning to think about their general education programs. One of the responses to reports from the first AAC&U conference was, "Hey, we're not doing so badly after all! What's the rush?"As we have said, one of the first steps in any successful timeline is summoning a campus-wide belief that change is both necessary and urgent, a belief that would take more time to coalesce at Franklin because of the history of the old program. The general education program review was scheduled to begin in 2002–2003, the year after the accreditation process had been finished. Missing the deadline for the reaccreditation process created the opportunity to conduct a thorough and intentional review of what was literally 30% of the college curriculum and rethink the whole "general education" idea at a deep and fundamental level. In hindsight, we now realize that our timeline really began at this point, even though ideas of serious reform manifested only as griping at faculty lunch tables and a twinkle in the dean's eye. Given our experience, we believe that any campus considering a major revision to its general education program should begin with assessment of its existing program and the campus culture surrounding it. The results of this assessment may indicate one of several things: the current program is solid and only needs minor tweaking; or, as happened at Franklin, the curriculum is in need of a major overhaul. Assessment not only helps identify the specific problem areas in a curriculum, but (General Education Councilor leaders with their eyes open) it may also reveal differences in opinion that could prove to be obstacles to progress later in the timeline.

Our recommendation is that if a college is planning to include program review as part of their curricular reform process, they should set aside at least a year or more, unless ongoing and comprehensive program assessment is already part of their institutional culture. At Franklin, just collecting institutional data and writing the self-study took the better part of a year (2002–2003). When it was finished, the self-study report was given to a review team composed of an "internal reviewer"—a faculty member outside of the general education program—and an "external reviewer"—Professor Jerry Gaff of the AAC&U. The review team conducted individual interviews, focus groups, and open meetings during the site visit in the fall of 2003–2004 (see Figure 2).

Despite evident differences in opinion among the faculty who participated in the discussions, both reviewers called for reform. The self-study had pointed to several issues needing attention: the rigidity of the program's structure, the over-reliance on adjunct faculty, inconsistency among course sections, and the need for better assessment and greater accountability. Gaff's report identified a number of additional problems with the program: it had grown too large (50 hours of course work for students without placement credit), too few departments contributed teaching faculty to the program, most students and many new faculty did not generally understand the purpose of the program, and the program was no longer an asset to recruitment and retention. Gaff's conclusion was unequivocal: Franklin College should "take a fresh look at its curriculum and devise a more distinctive program that could become the centerpiece of the education of all students and a 'signature program' for the College" (Gaff 2003, 1). The internal reviewer articulated a vision that, had we realized it at the time, signaled the need to build consensus first:

> I'd like to see . . . the owners of the FC [Franklin College] curriculum step outside of the comfortable confines of 'the way we've always done things' and meaningfully engage one another in a serious consideration of what might be learned and applied from the GE self-study and external review. . . . [I'd like to see] my talented colleagues focused as a community on what it means for *us* to say that we are a liberal arts institution and how our GE program might be improved to more authentically embody that meaning. . . . faculty from all departments [should be] clamoring

2003-2004	• External review team visits; reviewers recommend a full-scale reform. • Task force appointed to study the literature and some appropriate models of general education. • Task force gathers faculty input on the strengths and weaknesses of the current program and their desires for the revised one. • Task force begins to articulate the objectives for the program, building on the existing student learning plan.
2004-2005	• Task force develops a curricular plan, incorporating the information and ideas obtained during the previous year. • Faculty approves the plan in the late spring.
2005-2006	• Faculty designs and approves the courses, "fleshing out" the approved plan. • Admissions and marketing begin promoting the new curriculum.
2006-2007	• First year courses implemented.
2007-2009	• Remaining courses implemented.

FIGURE 2. First timeline

for the opportunity to teach in a vital, enriching GE program . . . that could shine through in our marketing, institutional advancement, and recruitment efforts. (Garner 2003)

The two reviewers' recommendations persuaded the dean's faculty advisory committee to endorse the idea of appointing a task force to investigate the possibilities for revision or reform. We should say at this point that the faculty as a whole was not convinced that the old program had to change; the groundwork to execute our timeline had not been laid.

Second Step: Build Consensus

Finding consensus among as diverse and independent a group as a faculty is not a simple, one-step process, but rather a multi-layered effort. Franklin did not yet fully appreciate the significance of several signs along the way pointing to the fact that widespread agreement was going to be difficult to achieve. To lead the task force, the dean appointed the chair of the GEC, who had written the bulk of the program review self-study and who had expressed a continuing interest in reform. The chair brought with her many years experience in the cooperative movement of the 1960s and 1970s and asked for several conditions before accepting the job: that the process be completely open, that it be as inclusive as possible, and that all decisions be made with the broadest possible input and support. The dean readily agreed and appointed a group of faculty, staff, and students to the newly named Liberal Arts Task Force.

It is difficult to overestimate the importance of the choice of a "cooperative" leadership style. Timelines only work when people are agreed about where they want to go. Discussions sponsored by Franklin's leadership program had made the faculty aware that leadership style is a matter of choice. Unfortunately, in the several decades prior to the general education reform process, many faculty felt that too many past decisions had been made at the highest levels (the dean, the president, the board of trustees), and that faculty approval was sometimes little more than a rubber stamp. At one point during the site visit, for instance, a faculty member commented that, even if they wanted to, the faculty was powerless to effect change at the institutional level. This comment revealed the feeling among many faculty that they had been disenfranchised by past years' decision-making processes and were suspicious of initiatives from the administration, fearing that yet again new programs would be "done deals" by the time they reached the faculty. When the task force announced that it would use a "cooperative" leadership style, the faculty was unimpressed. The so-called "timeline" was received with the same dubious lack of interest as were many other administrative announcements at the time.

The cooperative impulse informed the composition of the first task force and, we think, may have helped persuade onlookers that the leadership really *was* interested in hearing everyone's point of view. While not specifically representative, the initial 12-person committee included faculty from math and natural sciences, modern languages, history, sociology, physical education, and English, as well as two students, the director of admissions, and the dean himself (ex officio). Task force members were chosen primarily because of their perceived ability to contribute to an honest conversation about the general education curriculum, but the assembled group included some older faculty, some newer, some interested in change, others not. Defenders of the status quo were deliberately included in the committee to ensure a breadth of opinion. Especially at this delicate beginning, neither the dean nor the task force chair wanted to give the faculty the impression that a bunch of radical reformers were going to run away with the curriculum.

Seek Input from the Community

The original timeline called for an "information" phase, when the task force would gather input from the entire faculty and investigate models of general education. After that, so the thinking went, it would develop a set of goals and then develop a curricular model that the faculty would endorse. The dean's advisory committee had mandated that the first priority of the task force be to write a new student learning plan, a directive that clearly reflected their constituents' loyalty to the old program and a response to the report from the first AAC&U team. The advisory committee wanted the new program to preserve the "intentionality" of Franklin's old one. As it turned out, although the instinct to identify the goals of the new program first was a good one, ultimately the task force found that without a new program in place, it was unrealistic to write a student learning plan as detailed and course-specific as the original. Some might argue that the time spent on this early project was wasted, but the process did clarify the faculty's goals for the general education program.

The task force spent the spring semester of the first year of the original timeline, academic year 2003–2004, conducting one-on-one, face-to-face interviews with the faculty and staff, including long-term adjuncts and senior administrators. Once the interviews were complete, the task force collated the results and presented its results to the faculty in the form of a new mission statement and a set of top-level goals. At that point, the dean's advisory committee agreed with the task force that writing a more detailed version of the student learning plan would have to wait until a new curriculum had actually been put in place. Meanwhile, the task force proposed that it spend the remainder of the year investigating the kinds of programs in place in peer and aspiration institutions, particularly in four-year liberal arts colleges like Franklin. The task force shared the results of this research with the faculty at the May faculty meeting and recommended that it spend the following year developing "curricular models" that could be tailored to the goals expressed in their interviews.

The Beginning of the End of the First Timeline

At the beginning of academic year 2004–2005, we seemed to be on track with our original timeline. We did not anticipate the long-term implications of the survey of faculty and staff, however, which had exposed a wide chasm in opinion within the community. Most significant was the divergence of opinions about *what kind* of courses should make up the general education program. About half of the faculty was interested in topics courses that would "wake up" the students intellectually. The other half insisted that the core courses should be "basic skills" courses that would get the students ready for upper-division courses in their majors. Underlying the whole debate were the questions of who Franklin College students were and who they should be. Faculty frustration sometimes took the form of "blaming the students" for their inability to perform to standards. These faculty felt that the purpose of the general education program was to "fix" the students—that is, whip them into shape—before they declared their majors. Others regarded students as learners in various stages of development, many admittedly underprepared for college work, who needed the faculty to engage them and show them how to grow. What the face-to-face interviews revealed, then, was that the faculty was split over some of the most fundamental issues in education.

In an attempt to resolve some of these issues, the task force sponsored a series of monthly discussions, beginning with a half-day workshop at the opening faculty meeting. This initial forum yielded a number of common threads: a majority of the faculty wanted the new program to be smaller and more flexible, interdisciplinary, thematic, and integrated. A significant subset of the faculty also wanted it to include team-teaching, writing across the curriculum and other basic skills, and a capstone experience. In the original planning of the timeline, we planned to have community-wide general discussions, but at this point, those discussions became absolutely crucial.

In the meantime, the task force divided itself into three groups, each charged with designing a new curriculum, complete with courses that incorporated the goals from the previous year and the ideas that were emerging from faculty discussions and student focus groups. The three curricular models quickly became very different from one another. One was an only slightly changed version of the existing program. While its size was trimmed slightly, it remained skills-driven, developmental, and departmentalized. A second option, called "the seminar model," was composed of topics courses in many disciplines, which were team-taught and driven by student and faculty interest. The third option was a content-driven distribution model that had the feature of centralized oversight, an idea that the faculty quickly absorbed into its thinking and would incorporate into the curricular proposal it ultimately chose.

The three subgroups presented their proposals to the faculty in May 2005 and asked the faculty to indicate their preferences by a survey/ballot.

Despite the fact that the campus-wide interviews had already indicated deep divisions in the community, the results were startling— according to the institutional research officer, a textbook case of "bimodal" polarity. The two programs at the extreme ends of the spectrum—the "no change" program and the controversial "seminar" model—split the votes almost in half. Because of the design of the survey/ballot, the task force also learned that the two main viewpoints were directly opposed to one another and mutually exclusive. The year ended in an impasse. The original timeline was dead.

A New Timeline

At that point, the dean decided to send a second team to the AAC&U Institute on General Education to figure out what to do next. The second AAC&U team included the task force chair, the institutional research officer (the only such individual at the conference), several old members of the task force, and one new member. Almost immediately on arrival, the Franklin team learned that the "get a committee to write a curriculum" approach had caused many a reform effort to end in failure, just as it had at Franklin. In the same series of presentations, however, the task force heard a report from the chief academic officer of Salve Regina University about its unique approach to curriculum reform: Salve Regina's task force had invited each and every faculty member to write a curricular proposal to submit to the faculty, from which the faculty adopted the one that earned the highest number of votes at the end of the year. One key element of this approach was its one-year timetable. The proposals had to be written, circulated, debated, and voted on within a single academic year (Trainor 2004).

After initially rejecting this approach as impractical for its conservative campus, the Franklin team came to regard the Salve Regina approach as its best hope for resolving the stalemate at home. The curriculum selected by the faculty at Salve Regina was apparently operating successfully, so the question of whether the approach would work had at least one answer. The other consideration was the testimony of many schools at the AAC&U conference about having spent literally *decades* on the same curricular reform. The team was certain that the Franklin community did not want to prolong the process for decades. The one-year time limit, initially daunting, became one of the most appealing aspects of the idea.

Upon its return, the task force developed a timetable for the process and asked the faculty to endorse both the Salve Regina approach and the proposed timetable (see Figure 3). Initially the faculty was reluctant to endorse the suggestion and asked for revisions, but after a second reading, they approved the timetable. The most persuasive argument in favor of the timetable was the threat of potentially wasting years and years without results, as had so many other campuses. The deadline for proposals was set as December 1, 2005. The task force facilitated several general faculty discussions and assisted individual proposal writers during the writing period, the three months between September 1 and December 1. The student member of the task force asked if students might submit their own proposal, to which the answer was "yes." One member of the task force withdrew to write his own proposal. The timetable, which at first glance appeared to be a radical idea, for the most part worked smoothly, much to the surprise of both participants and observers.

Salve Regina had reported a last-minute attempt to subvert its reform process, and Franklin experienced its own form of resistance that, curiously, was frequently "parliamentary" in nature. Toward the end of November, several proposal writers asked for an extension of the December 1 deadline. The task force did not see any reason not to give the writers another week or so, but the change of deadline became a saliva-soaked sock in a ferocious tug-of-war over control of the process. Opponents to the one-year timetable—who were generally those most vocally opposed to reform of any kind—claimed that the change of deadline meant that the whole timetable had to be resubmitted to the faculty for approval. The December 13 faculty meeting was tense and fractious; eventually the faculty decided that the task force had acted in good faith and had not broken its covenant with the community. The extended deadline was allowed to stand.

A total of eight proposals were received, including one written by students, and were posted to a universally accessible web site. The college canceled classes and held a retreat one afternoon in February. Each proposal writer presented his or her proposal to the entire group and then retreated to a classroom to answer questions. The faculty rotated through all eight proposal rooms in groups of ten. By the end of the retreat, all of the proposal writers had specific feedback from the faculty, and the faculty better understood the choices they had.

A built-in "revision period" followed the retreat, giving proposal writers the opportunity to change their programs in response to suggestions from the faculty. As a result of the retreat, one proposal was withdrawn, several incorporated ideas from other proposals, and two proposal writers

25	Aug	Faculty meeting: (survey results); (timeline proposal)
	Sep	General discussion of process idea
13	Sep	Faculty meeting: Amend/approve process
	Sep	General discussion
	Oct	General discussion
	Nov	General discussion
1	Dec	Deadline for proposals
13	Dec	Faculty meeting: Formal presentation of proposals (first reading)
	Feb	Half–day retreat: Discussion of proposals
14	Feb	Faculty meeting: Task force presents criteria (first reading)

FIGURE 3. Franklin College: One–year timetable (2005–2006)

joined forces to produce the curriculum that would eventually be chosen by the faculty (see Figure 4). The ideas that seemed to unite most of the faculty were interdisciplinarity, flexibility in scheduling, and topics courses. In the end, there were seven proposals on the ballot, including the student proposal and the old general education program. The winning proposal, written by a professor of history and a professor of math, was titled "Opening a World of Possibilities." While there was significant support for several other proposals on the ballot, especially the option of retaining the old general education program, the voting method had made it possible for a clear winner to emerge. Surprising nearly everyone involved, the college had stayed on track and had written and selected a new curriculum in less than a year.

Implementing the New Program

Implementation of the new curriculum was not part of the one-year "timetable." The implementation period was given a year to complete. At any rate, the dean appointed a new task force to lead the implementation effort (the Liberal Arts Implementation Task Force, or LAITF), led by the chair of the previous task force, including faculty and student representatives,

Year 1 (2002-2003)	• First team sent to AAC&U general education conference • Faculty writes self-study documents for general education program review
Year 2 (2003-2004)	• External review site visit • Dean appoints Liberal Arts Task Force • Task force interviews faculty and staff • Task force presents "goals" for a revised program to the faculty
Year 3 (2004-2005)	• Task force divides into three design subgroups • Subgroups present three curricular proposals to faculty • Faculty vote ends in impasse • Dean sends second team to AAC&U conference on general education
Year 4 (2005-2006)	• Faculty endorses "Salve Regina" approach • Faculty and students design proposals • Faculty retreat provides forum to discuss proposals • Proposals revised and resubmitted • Faculty chooses "Opening a World of Possibilities"
Year 5 (2006-2007)	• Faculty curriculum committee vets the new LA courses • Faculty approves core courses • Faculty approves exploratory courses • Freshman courses online for fall registration • New curriculum added to catalog; freshmen register for fall 2007-2008

FIGURE 4. Second timeline

one of the proposal writers, the registrar, and the new Liberal Arts (LA) coordinator, something the general education program had never really had. The business of the LAITF was to get the new curriculum fleshed out so that it could be put in the 2007–2008 catalog and incoming freshmen could register for the new Liberal Arts courses in the fall of 2007 (see Table 1).

The task of turning ideas into courses took the time and energy and cooperation of all departments and divisions. Departments that had traditionally offered the core courses in the general education curriculum took

CORE COURSES			
Freshman	LA 101	Reading/composition	4
Freshman	LA 102	History	4
Freshman	LA 103	Mathematics	4
Freshman/sophomore	LA 111	Speech	3
Freshman/sophomore	LA 112	Contemporary issues	3
Sophomore	LA 201	Literature	3-4
Junior	LA 301	Capstone	3-4
EXPLORATORY COURSES			
Freshman/sophomore		Fine arts	3-4
Freshman/sophomore		Social science	3-4
Freshman/sophomore		Laboratory science	4-5
Freshman/sophomore		Philosophy & religion	3-4
Freshman/sophomore		Intercultural	3-4
Freshman/sophomore		Intercultural	3-4

TABLE 1. Opening a world of possibilities

the responsibility of writing the course descriptions for the new LA courses. The task force and departments first completed the core courses that incoming first-year students would take in the fall (composition, history, math, speech) followed by the writing-intensive sophomore literature course. All of the new courses had to go through the normal curriculum approval process—first vetted by the Faculty Curriculum Committee (FCC) and then presented to the faculty for two readings before a final vote. The core courses earned FCC and faculty approval relatively smoothly, but two other core courses that represented relatively unfamiliar territory for the college—a first-year topics course titled "Contemporary Issues" and the capstone experience—took longer to achieve faculty approval. Global descriptions of the "exploratory" courses—content courses in specific disciplines—involved many different departments and also took several revisions to adopt. While the implementation process stayed within the one year allotted to it, the final approvals came only during the last faculty meeting of the year.

One of the most controversial elements in the new curriculum was its inclusion of "topics" courses. A majority of the faculty liked the idea of being able to develop courses around topics of particular interest. Although all sections of a single topics course (LA 101, for example) would ideally produce similar learning outcomes, individual faculty instructors would have the freedom to choose their own themes and course material. The thinking was that topic-driven courses would give students more choice in what they were studying and at the same time relieve some of the "burn out" suffered by many general education faculty, who had been teaching essentially the same courses for many years. The college was already familiar with the problem of inconsistency among sections of the same course, however, so the task force wrote global "course criteria" for all of the new LA courses to ensure that every course bearing the same label would meet the same set of expectations. The writing of the criteria was a time-consuming and painstaking process and often drew fire in faculty meetings. The delay in approving LA 112 "Contemporary Issues" and generic descriptions of the exploratory courses orbited around disagreements over the criteria (see Appendix B for an example of course criteria).

A Mistake in the Timeline?

By the end of the fifth year (2006–2007), all of the new LA courses had been approved, although, at this writing the capstone course, LA 301, has not yet been offered and will likely create as much, if not more, controversy as did the other courses. The instincts of the task force and the dean that the faculty at Franklin could not have tolerated a long, drawn-out process will probably prove to have been correct in the long term, but like any radical idea, the one-year timetable, especially followed by a relatively short implementation period, has had its benefits and its drawbacks. The benefits are that the new curriculum was written quickly and implemented immediately, before the process could exhaust the energy and the will of the people. The compressed time frame shortened the duration of the conflict and may have prevented certain kinds of hard feelings. The college was able to get "instant gratification" of its desire for change ("instant" being defined as five years instead of thirty).

The main drawback was that many faculty felt rushed. The task force, the dean, and the LA coordinator all heard cries of pain during the process of writing and teaching brand-new courses within just a few months of their approval. Many still feel that the expectations for the new courses have not yet been fully worked out. There are still some pockets of resistance to the new courses, which express themselves as, "This isn't working. We need to go back to what we had before." We do not yet know whether we should have allotted more time for implementation or not. The true test of a timeline is whether or not the curriculum that is adopted stays adopted. We hope that, as time passes and the faculty works the kinks out of their new courses, the desire for the old and familiar will draw fewer into its embrace. We also hope that the faculty will allow the curriculum to behave as a living organism that can adapt and evolve, rather than as a fossil trapped in sediment. But only time will tell.

Franklin's timeline—more precisely, two timelines and a timetable—successfully brought about a significant set of changes to the liberal arts curriculum. The new program preserves many of the best aspects of the old one, but it is simpler, more coherent, and more flexible. It reflects the institution's need for greater intercultural awareness, a broader commitment to service, and an earlier exposure to the way disciplines interact. Equally important for the community culture is the fact that the reform process engaged the faculty and students in a sustained conversation about learning. As a result, there is new energy and commitment to the teaching of the liberal arts at Franklin College. Both old and new faculty now have equal stakes in the success of the program.

The last piece to fall into place in the Franklin reform will be systematic program assessment. It may be that the final pieces of program assessment will have to wait until the last course is implemented into the cycle, but the college has begun participating in the Wabash National Study of the Liberal Arts, which will provide meaningful data about how well the program achieves the goals currently articulated in the course criteria. Once all of the new LA courses are in place, the LA coordinator will oversee the writing of a new student learning plan and present it for faculty approval. The two most important factors in Franklin's reform process—time management and consensus building—will also guide the campus toward general assessment.

Successful Timeline: A Chicken or an Egg?

What is less clear is the reason for the cultural changes we see at Franklin. It is hard to know whether they are the *result* of using timelines or the *reason* they worked. It is difficult to separate the effects of a collaborative reform process and the quick delivery brought about by the timeline from other factors affecting the campus climate. Despite the economic downturn of recent years, the college is experiencing the best financial and enrollment condition in its history. The administration recently invested in a more equitable and competitive salary scale for both faculty and staff, which raised morale considerably. While faculty members still express disagreement with some administrative decisions, they have demonstrated greater willingness to work with administrators and appear to be less suspicious of administrative decision-making in general. The "blame-the-student" philosophy still shows itself occasionally, but general discussions now more often include ideas about ways to challenge students and provide the support they need to meet the challenge.

It is also true that, despite a lack of consensus at the beginning of the timeline, the seeds of change must certainly have existed in the faculty culture for the curricular revision to gather sufficient momentum. Because it challenged long-established inequities in workload and called for more equal participation in general education, the reform process itself represented a major risk which the faculty—albeit some begrudgingly—agreed to take on. Loud voices of dissent frequently dominated pre-vote discussions at faculty meetings, but the votes themselves were consistently in favor of change, often 3:1—strong evidence that an overwhelming majority of the faculty quietly but firmly supported the process. It is our belief that the consistent efforts of the LA task force to solicit input from the faculty helped establish greater trust among faculty colleagues as well, and that the timelines, especially the one-year timetable, despite their demands on people's energy, represented a sort of security as well. The timetables served as a pledge that the risk-taking would not last forever, that there *was* light at the end of the tunnel.

Lessons Learned

We have come to believe that a timeline is essential to ensure that a curricular reform effort makes the most efficient use of people's time and energy. Franklin's timeline cut short an effort that potentially might have dragged on for decades. An appropriate timeline helps people distinguish between issues that must be addressed during the change process and issues that can be worked out during or after implementation. Once we had agreed on a broad structure for the new curriculum, for example, a sizeable minority of faculty wanted to delay implementation until all of the courses had been worked out in detail. Had we chosen to extend the timeline another year, we might (or might not) have eliminated all of the wrinkles we are ironing out now, but it would have been anti-climactic at best. More importantly, however, we would likely have remained mired in the traditional paradigm the reform was trying to change—focusing on the input (what faculty were teaching) rather than outcome (what students were learning). To keep up with our students' needs, which change faster now than they ever have in history, a curriculum must be a living, breathing, adaptive system that we continually assess and revise. Our commitment to the timeline actually forced us to change some of our most basic ideas about curriculum.

Not all timelines are appropriate for every institution, of course. Forcing a timetable on an institution that has not been prepared for change will result in a backlash and probably end up using more time rather than less to achieve consensus around a new program. Franklin began its work with a timetable based on the assumption that the campus was close to consensus about the basic issues, an assumption that turned out to be wrong. A timeline alone cannot create agreement, but it can help an institution that has reached consensus turn its ideas into a concrete program. Not every college or university will need to spend as much time getting input as Franklin did. Those designing the timeline need to understand the culture of their community and design it with that culture in mind. Our advice to those beginning a reform effort is:

1. ***By All Means, Use a Timeline!*** After having heard stories of decades-long reform efforts at AAC&U and having weathered our own bumpy reform process, we strongly encourage every campus to use a timeline to structure their efforts. Begin with a realistic understanding of your own institution, and then build a timeline around it that is both aggressive and flexible. The psychology of change is curiously contradictory. Without any pressure to finish, people will debate endlessly and you may never get done. On the other hand, if people do not have a sense that there actually is progress, they will become discouraged and uncooperative. On one hand, people do not want change, but on the other, they want it quickly and painlessly.

2. ***Choose Your Leadership Carefully.*** The leadership you choose will set the tone of the whole endeavor. You need people who understand the faculty and their thinking about curriculum, who are ambitious, but also realistic about what can be expected. It is important to have a strong committee that can manage the process, ensure broad participation and input, and hold

the faculty to the timeline. On the other hand, our experience (and that reported by many other institutions) is that a committee working in isolation from the rest of the community—even a committee composed of the very best people available—can rarely, if ever, design a curriculum that the full faculty will accept. Entrust the process to the committee, but decision-making to the people who will have to live with the program.

3. *Know Where You Are at the Beginning.* Every institution has a different history—more or less experience with general education, greater or fewer numbers of faculty committed to change. A campus that is just beginning to write its first general education program will start in a different place than one which is revising an existing program. Before you do anything else, assess the campus climate for change. Determine as well as you can what broad areas of agreement exist and where the disagreements are—this in itself may take time, depending on whether you conduct individual interviews, as we did, sponsor faculty discussions, or administer surveys. On the assumption that every campus has its disagreements, consider which might be the best ways to bring your campus closer to consensus on the broad issues that divide it. Then allow time for consensus building on the timeline.

4. *Stick To The Deadlines (Or Not).* If the proper groundwork has been done, our advice is to stick to the timeline. When it comes right down to it, this may be the most difficult part of using a timeline. Especially as the process approaches its end point, you will probably hear requests (pleas, demands) to change the deadline, extend the process, "give us another year." This is where the leadership needs to be at the top of its form. Is there a true and genuine need for more time, or would more time just give people time to obsess about all the things that might go wrong and try to solve all the problems that could possibly arise? By its very nature, curriculum is an organic being, an organism that evolves, grows, changes, and matures. No one can answer all of the questions in the abstract, in isolation from an actual program. Only by jettisoning the first timeline could we break a real impasse, once we recognized it as such. But only by refusing to allow an extra year before implementation could we

give the faculty a sense of having achieved a success and shift our emphasis towards creating a cycle of assessment and improvement. The best we can tell you at this point is to think through your timeline in advance as carefully as you can, be aware that you will be asked to change it, and be prepared to decide whether to stop or to keep moving.

5. ***Be Prepared to Start Over.*** On the other hand, precisely as happened at Franklin, sometimes the first attempt does not work. Sometimes you reach a point where you have to say, "This isn't going to work." Looking back, we realize that Franklin was very, very lucky. We were able to change course after two years without much backtracking. Some might argue that we actually spent the first two years laying the groundwork we should have laid before we began. We took some hits from starting over. During that fretful faculty meeting where the task force presented its new timeline, we heard comments like, "What?! You're going to start all over again? What the hell have you been doing?" Hopefully, the experience and advice contained in this chapter will help you avoid having to start over. If it happens — or if you are already in the middle of starting over — do your best thinking about *why* your first approach is not working and see if you can devise a new approach that corrects the defects. Once you have come up with your new plan, then it's time to be honest. Go to your faculty and tell them the truth: "We've realized that the path we are on will not lead us to where you want to go. Based on what we're hearing from you, we think we've finally found the right way." Of course, you can only do this once.

There are still those who debate the merits of the new program, but the fact remains that a new curriculum is now in place and the faculty are engaged in delivering it. Looking back at the process, we find three primary reasons for this success. The first — the precondition for the other two — was our recognition that we had to set aside time for consensus-building in our planning. Second was understanding that the campus climate necessitated an open process and cooperative decision-making. And last, the primary focus of this chapter, was time management in the largest sense: using timelines as visible, concrete proof of our commitment to respect our faculty's time and energy. The decision to keep the process open and cooperative gave every member of the college community the opportunity to contribute to the form and content of the new curriculum, essential to any consensus-building process. Understanding the need to avoid a time- consuming, labor-intensive process persuaded an already fully committed faculty to stay the course. And finally, knowing when to pivot and turn in a different direction allowed us to recover from a false start and ultimately achieve our goals.

Time, as Shakespeare knew, controls the lives of human beings. As Brutus says in *Julius Caesar,* "There is a tide in the affairs of men / Which, taken at the flood, leads on to fortune" (4.3.218–219). What Shakespeare meant was that if people understand the dynamics of time, they can turn it to their advantage. Agents of change can control neither the circumstances nor the external forces at work in an institution at any given moment, but they can manage time. Using a timetable was a key factor in Franklin's success. We also benefitted from a serendipitous role model and what turned out to be good judgment about when to slow down, when to press forward, and when to change direction. Our experience revealed a truth about managing change on a college campus — the real power of the faculty lies not in blocking change, but in taking charge of it.

APPENDIX A: An Excerpt From the Original General Education Student Learning Plan

GOAL 1: STUDENTS WILL DEVELOP A PERSONAL ETHICAL FRAMEWORK

Objective 1. Students will critically analyze their values, and those of the college, and those of their culture.

GE 101–102 criteria:

1. Students will read and discuss essays and novels that raise significant questions of value.

2. Students will write essays in which they are asked to respond personally to the values question(s) raised in their readings and discussions.

GE 304 criterion:

Students will cite examples of how their values and those of our culture influence decisions about ideal family size and the methods employed to attain the desired family size.

GE 307 criteria:

1. Students will explore values in various cultural contexts, and will do so with sufficient accuracy to make connections between values and consequences, in fictional and nonfictional works.

2. Students will present analyses of their own values with sufficient clarity to comment on the advisability of holding various of the values systems explored in the course; and distinguish their values from those of other classmates and those of works presented.

Objective 2. Students will evaluate a variety of perspectives on issues relating to race, class, and gender.

GE 101–102 criterion:

Students will encounter readings that focus specifically on issues of race, class, and gender.

GE 205–206 criterion:

Students will relate the significance of historical issues to contemporary discussions of race, class, and gender.

GE 307 criterion:

Students will explore a variety of perspectives on race, class, and gender, in various cultural contexts, and will do so with sufficient accuracy to make connections between values and consequences, in fictional and non-fictional works.

Objective 3. Students will evaluate a variety of perspectives on issues relating to the environment.

GE 304 criterion:

Students will compare and contrast the methods and philosophies of population control programs in at least three different cultures.

Objective 4. Students will analyze a number of religious/philosophical value systems.

GE 205–206 criteria:

1. Students will accurately describe/identify the fundamental characteristics of major pre-modern religious and philosophical traditions (e.g., Judaism, Christianity, Islam, Buddhism, Hinduism, Confucianism, Daoism, Greek philosophy).

2. Students will accurately describe/identify the fundamental characteristics of the major modern secular ideologies (e.g., Marxism, classic liberalism, nationalism, fascism, social Darwinism).

Objective 5. Students will evaluate examples and philosophies of leadership.

GE 205–206 criterion:

Students will cogently describe philosophies of leadership or ruling from pre-modern (e.g., Chinese legalism, Confucianism, Daoism) and modern (e.g., nonviolent resistance, "personality cult" dictatorship) eras and how they were embodied in selected historical individuals.

Objective 6. Students will complete a service project.

GE 307 criteria:

1. The projects will be supervised and at least 20 hours in length.

2. The projects deal with the clients, the leadership of service agencies, or with a specified social problem.

3. The projects will allow the students opportunities to observe development in the clients served.

4. Students will document their projects in a journal, with supervisor's certification of the time commitments.

APPENDIX B: An example of "Course Criteria"

LA 10. THE SELF IN SOCIETY: THINKING, READING, AND WRITING CRITICALLY (4 CR)

A writing-intensive topics course focused on the self in society. Introduces critical thinking, reading, and writing, and the art of argumentation. Fall and spring.

Course Criteria: After successfully completing LA 101, students should be able to

Disciplinary Literacy: Write a coherent, well-organized essay that develops its ideas; evaluate and produce valid logical arguments; understand plagiarism and how to avoid it.

Lifelong Learning: Articulate the importance of coherent writing to their future life.

Global Perspective: As the first step toward understanding cultures other than their own, examine the diversity of values represented by their classmates and the course material they study.

Experiential Learning: Debate a variety of topics in large and small groups; work effectively with other students in small groups; give and receive feedback about written work.

Interdisciplinary Focus: Connect course materials with their own prior experience and knowledge of other topics; transfer critical reading and writing skills across disciplinary boundaries.

References

Gaff, J. G. 1980. Avoiding the potholes: Strategies for reforming general education. *Educational Record* 61(4): 50–59.

Gaff, J. G. 2003. *Report to Franklin College general education program review*. Report to Franklin College, Franklin, IN.

Garner, T. 2003. Franklin College general education program review: Internal review. Report to Franklin College, Franklin, IN.

Shakespeare, W. 1984. *Julius Caesar*. Edited by A. Humphreys. Oxford and New York: Oxford University Press.

Trainor, S. L. 2004. Designing a signature general education program. *Peer Review* 7(1): 16–19.

Zolner, J. 2007. *Curriculum change at Babson College*. Case study, Harvard Institutes for Higher Education: Cambridge, MA.

CHAPTER 5

From Concept *to* Commitment

USING NATIONAL RESOURCES and DATA to EFFECT GENERAL EDUCATION REFORM

by Suzanne Beal *and* Kelly Trigger

Frederick Community College (FCC) is a comprehensive community college that serves the citizens of Frederick County, Maryland. Like many of its counterparts, FCC has spent much of the last fifteen years engaged in various forms of general education transformation. Our college has not only reorganized the general education curriculum, but more importantly has modified pedagogical practices to meet the demands of twenty-first century learning. FCC's experience is both a model of reform and a cautionary tale. We have learned that major curricular reform necessitates profound cultural change. Initiatives that focus on the structure of the curriculum are often doomed to failure because the forces that drive reform paradoxically create barriers to it. This is especially the case at community colleges where external constituents have a substantial voice in determining the program. While our current general education program shares much with that of the past, the academic culture in which it exists has been altered radically in large part by the efforts to transform general education. This dramatic shift in institutional culture was facilitated by an administrative reorganization and motivated by national reform models.

In the fall of 1995, the college appointed a new chief academic officer for the first time in twenty-six years. To break through the obstacles of insularity, complacency, and resistance, she reorganized the academic administration from three permanent associate deans to seven, faculty-elected department chairs. This reorganization instituted a process of shared decision-making that embodied collegiality. Anyone who has worked in academia realizes that change does not come about by administrative fiat, but is driven by the internal imperative of the classroom. Consistent with the collegial nature of academic life, the new leadership implemented a change process we have come to describe as the four C's. For us, cultural transformation and curricular reform occurs in stages—from concept, to conversation, to critical mass, to commitment. Our transformative agenda has deliberately focused on creating a climate in which new ideas are encouraged (concept) and shared through a vibrant faculty development program (conversation) until such time that a critical mass of faculty have endorsed the ideas, and we can establish guidelines and expectations for the faculty as a whole (commitment). The four C's has shaped the process by which FCC has altered the general education curriculum both in terms of content and pedagogy. For us, our growing knowledge of national frameworks for leadership and learning in higher education formed the foundation for our transformation of general education from a focus on presentation of content to student learning.

Contextual Constraints and Considerations

The focus on general education in community colleges is an exploration of community college identity within higher education as well as a site for reconciling the discrepant missions of transfer students and career preparation. General education curricula, often criticized for lack of coherence, have remained pretty much intact from the 1940s to the present day. Overwhelmingly, these curricula have consisted of a menu of distribution requirements. Why is it that a structure universally seen as inadequate has been so persistent? At least three specific barriers impede general education reform at community colleges. First, external constituents, to a large extent, determine the programs. Second, for career and transfer programs, general education requirements fulfill relatively distinct needs. Finally, the intermittent enrollment patterns of community college students, accompanied by the disparate goals and needs of students, make curricular coherence difficult. An overview of FCC's experience of these three barriers suggests that general education reform is a daunting task.

First, general education is regulated by Maryland legislation and administered by the Maryland Higher Education Commission (MHEC). Changes to Maryland's law in 1991 and again in 1996 seemed to provide community colleges with more flexibility in curriculum design and greater assurance of transfer (Maryland Chief Academic Officers 1997). Ironically, the initiative inscribed distribution requirements into the law, thus substantially limiting community college autonomy.

Another issue for community colleges is the degree structure that separates career from transfer programs. The bifurcated community college mission exacerbates the traditional tension in higher education between liberal arts and vocational courses. The role of education in economic development is a hallmark of community college workforce preparation. At the same time, for students seeking a baccalaureate degree, the general education program at the community college constitutes their primary exposure to liberal learning prior to engagement with their major. The pressure to reconcile the two missions is particularly acute in Maryland, where the difference in general education between career and transfer programs is delimited by the percentage of general education in them, as mandated by law. Since all of the general education courses must meet the needs of both career and transfer institutions, consideration of the skills and competencies imbedded in general education becomes as much of a concern as content. Critical thinking, communication, cultural competence, technology, and quantitative reasoning have been the raison d'être of career program general education. Where transfer programs tend to conflate liberal and general education, career programs see the role of general education as providing necessary "soft skills" to navigate successfully the world of work. Unfortunately, the general education curriculum, rather than bringing the two missions of the college together, is often a battleground in the struggle for primacy of one mission over the other.

Perhaps the most daunting challenge to curricular reform, however, is the nature of the community college student. According to community college theorists Cohen and Brawer (2002), "Two words sum up the students: *number* and *variety*. To college leaders the spectacular growth in student population, sometimes as much as 15 percent a year, has been the most impressive feature of community colleges" (37). Cohen and Brawer reported that community college enrollments have grown from about 500,000 in 1960 to almost 5.5 million at the end of the 1990s (37). As enrollment continues to grow, Maryland community colleges particularly have been affected by a tripartite funding structure of tuition, state support, and county support. In recent decades the state support has eroded, and colleges have been forced to rely more heavily on tuition and county support. In addition to tuition increases, which beg the question of affordability and access, the two effects of this fiscal climate have been severely restricted resources for program development and an increasing reliance on adjunct faculty to teach general education core courses. Both circumstances impede general education transformation.

Even more than the numbers of students in our college, their variety affects how our programs are structured. In Maryland, as previously noted, courses in the general education core must serve the needs of both the transfer and career student. In practical terms, this means that both the four-year college professoriate and the employer equally must conclude that the community college core general education curriculum is sufficient preparation for students' next steps. Furthermore, both types of students must see the curriculum as relevant to their transfer or career program goals.

In addition to divergent program and student goals, the age range, part-time status, academic preparation, and diversity of students shape the core curriculum. The stereotypical community college student is an adult, working female in her late twenties who attends school part-time. However, this profile is somewhat misleading. Although the average age of FCC students is 26, this age has declined steadily as the enrollment of 19 year-olds outnumbers students of other ages. Still, a substantial population of highly motivated, upwardly mobile working adults enrolls in FCC because it is accessible, affordable, and available part-time. They demand courses and services that recognize their life experiences and further their career aspirations. At the same time, a somewhat larger, growing population of recent high school graduates enrolls in FCC seeking a traditional collegiate experience. Many attend FCC because they cannot afford the tuition and living expenses of the four-year institution. Some are first generation college students insecure in their ability to manage the world of higher education, and our connection to the community makes us seem more familiar and safer. A growing number of others lack the necessary academic skills to be admitted to a four-year institution. Given our open door admission policy, a quintessential characteristic of community colleges, we admit students regardless of academic preparation. Hence, developmental or remedial education is a central component of the curriculum. For underprepared students who aspire to post-secondary education, yet lack the necessary skills in reading, writing, and mathematics to access the college curriculum, the community college is a last, best hope. At FCC, we have been quite successful in creating the academic bridge to the college level. However, our mission to provide developmental education places an additional burden on the curriculum, for while we admit students who may not be academically prepared, we must graduate students who can succeed at the upper division. As such, the general education core must be comparable to that of the four-year institution. Regardless of what guides students to enroll at FCC, the same core curriculum must be tailored to students with diverse enrollment patterns, resources, goals, and academic preparation.

Harbingers of Change:
The Learning College Movement and the Four C's

Our capacity for transformation has been facilitated as much by national conversations in higher education as by our own collegial process. While changes in state law and accreditation standards put pressure on the college to change curricula, the Learning College movement (Barr and Tagg 1995) and the publication of *Greater Expectations: A New Vision for Learning as a Nation Goes to College* (AAC&U 2002) offered academic leaders an authoritative framework for implementing curricular and pedagogical change and provided faculty with a language to express new classroom practices. We describe the specific impacts of each of these national initiatives as we trace FCC's journey of academic renewal and the ways in which external imperatives intersected with national trends to provide an atmosphere in which our four C's process resulted in permanent cultural shifts.

At FCC, implementing the Learning College vision significantly changed the communication structure and redefined the stakeholders in our college strategic planning. A turning point in FCC's history was a college-wide "visioning day" held in 2001, wherein all college personnel, from physical plant staff to faculty to the Board of Trustees, attended a strategic planning session to draft FCC's mission, goals, and initiatives. Heterogeneous groups wrote specific goals and objectives, and acknowledged strengths and weaknesses in the college's organization and processes. This change in communication recognized all college personnel as stakeholders in the college's direction and in our students' success. This shift was reflected in the parallel emergence of the four C's process in the academic realm of the college. Notably, communication and decision-making shifted from a top-down implementation of ideas by leadership to a feedback loop of ideas among academic administrators, faculty, and staff. Further, the Learning College concept that all college constituents were learners suggested that change, experimentation, and failure were part of the process of improving student learning. The power of faculty to take risks was essential to the general education reform process. Under the auspices of Learning College ideology, stakeholders were offered a place at the table to voice ideas and concerns and could legitimately take risk to make change. In sum, the Learning College philosophy, paired with the four C's model, allowed faculty to take a hold of what they could control: the process.

While various college groups were making decisions about legislated distribution requirements, goals and objectives, and outcomes assessment, individual faculty members were talking about the need to change their courses to better meet the needs of students. Unlike mandate-driven change, the impetus for these conversations came from experiences in the classroom and conversations with colleagues. Framing this new dialogue about classroom practice was Barr and Tagg's article, "From Teaching to Learning: A New Paradigm for Undergraduate Education," published in *Change* magazine in 1995. They proposed a shift in emphasis from faculty performance to student learning. At FCC, faculty discussions began to emphasize the organization and delivery of instruction. As individual educators and as an academic program, we began to realize that changes in demographics, the advent of technology and tech-savvy students, the globalization of the workforce, and the appearance of distance learning significantly influenced the facilitation of student success. At the risk of reiterating a cliché, we began the shift from the "sage on the stage" to the "guide on the side."

By the end of the 1990s, there were really two conversations about general education at FCC. One involved the formal process of approving courses, refining goals and objectives, and creating assessment projects, a process to which we devoted considerable time, energy, and college resources without, some would argue, commensurate result. The other conversation, percolating below the surface, was an informal, grassroots movement to modify pedagogical practices to better meet the needs of a changing student population and altered societal landscape. Pockets of change cropped up as faculty began experimenting with course delivery and design. Learning communities, linked courses, online classes, and alternative formats were being developed and evaluated at the course level. Some models were implemented within disciplines and among special programs such as the Honors College, known at FCC as an incubator for innovation. Yet, on a broader level we had no systematic framework to facilitate widespread reform.

Energy generated by the introduction of the Learning College philosophy, introduced in 2000 and implemented in 2001, repositioned the academic decision-making from a hierarchical, mandate-driven process to an inclusive faculty-driven, collegial conversation. The recently reorganized academic administration implemented the four C's process as the routine for engaging faculty and making change. In essence, the communication culture had shifted to enable faculty to have not only a stake, but also a voice in shaping the academic goals and direction beyond the classroom.

As faculty shared their classroom experiences among themselves and through the streamlined communication with administration, they also were aware of the external pressures from legislative mandates and new accreditation standards. Conversations, ideas, concerns, and anxieties traveled through the communication channels. The conditions were in place for substantially rethinking general education. What was missing was a framework to wed the grassroots faculty-driven classroom changes with external forces that called for formal assessment and curricular change. Enter *Greater Expectations*.

Informing Change: *Greater Expectations*

The publication of *Greater Expectations: A New Vision for Learning as a Nation Goes to College* (AAC&U 2002), referred to herein as *Greater Expectations*, was the catalyst for authentic transformation of our general education program. The publication's panel of education, business, public policy, and community leaders spent two years analyzing higher education, then offered a call to action that acknowledged "the emerging challenges in the workplace, in a diverse democracy, and in an interconnected world" and endorsed "a series of specific actions and collaborations to raise substantially the quality of student learning in college" (1). For community colleges the most important implications of *Greater Expectations* involved the general education curriculum. The report proposed that higher education must:

> help college students become *intentional learners* who can adapt to new environments, integrate knowledge from different sources, and continue learning throughout their lives. To thrive in a complex world, these intentional learners should also become:
>
> - Empowered through the mastery of intellectual and practical skills;
> - Informed by knowledge about the natural and social worlds and about forms of inquiry basic to these studies;
> - Responsible for their personal actions and for civic values. (2002, xi)

In addition to the succinct, elegant outline of the learning students need, the document proposed academic experiences that promote twenty-first century learning and described the roles of all of the stakeholders in achieving reform. *Greater Expectations* had a profound effect on FCC, because it presented an unequivocal argument for curricular change and a clear blueprint for systemic transformation, and because the academic leadership of the college committed to the implementation of the report's recommendations.

Why and how did *Greater Expectations* become the blueprint for change at FCC? First, the goal of producing intentional learners who are knowledgeable, empowered, and responsible was an effective and clear summary of the college's general education goals and objectives as well as the state's graduation requirements. In its simplicity, *Greater Expectations* reconciled what had seemed like a competition between external requirements and internal goals. Even more importantly, its emphasis on developing competencies in communication, critical thinking, and cultural competence, the recognition that co-curricular activities and undergraduate research opportunities significantly reinforced content mastery, and the introduction of team projects and learning communities as preparation for the twenty-first century workplace reinforced the emerging pedagogy of our forward-thinking faculty. Finally, the document spoke to external stakeholders such as our Board of Trustees and our K–12 and four-year partners. For us, *Greater Expectations* provided a cogent argument for curricular transformation and a road map for achieving it. As a result, it became the catalyst that integrated faculty-driven pedagogical reform with administrative imperatives. A concise timeline reveals how our commitment to *Greater Expectations* evolved over several years.

In November 2001, college faculty and academic administrators were introduced to the ideas later published in *Greater Expectations* at a regional general education conference at the University of Maryland at which executive director of AAC&U, Dr. Carol Geary Schneider, spoke. The University System of Maryland and the Maryland Higher Education Commission organized the conference as part of a series of initiatives prompted by changes in state law governing general education. For those of us in attendance, Dr. Schneider's overview provided the framework we had been looking for to facilitate our own transformative agenda, for *Greater Expectations* spoke to the disparate elements of our general education effort, including accreditation mandates for outcomes assessment, statewide concerns regarding transferability, and faculty focus on student engagement. To introduce the concepts found in *Greater Expectations* we invited Andrea Leskes, the director of the project, to speak on our campus on several occasions—a faculty retreat, a joint meeting with Frederick County Public School administrators and department chairs, and a regional general education conference among the community colleges, public and private four-year institutions in the western Maryland region. In addition, we disseminated the executive summary widely, including copies to our entire faculty.

Administratively, we included the implementation of the recommendations of *Greater Expectations* as a part of the college's strategic plan. In 2003, the college underwent a major reorganization, the result of which was influenced by the recommendations of *Greater Expectations*. And while some of the original organizational changes have been modified since that initial reorganization, the impact on institutional practice has remained. For example, we created a division of Arts and Sciences to focus institutional attention on the general education program. The Office of Student Life, recently renamed the Center for Student Engagement, was moved into the Arts and Sciences division in recognition of its primary role in facilitating co-curricular programming to enhance student learning.

In addition, we sent teams of faculty and academic administrators to two different AAC&U institutes to refine our transformation efforts. Faculty attendance at AAC&U's General Education Institute was particularly vital for several reasons. First, the faculty team, primarily consisting of general education committee members, was exposed to the viability of general education reform and a common language of change. Second, the team itself was interdisciplinary. The combination of student-focused change and a cross-discipline team of faculty offered fertile ground for conversations about what constitutes a generally educated person in the twenty-first century and which learning strategies promoted liberal learning. Using the common language of student success promoted by *Greater Expectations*, the cross-disciplinary team could talk from within and at the same time transcend their disciplinary boundaries to find common trends in students' educational experiences, offering a systemic look at students' exposure to general education at FCC. The faculty team returned to FCC to share their insights with peers, further reinforcing the language and model of general education renewal offered by *Greater Expectations*. Their conversations with colleagues facilitated movement toward the critical mass necessary to implement reform.

Building consensus in support of the recommendations in *Greater Expectations* was essential because it enabled us to fully realize the model's benefits. As the framework for our reform initiative, and because of its emphasis on the kind of learning students need, *Greater Expectations* helped us refocus our efforts from the structure of the general education curriculum (i.e., goals and objectives and distribution requirements), over which we had limited control, to its implementation, over which we had considerable control. Specifically, *Greater Expectations* made explicit recommendations for curriculum and classroom practices that, because of widespread faculty exposure to the document, have framed the work of the general education committee for the past several years. According to *Greater Expectations*, a twenty-first century curriculum:

- Prepares all students for successful careers, enriched lives, and engaged national and global citizenship.
- Develops self-directed, integrative, intentional learners who are empowered, informed, responsible, and thoughtfully reflective about their education.
- Is based on a practical liberal education in which students learn and apply their learning in multiple ways to complex problems and is characterized by a diversity of perspectives.
- Is informed by technology and develops information literacy.
- Sets high standards of performance, but without prescribing a standardized path.

To facilitate student success in this new curriculum, we must promote classroom practices that:

- While teaching knowledge, also ask students to apply it.
- Stress inquiry and engagement with unscripted and contested problems, including those drawn from real life.
- In an intentional way, employ the diversity of the student body as a learning tool.
- Develop and value collaborative as well as individual achievement. (AACU 2002, 48)

Although *Greater Expectations* provided our general education committee leverage to implement best practices and to assess discernable changes in student learning across the general education curriculum, the challenge for the academic administration and faculty involved in this effort was to institutionalize what had been boutique projects and initiatives. Within a collegial organization in which individual faculty make decisions about content and practice, a central question for our general education committee arose: how do we ensure that identified best practices are implemented across the curriculum and that students encounter the learning experiences that prepare them for the challenges of the twenty-first century? For us, the answers to this question involved a process of change. Although change to the structure of the program can be mandated, change to academic practice must be internally driven. Despite externally determined distribution requirements and required outcomes assessments, our general education program has been reformed primarily by the widespread adoption of classroom best practices implemented using the framework of *Greater Expectations* and the four C's approach.

The change in the purpose and activity of the general education committee is emblematic of our four C's initiative. Prior to 1993, there was no college-wide general education committee; oversight of the program was under the control of three academic division deans. The first general education organization was a task force who reported to the chief academic officer of the college. In 1996, the newly appointed chief academic officer recommended that a recently created task force become a standing committee of the curriculum committee and oversee the implementation of state requirements. The general education committee remained a subcommittee of the curriculum committee from 1998 through 2007. Then, in recognition of the college's understanding that real change must come from classroom practice, the general education committee, with the endorsement of the college governance structure, reconstituted itself as a policymaking body whose functions were to establish guidelines for classroom practice within general education courses and to promote best practices.

One pertinent change that resulted from the committee's shift in purpose was the creation of a "Statement of Expectations for General Education Courses," which guides the curriculum committee in approving new general education courses and specifically delineates the inclusion and assessment of college-level communication, the use of common critical thinking language, the employment of active student engagement strategies (e.g., co-curricular experiences, original research), the promotion of interdisciplinary thinking, and the integration of multiple perspectives. Charting the progress of two specific general education reforms included in the "Statement of Expectations" illustrates how the four C's approach, with the support of *Greater Expectations*, has transformed our curriculum. FCC's co-curricular program and the adoption of common critical thinking language are among the most profound changes to classroom practice to occur.

Realizing Change: A Closer Look at Co-curricular Programming and Critical Thinking

Greater Expectations promotes the inclusion of out of classroom experiences as an important strategy for creating authenticity and relevance to the curriculum. The integration of co-curricular experiences has been a signal feature of FCC's general education reform since the mid-nineties. The initiative has grown from an effort of a handful of faculty to an institutional expectation for general education. During the fall of 1995, FCC implemented the co-curricular mini-grant program, through the Office of Student Life, to address poor attendance at college-sponsored events. The program was founded on this basic premise: if faculty played a greater role in shaping the co-curricular offerings, attendance would increase and the programming would have greater academic appeal. Further, as a supplement to in-class instruction, co-curricular programming would allow students the opportunity to experience, on a more personal and active level, what they were learning in class. Enabling faculty and staff to share in the design of co-curricular programs and events would assure that event programming had cross-discipline appeal, topical relevance, and expected educational outcomes—as well as a guaranteed audience. Mapping the evolution of FCC's co-curricular mini-grant from its inception to the current co-curricular programming reveals a process of concept, conversation, critical mass, and college commitment.

During its initial three-years, from 1995 to 1998, the program provided over $25,000 in support of co-curricular programming that spanned virtually every division of the college. Then, in January of 2001, guided by the Learning College principles, FCC underwent college-wide strategic planning. From cross-campus conversations among faculty and staff workgroups emerged a strong institutional vision, mission, and strategic plan, including assessable goals that specifically and explicitly connected co-curricular activities and planning to the curriculum. The release of *Greater Expectations* in October 2002 coalesced with on-going refinement of the college's strategic plan and offered a model for creating intentional learning opportunities. The timing of this report, coupled with the task of developing an outcomes assessment plan for the college and our accreditation body's support of co-curricular integration (Middle States Commission on Higher Education 2002), allowed work-teams to revisit the strategic objectives outlined in the institution's strategic plan. Further, repositioning the Office of Student Life within the newly formed Arts and Sciences division in 2003 provided greater opportunities for faculty and staff to work together on strengthening co-curricular offerings. This administrative shift illustrated that the integration of co-curricular experiences had moved through the four C's process to college commitment. As a result, faculty and staff interest in the mini-grant program continued to grow, and by May of 2003, over $28,000 was spent on co-curricular programs.

In addition to the change in administrative structure, one of the most significant steps in institutionalizing integrated co-curricular programming was the creation of a diverse co-curricular planning team comprised of faculty and staff from all academic disciplines and areas of the college. The committee met in June 2003 and determined a full semester of collaborative co-curricular programs, which were shared with all faculty and staff in August, allowing faculty to include programming in their courses. Attendance at co-curricular events increased dramatically, and the discussions that followed each event became much richer, having engaged a variety of disciplines. Building upon the momentum to create intentional learning opportunities outside of the classroom, events were designed with core learning outcomes in mind and a campus theme to unite all disciplines. By the end of the 2005 academic year, the results were astounding: 146 co-curricular events had been planned—46 supporting arts literacy, 19 supporting community building and celebration, 32 supporting leadership and career development, 11 focusing on volunteer service and environmental activism, and 38 showcasing social and cultural values.

In the summer of 2007, the general education committee held a retreat to integrate co-curricular programming into general education courses more fully and to assess the programs' impacts on student learning. Advanced distribution of information, program promotion, faculty development about the co-curricular program and its cross-discipline connections, and ideas for assessing student learning strengthened the program and it continued to flourish. By the end of the 2008 academic year, the co-curricular mini-grant program and sponsorship of out-of-the-classroom learning opportunities accounted for more than $45,000 of the annual budget and netted the production or promotion of 292 faculty, staff, and student events, in addition to student club and government activities. Clearly the concept of co-curricular programming's relevance to general education had achieved critical mass and college commitment.

The national model for liberal education reflected in *Greater Expectations*, accompanied by leadership that welcomed college-wide conversations to understand, plan, and implement intentional learning that permeates across campus structures, established the foundation for cultivating collaborative opportunities for faculty and staff to influence student learning beyond the classroom. While the college commitment to the co-curricular model offers modest funding to finance events and create cross-discipline materials, planning retreats provide a place for faculty to shape co-curricular themes and activities and share ideas for incorporation and assessing co-curricular activities within general education courses.

As we have demonstrated, general education curriculum renewal and reform requires critical mass, specifically faculty buy-in, in order for appreciable course-level change to occur. Unlike the seemingly natural evolution of co-curricular programming's integration into the general education curriculum, the reform of our critical thinking pedagogy has been more complex. Our critical thinking initiative demonstrates what happens when, given the *Greater Expectations* framework that supports a culture of continuous improvement and reflective, intentional teaching and learning, multiple activities can converge to develop critical mass and enable sustained change (i.e., commitment).

The ability to think clearly and critically is a central component of all general education programs, and all stakeholders mandate its assessment. At FCC, our challenge has been two-fold: to ensure that our graduates have robust analytical skills and to help our students understand critical thinking when they are asked to engage in it. In December 2002, a critical thinking assessment workgroup was tasked with defining critical thinking and developing strategies and assessment tools to measure students' critical thinking. As the committee reviewed models, language, and methods of assessment, struggles over defining, teaching, and assessing critical thinking emerged. The committee consulted with Dr. Linda Suskie, currently executive associate director of our accreditation commission, about specific outcomes assessment processes. Using Dr. Suskie's recommendation to gather baseline information about the status of critical thinking teaching and learning in general education courses, the committee developed two pilot groups. The first pilot group examined their courses to determine the critical thinking skills taught most often in core general education courses and the kind of assignments used to teach these skills. The second pilot group analyzed their courses to determine how students in core general education courses were actually evaluated. From the groups' collective conversations about their results emerged a critical thinking rubric with specific indicators that faculty could use to evaluate student learning in course assignments. With the formulation and implementation of curriculum-wide outcomes assessment beginning, the critical thinking rubric was soon put to good use.

In fall 2005, we formalized our outcomes assessment process by creating the Outcomes Assessment Council, a group comprised of faculty from across disciplines, our chief academic officer, and the executive director of assessment and research. The primary goal of the council was to oversee the formal assessment of student learning in general education courses. The outcomes assessment model adopted by faculty outlined a three-year process of evaluating high-enrollment general education courses, identifying areas of weakness in student outcomes that arose from the evaluation, and employing corrective actions to improve student outcomes. Faculty struggles with outcomes assessment were evident as questions and proposed barriers to instituting a productive outcomes assessment model surfaced. Despite lingering questions, academic departments began formulating their three-year assessment projects. They focused their projects on critical thinking in large measure because a critical mass of faculty had accepted the rubric piloted in the previous two years. Upon completion of the first three-year outcomes assessment cycle in spring 2008, faculty teams assessed multiple high-enrollment general education courses for student critical thinking outcomes, analyzed the results, and currently are in the process of implementing changes to improve student critical thinking outcomes.

While the rubric proved invaluable to the outcomes assessment process, a significant ancillary concern arose: how do we make acts of critical thinking more readily recognizable to students? To explore this question, a cross-discipline committee of faculty convened during the summer of 2007 to analyze course assignments that professed to promote critical thinking. The committee recognized overlaps in language use, studied models of critical thinking including our critical thinking rubric, and then offered the following recommendation: to promote critical thinking across disciplines, course assignments should adopt common language when formulating and discussing assignments that use critical thinking. They offered five assessable, action-oriented statements that could be tailored to specific disciplines. In fall 2008, after soliciting feedback from faculty, the general education committee supported the committee's recommendation and advised the college governance structure to adopt the common critical thinking language. The recommendation was approved. Today the common critical thinking language is part of the general education "Statement of Expectations" and is used across disciplines in the creation of course assignments that intentionally focus on developing students' critical thinking. In addition, the critical thinking rubric is available for faculty use as they create their assignments and assess student outcomes.

While the critical thinking initiative clearly reflects the four C's process, the recent incarnation of our general education committee and newly created FCC General Education Institute illustrate how fully engaging a national model can bring about dynamic, sustained commitment. By 2008, the general education committee's function had evolved beyond its position as a policy-maker to an organization that supported, developed, and implemented best practices. Informed by national frameworks for change, the committee's process has become the apotheosis of the four C's. Members and supportive administrative leadership have created a communication structure that introduces concepts, facilitates conversation, supports the movement toward critical mass, and follows through with commitment.

Influenced by the college's concept of continuous improvement, the general education committee, with the support of our chief academic officer, sponsored its first General Education Institute in the summer of 2008. Inspired by feedback from FCC faculty participation in AAC&U's Institute on General Education, the FCC institute goal mirrored the national institute's mission to support the on-going growth and renewal of general education. The theme for the first General Education Institute was critical thinking.

Six fellowships were awarded to faculty who submitted proposals to substantively change the critical thinking assignments and assessment in specific general education courses. In exchange, faculty fellows earned a stipend to develop their expertise in critical thinking, collaborated with other fellows, created course changes, shared their curriculum projects, and agreed to work with other faculty to implement critical thinking curriculum changes. Feedback from the fellows indicated that the General Education Institute empowered them not only to make course changes, but also to enrich their critical thinking theory and practice. Fellows have infused clearer critical thinking assignments into their general education courses using the common critical thinking language, and they have collaborated with other colleagues within and beyond their disciplines to improve critical thinking assignments and student outcomes in various general education courses. The success of this initiative has prompted us to continue the General Education Institute. Having adopted a culture of assessment and continuous improvement that supports intentional teaching and learning, we are embracing our next renewal effort: cultural competence. In support of our collective efforts to assure that students can demonstrate cultural competence, the 2009 General Education Institute will offer fellowships for faculty to transform their courses and collaborate with peers to create learning experiences that develop students' global and cultural knowledge and skills.

Collective faculty input about the growth and shifts of general education over the past fifteen years indicates that the four C's process of concept, conversation, critical mass, and college commitment, while replete with false starts, uncertainty, and periods of slow progress, offers an approach that promotes faculty resourcefulness in making changes at curricular and classroom levels. Paramount to this process is not only faculty empowerment, but also the shift from teaching to intentional learning brought forth by *Greater Expectations*. The tendency towards insularity and parochialism create powerful barriers to authentic general education reform. This may be particularly true of community colleges because of our community-focused mission. National resources such as *Greater Expectations* can be powerful antidotes to institutional lethargy and resistance by providing a framework for renewal.

We began our discussion of FCC's journey with the notion that our experience can be seen as a cautionary tale. Considerable time, energy, and angst have been focused on the structure of our general education program: which courses will become a part of the general education, whether the optional categories should be included, and in what format the syllabi should be presented. In the end, these conversations did not yield substantive change in part because external constituents and the nature of our student population limit our choices. However, our program has changed dramatically. The learning experiences of students enrolled today are significantly different from those of ten years ago. We have realized that authentic change occurs when faculty members alter the way they think about student learning. *Greater Expectations* had such a profound impact on our campus because it so eloquently articulated both a blueprint for administrative implementation and a philosophy of classroom practice that resonated with faculty's understanding of students. According to *Greater Expectations*, the purpose of twenty-first century liberal learning is to produce intentional learners – a result for which faculty, campus administrators, policy makers, and students themselves bear responsibility. The focus on learning outcomes puts classroom practice at the center of that endeavor. Authentic transformation of classroom practice originates in conversations among faculty that grow until a critical mass of teachers come to consensus around best practices that the college commits to implement through policy and the allocation of resources. The national conversation can provide institutional policy-makers with an intellectual road map for change.

References

Association of American Colleges and Universities (AAC&U). 2002. *Greater expectations: A new vision for learning as a nation goes to college.* Washington, DC: AAC&U.

Barr, R. B., and J. Tagg. 1995. From teaching to learning—a new paradigm for undergraduate education. *Change* 27 (6): 12–25.

Cohen, A., and F. Brawer. 2002. *The American community college.* San Francisco, CA: Jossey-Bass.

Maryland Chief Academic Officers. 1997. General education implementation guiding principles. Retrieved March 7, 2009 from http://mdcao.usmd.edu/guid.html

Middle States Commission on Higher Education (MSCHE). 2002. *Characteristics of excellence in higher education: Eligibility requirements and standards for accreditation.* Philadelphia, PA: MSCHE.

CHAPTER 6

Putting Learning First

HOW COMMUNICATION SHAPED
ONE CAMPUS'S REFORM

by Anne Kelsch, Joan Hawthorne,
and Thomas Steen

Creating change in higher education depends on a mix of factors—some
intentional and strategically planned, others improvised and invented
along the way, some responsive to particular needs and problems, and others truly serendipitous. This is especially true for change in general education, given the breadth of the program and multiplicity of constituencies.
Change in general education programs is further complicated by aspects
of institutional culture that block, rather than facilitate, conversations
across disciplines, programs, and colleges, and among students, faculty,
staff, and administrators. Yet unless those conversations take place, productive and effective reform may be impossible.

Critical among many factors contributing to success in our own re-
cently-completed process of general education reform at the University of
North Dakota (UND) was a commitment to clear, forthright, and open
communication with stakeholders. That commitment was consciously
adopted early in the reform, and it served as a guiding principle throughout
the process, shaping subsequent decisions. From the very beginning, we
saw that progress would be difficult or impossible without serious conversations involving as many people as could be engaged and representing as
many corners of campus as could be reached. Mechanisms that permitted
only a one-way flow of information would be inadequate. We recognized
that communication needed to be a two-way process in order to foster dialogue that could support and guide our work. The processes needed to be
transparent, and we had to be prepared to listen to concerns and engage in

conversations with partisans on all sides of every general education question. However appealing the thought, we could not simply adopt favorite ideas or even best practices from other programs. Our communication processes needed to cultivate a broad sense of program ownership. All interested parties—including stakeholders without strong intrinsic interest in general education—needed to feel that their ideas were represented and considered.

Furthermore communication could not be "done" all at once. It needed to be iterative, embracing multiple voices and perspectives at every step. We needed cycles of conversation that would begin with a look back at the data regarding successes and failures of the old general education program, continue while collecting information and soliciting ideas that might shape the revised program, and reach a culmination when moving toward consensus on the final proposal. In retrospect, this commitment to communication, which guided the entire process, was a major key to the success of our reform.

Catalysts for Change

With the goal of improving our general education program, we spent four years, first, reviewing the program and, later, developing a proposal for revising it and planning the transition. The proposal was approved in the spring of 2007, and the new program was first implemented for incoming freshman students in fall of 2008. The heart of the process to reform general education at UND occurred over a two-year period (2005–2007), but in some ways, the seeds of change had been sown long before the decision to revise our program was made. Collection of data about the current program and the communication of that data to the campus was a critical first step.

Our data collection efforts began in 2000 when a team of ten faculty members from across campus began a longitudinal study of the cross-disciplinary goals of our general education program (the General Education Longitudinal Study or GELS). Designed by the Associate Provost and funded by the Bush Foundation, the project employed qualitative methods of in-depth interviews and inductive analysis, and it aimed at capturing students' perceptions of their learning around the general education goals across their entire career at UND. The study team followed 120 students throughout their time at UND. Each student was interviewed once a semester by a member of the faculty research team, and the final data set comprised over 500 interview transcripts. Faculty involved in the project analyzed the interviews and reported findings in a formal yearly presentation to campus. A comprehensive analysis of the project was prepared and presented at the end of the fifth year and generated extensive dialogue on campus (for a more detailed description, see Kelsch et al. 2004).

Among the most important—and discouraging—findings shared during those early reports was that freshman and sophomores, with great consistency, said that they perceived their general education experience as mostly "hoop jumping": they sought to get through the courses as quickly as possible in order to "check off the requirements and get them out of the way." Faculty seemed to be similarly disengaged from general education, teaching their courses as introductions to the major and rarely if ever mentioning the general education program or its goals. Upper division students increasingly valued the cross-disciplinary goals of the program, but usually that took place in the context of their majors, not in the courses they had actually taken to fulfill general education program requirements. Additionally, the majority of students found the language of the program odd and confusing, which led to frequent misinterpretations. For example, queries about "recognizing and evaluating choices and their consequences" often prompted responses about personal choices concerning drinking and socializing, rather than intellectual or professional choices. When asked about "creative thinking," students felt that if they were not in a fine arts course, they did not have the opportunity to develop this skill. On the whole, students definitely did not perceive the general education program as something to be valued for its own unique contribution to their university experience.

When the GELS team discussed their findings with the campus, it was clear that study results indicated a strong need to re-think the general education goals and program. The team, in their final report, articulated an unfulfilled ideal that "The goals of General Education describe the expectations we hold in common for the university graduate" (Kelsch et al. 2004, 42). Given that students (and many faculty) did not experience this ideal, the team stressed the need "to reaffirm these common goals and bring new life and meaning to the ways we address them within the University." The final recommendations articulated multiple ways to make general education, and its purposes and meaning, "more visible and more fully embodied in the culture of UND."

At the same time that the GELS group was interviewing students and reporting back to the campus, the General Education Requirements Committee (GERC, a standing committee of our university senate) found itself struggling with the annual revalidation process in which it reviewed courses included in the program. With a distribution model that included more than 300 distinct courses, housed in over 35 different departments, handling the revalidations was a lengthy, time-intensive process. And it was a process that inevitably involved discussion and decision-making that reflected confusion over the philosophical underpinnings of the program itself.

Over time, the GERC had come to see that its concerns and struggles with individual instructors and departments were actually rooted in a recurring concern for the program as a whole. On an individual basis, the typical problem was that revalidation requests lacked a connection to the general education program's goals and purposes. Without an understanding of how these courses contributed to general education, committee members regularly found themselves frustrated in their efforts to decide whether or not the course in question deserved to be revalidated. If they said "no" to revalidation, the departments and faculty members bringing forward the request cried, "foul." If the committee decided to approve revalidation, some members felt that the GERC was not doing its job in making sure that the courses contributed as much toward students' general education as to the disciplines housing the courses. After some years of frustration, the GERC decided that something had to be done—that revalidation requests must be more thoughtful and more intentional about their contribution to general education. The committee also determined that it must more actively communicate with faculty about general education. Committee members needed to (a) educate faculty and departments about revalidation, (b) initiate discussions to help them see the need for improvements in the process, and (c) revise the revalidation system itself.

This—the work of the GERC in the struggle over the revalidation process—became the second catalyst for UND groups reporting to the rest of campus on their concerns. The problems they raised did not generate action toward change, although they clearly did raise awareness that we could do better in our general education program. A third factor, external to the campus, proved to be the tipping point.

In 2003, the Higher Learning Commission (HLC) of the North Central Association conducted our accreditation review. Following their campus visit, the accreditors charged that UND's assessment of student learning was weak, warranting a "focused [follow-up] visit." Among the HLC's criticisms was their view that our assessment of student learning in general education was especially problematic. We over-relied on indirect assessment information, which was useful in some ways, but did not provide us with concrete evidence to indicate whether or not UND students actually learned what we intended them to learn with respect to our stated goals for the program.

The HLC's criticism pointed back to the problems raised internally by the General Education Longitudinal Study and the General Education Requirements Committee. If, as the GERC had noted, our general education goals were neither well-known nor well-used by faculty, then it stood to reason that meaningful assessments of what students were learning (and discussions of the findings) were also missing. Likewise, if students were not part of conversations about general education, in the classroom or out, then it was hardly surprising that students perceived general education as something to "get through" as quickly as possible, rather than as a potentially meaningful part of their university experience. In a sense, the two campus groups had set the stage so that when the HLC voiced their concerns, our general education reform efforts were set in motion.

Considering Constraints on Reform Processes

With all of these forces propelling the campus toward significant change in general education, such change might have seemed inevitable. But in fact, on every campus there are countervailing winds, forces that make change seem difficult or impossible. Decisions about how to respond to these forces inevitably shape the reform process. One constraint at UND was its status as one institution within the larger state university system. Several years earlier, at a time when general education reform had most recently been attempted, a task force had been appointed. Members proposed ideas and debated them enthusiastically. But after a promising beginning—and before agreeing to any concrete proposals—a state mandate was announced in response to heightening concern over issues of transfer and articulation. The system office, at the behest of members of the state legislature, imposed a common distribution system for general education upon all state institutions of higher education.

Although there are clear advantages to such a state-wide system from the perspective of today's increasingly mobile students, the mandate had caught members of the previous task force off guard, entirely deflating them. Their best and most creative ideas, they believed, had essentially been made moot by the new system required of all state institutions.

In retrospect, of course, many potentially productive options for general education reform remained open to individual campuses. But the carryover sense of futility that still existed among those who recalled that effort was an impediment to reform. It left a residue of cynicism among some faculty: Could we really create substantive change within system mandates? Should the system requirements be challenged? Would such a challenge be hopeless, resulting in the waste of additional years of effort? The skepticism reflected in such questions was a serious concern. No one wanted to commit the time if there was no realistic possibility for genuine reform. Fortunately, it proved possible to address this concern through honest communication among parties, including those who had felt "burned" by the previous reform attempt.

Another constraint, given our status as a mid-sized state university, was money. Most of those with an interest in general education reform were faculty, people who did not routinely manage budgets, but who did regularly find that the difficulty of obtaining dollars always limited implementation of great new ideas for the classroom or the curriculum. With little or no new funding available, which most faculty on campus assumed to be a given, there was concern about the possible effectiveness of any real reform. If implementing a new program required money, where would it come from? Were there any means of significantly improving general education without spending additional money? Was the administration honestly prepared to provide even incremental amounts of new funding? The issue again proved resolvable through conversation, this time with top administrators. "Money will not be an insurmountable impediment," was the message communicated to campus. Getting the program right was to be a priority, and justifiable reallocations would be possible.

The variety of undergraduate programs offered at the university created other issues. Traditional arts and sciences majors like chemistry, biology, music, and history were fairly flexible. Large portions of undergraduate degree requirements were left to a student's own choice. But within majors like engineering, aviation, and nursing, degree programs were seriously constrained. The state board of education exerted pressure to keep the credits required for graduation at a level where degrees in such programs could be attained in four years. Professional accreditation standards mandated topics and courses to be included within the major, but they also specified skill and knowledge areas outside of the major for coverage within the program's curriculum. For students in professional fields, the entire degree program functioned a bit like a house of cards: each piece was dependent on the others, and trying to adjust any card would have an impact on the entire structure. Could we change general education without creating massive headaches, and an impossible dilemma, for faculty and students within the professional degree programs? Extensive two-way communication with key departments resolved the dilemma. The engineering faculty, for example, revealed themselves to be enthusiastic supporters of general education. Skills like effective speaking and writing were highly valued in their fields, and, through extensive and iterative discussions with faculty in such disciplines, it proved possible to make significant revisions to the general education program within existing curricular constraints.

Finally, inertia and conservatism are real forces that constrain reform in higher education. It is easiest to do what has been done in the past. Generating and harnessing creative energy for change is difficult. Any change would ultimately need to be accepted in at least four stages (being approved by the group that developed the program proposal, as well as receiving endorsement from the GERC, the university senate, and the administrators), any one of which could derail the entire effort. Was this possible? Would it be all sound and fury, signifying nothing? Was it a worthy use of faculty time and energy?

We were reminded of a multi-institution research project of general education reform that several members of our university community had recently examined in a study seminar (Kanter, Gamson, and London 1997). Many of the case studies in the book dramatized the difficulty in prevailing against inertia. At a number of the institutions that Kanter's team studied, general education reform was either totally unsuccessful or of minimal value because they could not find a way to break loose of their campus traditions and "the way it's always been here in the past." Would our attempts at reform be equally unproductive? Yet, campus-wide interest in the GELS findings had been high, and ongoing conversations across campus persuaded us that, done with extensive discussion and great openness, reform could succeed.

These questions and concerns, well-recognized by both faculty and administrators, meant that the success of any reform effort could not be taken for granted. It would be difficult in ways both unique to UND and common across higher education. With that recognition, our reform effort was launched.

Moving Forward: The Reform Process

No one would recommend that a general education reform effort begin without a permanent provost in place, but ours in fact did. Our provost had just left to take a new position, so the dean of Arts and Sciences was asked to step into the interim role. With encouragement from the president to respond to the HLC's concerns, she started asking questions about our current general education program and its operation. This led to the first formal step in our reform process: organizing a team to attend an institute on general education sponsored by the Association of American Colleges and Universities (AAC&U).

The team's members included the assistant provost for assessment, the leader of the GELS study, the chairs of the assessment and general education requirement committees, and the interim provost. Besides attending sessions and meeting with consultants and teams from other institutions, the group spent a significant amount of time at the Newport, Rhode Island institute designing a plan for how UND might go about a full-blown review and revision of its existing program. In fact, based on advice from the institute's experts, the team found itself focusing more on the process of program review than on specific curricular changes that UND might adopt down the road. By the time members of the "Newport group" returned, they had a concrete plan for the next steps that would put the campus on track toward general education reform.

Among these steps was the immediate collection of data to enable thorough examination of the current general education program. This idea came directly from the AAC&U institute where several national experts recommended starting any campus reform process with a careful collection and review of program data. Based on that idea, our plan was to begin by collecting data that could be easily accessed. Course frequency counts were one such piece of information. Staff in the registrar's office provided counts of the number of students per year who enrolled in each general education course, allowing identification of the courses that were most frequently taken for general education credit. A second step was to request (in concert with the GERC) information from departments about the general education goals that were addressed within the individual courses that made up the program. Using this course-goal alignment information, in tandem with a set of randomly generated transcripts from graduating seniors, it was possible to find out how many "hits" each senior had on each of our six general education goals during their career at UND.

This additional data, collected to supplement what was known from the GELS, supported the findings of that original study. For example, the cultural familiarity goal was not only the least valued by students, it was also the least emphasized on their transcripts. We learned that, based on program-specific recommendations or requirements, most students took a common set of courses for general education. At the same time, flexibility in the distribution requirement meant that, for any given student, some portions of the curriculum would vary unpredictably. Our increasing understanding about how our general education system worked further fueled the sense of urgency around program reform.

Using these data, coupled with the push from the HLC to improve our assessment of general education and the earlier recommendations that grew from the work of the GELS and the GERC, the Newport group (now evolved into a steering committee) determined to go forward with a campus-wide discussion and review of the program. Although the time was right to move forward with reform, there was some delicacy about how to do so. A key problem was the time-consuming nature of the task. As at many institutions, our University Senate charges the GERC with responsibility for all aspects of the program, including oversight. That meant that the work of conducting the reform process could be properly viewed as within the purview of that standing committee. But the committee typically needed to direct its energy toward the time-consuming course approval and re-approval process (validation and revalidation), along with student petitions. Also at this time, the committee had asked departments to assess learning related to general education goals as part of the revalidation process (another institutional response to the HLC's concern about our campus assessment work). Therefore, the revalidation portion of the committee's work had been made significantly more challenging by a new policy that required, in the first year after enactment, submission of plans for assessing learning around general education goals addressed in the courses. In subsequent years, revalidating departments were told that they would be required to submit data demonstrating learning, as well as analysis of the data, a description of how it had been collected, and reflective commentary regarding changes that might be made as a result of the findings. Not surprisingly, GERC members now had the much more complicated role of liaisons and mentors to departments and faculty adjusting to requirements that had previously been entirely pro forma. So even though the charge of the GERC included program revision, members realistically did not have the time to undertake it. That led the steering committee to consider proposing an ad hoc group to review the general education program and propose revisions.

There were other reasons to appoint an ad hoc group as well. National recommendations advised campuses to consider general education as a program that is not limited in scope to the academic arena. Advising, extra-curricular programs, campus housing, student affairs, and academic support units all influence a student's experience in higher education, and this included general education. Involving people from these areas in conversations about general education reform made a lot of sense, and they were not were part of the GERC, an academic entity comprised primarily of faculty members. Furthermore the creation of a new group afforded the opportunity to incorporate more stakeholders in the process. Between the reality of the GERC's workload and the desire to include both non-academic players and a larger circle of academic players, an *ad hoc* group was clearly the best option.

With input from the steering committee, the interim provost invited people from across the campus to join what became the General Education Task Force (GETF). The 25-person group that resulted included faculty from a wide range of disciplines and perspectives, student leaders, deans and department chairs, and key staff members from academic support areas (e.g., advising, international programs, American Indian student services, and the library). Their charge was to review the current program and, in the light of national trends in general education, make recommendations for reform so that the future program would be effective, clear, and assessable. From the outset, there was widespread agreement among task force members that any proposal for change must address four needs: first, the program needed greater intentionality; second, student learning must be the focus; third, the program must be assessable; and fourth, an ongoing review process needed to be built in.

Although originally asked to serve for one year, task force members ended up working for two full years (2005–2007). Members took on a significant commitment that included retreats, bi-weekly meetings of the committee of the whole, and subcommittee work that included departmental outreach to solicit input from faculty who might not show up at campus-wide meetings. Communication with the larger campus dominated the project from beginning to end. The kick-off activity was a "summit" that opened campus-wide conversations about ideas surfacing in national discussions of general education. Additional open meetings, in a range of formats and venues, kept the work visible while providing a means of both generating and testing ideas for possible inclusion in the revised program.

Our commitment to open communication with all campus constituencies led to a reform process that was both lengthy and challenging. Every idea with a champion on campus, whether that champion sat on the task force or not, was debated and considered at some point during the group's work. And each idea was handled similarly: someone (either on or off the GETF) submitted an initial "idea," an individual or subcommittee developed the idea into a fully-articulated proposal, and GETF as a whole reviewed and debated the proposal. By the end of the voting, every member of the task force, including those in leadership roles, had "won some and lost some" as items were selected or rejected for inclusion in the new program.

Once individual proposals had been accepted and incorporated into an emerging "program plan," drafts of the program were brought back to the campus at large for more response and input. By the end of the iterative process, all members of the task force were able to serve as advocates for the proposal because of satisfaction with the process, although no individual would have supported every feature of the new plan. The result—a proposal to revise the program goals and modify the requirements—went to the GERC and the university senate for endorsement at the conclusion of that two-year period (University of North Dakota, Office of the Registrar 2008).

In anticipation of likely disagreements over small details within the program, each of which members of the GETF viewed as contingent on and in relationship to other program details, both the GERC and the University Senate were asked to vote on the proposal as a whole, rather than amend and revise on the spot. They agreed to do so, and, by the conclusion of lengthy and sometimes heated discussion, both groups had approved the proposal—paving the way for a year of transition planning and a two-year phase-in implementation process, which is currently underway. General education reform would be a reality.

Looking Back: Principles for Progress

In retrospect, some clear principles guided our work. Some of these principles derived from the national conversation on general education reform. In particular, members of the Newport group came home with lessons learned from both failed and flourishing reform efforts at other institutions. First and most notably, we learned that communication with and engagement of various constituents was essential if the campus was to embrace any change. In response to this idea, the GETF sought to engage people in a number of conversations focused on gathering and dispersing information. In many ways our engagement strategies took advantage of obvious interdisciplinary communication structures within the institution:

we held open forums, gave box lunch presentations on our progress, and held a series of general education summits featuring national figures in higher education.

We also knew that these efforts would most likely reach people already predisposed to take part in the conversation, so we looked for ways to reach out to those less inclined to come to us. This meant establishing new lines of communication about general education. Perhaps the most effective way we did this was by embracing traditional structures. Departments, for example, wield considerable power on campus. So rather than just inviting faculty to join us, we pulled departments into the conversation by going to them: we arrived at their door, visited with them during a faculty meeting, and asked for their ideas. At several junctures we scheduled time in regular department meetings to survey faculty about what needed changing, what was working well from their perspective, and how they viewed the new program as it was constructed. In total, we visited 23 different departments (often more than once), intentionally including the major "providers" and "consumers" of general education, as well as anyone else who responded to our offer of a visit. This investment in "shoe leather" yielded valuable insights that most likely would have been missed without the outreach, as well as a measure of good will and greater credibility.

We documented the outreach work we did in pursuit of wider involvement, and we used that list to communicate the extent of our outreach. As we approached a final version of our new program, it was helpful to have a list of the forums, departmental visits, and invitations for discussion which had been offered throughout the process when, inevitably, some objected that their input had not been adequately sought. To faculty who suddenly felt rushed when we brought the new program to the university senate for approval, we could point to several years' worth of opportunities for their ideas, questions, and concerns to be expressed. This list of our efforts made clear that we genuinely sought input from and communication with the whole campus, and our push forward at that particular instant was not intended to silence dissent, but to maintain momentum.

Other key principles of process that we developed from the discussions at the AAC&U Institute were consensus, transparency, and inclusivity. In the spirit of consensus we agreed that, given the diversity of perspectives represented, the GETF would move forward only with a two-thirds majority, rather than a simple majority, on all decisions—if we could not reach a super-majority among ourselves on a particular idea, we reasoned, we would be ill-prepared to be persuasive with others who had not participated in our study and discussion. To enhance transparency, we held formal sessions to discuss our work, but we also posted to the web all proposals considered, along with the draft of the new program and our readings, meeting notes, and other pertinent information. Strategies of engagement (with multiple venues and forums for two-way communication) also enhanced transparency and inclusivity and helped us move towards consensus.

Another key principle, that reform must be data-driven, grounded our efforts firmly in our home context. From the start, assessment data from and about our students had prodded and inspired us. In fact, data had been a powerful initial impetus for undertaking reform. Commitment to a data-driven reform process often required the additional work of gathering that data. Our collection of information around general education followed an organic process of inquiry: knowledge acquired led to more questions and the need for further study. Our original data, student perceptions gathered in the GELS, had conclusively detailed many weaknesses in our program and suggested specific areas that needed to be addressed. This led to additional assessment projects, which in turn provided more focused information to guide our path.

Our consideration of our cultural familiarity goal provides a good illustrative example. As noted earlier, we knew from the GELS that our students did not perceive significant learning around this goal and valued it least among the six existing general education goals. We also knew from the transcript analysis that value and exposure correlated: our students had the least exposure to cultural familiarity, and they valued it least. This finding inspired another project designed to assess the quality of student learning around the cultural familiarity goal. Developing a meaningful assessment required an innovative approach. Led by our assistant provost, a faculty team developed and conducted a direct outcomes assessment based on semi-structured group interviews. Using a rubric they created that identified key criteria, faculty scored the responses of randomly selected graduating seniors to probes concerning their conceptual understanding, application, and self-awareness of diversity-related knowledge and skills. The results of this study further reinforced a high level of dissatisfaction among faculty with student learning around diversity.

These assessment projects, which connected general education reform directly to the work teachers were doing, proved to be another means of creating opportunities to communicate directly with faculty, thereby deepening faculty engagement. The fact that our assessment efforts were

largely homegrown and sought answers to questions faculty found interesting and important about their students' learning was key. Our campus
culture, and UND faculty in particular, cared deeply about student learning and wanted to know what needed their attention in regards to improving it. As we proceeded, it became clear that information that showed
where improvements needed to be made captured people's attention and
engaged them in the reform process. Rather than reform being about seemingly abstract ideals in higher education, it was about our students and our
classrooms, and faculty themselves had been participants in the conversations about student learning around general education goals. Such projects
gave the GETF a clear sense of existing problems and potential solutions,
and a broader, more engaged group of faculty to draw on in their work. In
the case of the cultural familiarity goal, assessment data led to the conclusion that not only did our goal require serious reconsideration in terms of
its language and meaning, but students also needed more intentional opportunities for learning related to this goal. Ultimately, UND instituted a
six-credit hour requirement (split between U.S. and global perspectives)
for a newly articulated social and cultural diversity goal. This change, from
a vaguely worded exposure goal to a rigorous two course requirement,
constituted a serious commitment to student learning on the part of our
faculty. This example also illustrates the reality that many of these process
variables mutually reinforce one another. Gathering data through projects
that included faculty from across disciplines broadened communication
across campus, engaging more people in the process and making it more
transparent and inclusive.

One last principle became our touchstone. The GELS had allowed us
to listen to our students and better understand the program from their perspectives. The study had captured student language and the faculty research team had worked conscientiously to incorporate those student
"voices" in their reporting. For our campus, it was very powerful to "hear"
from students that the claims we made for our general education program
often failed to relate to students' experience of it. Students had stated time
and again that the general education learning goals that we as an institution
held as foundational were not accomplished in the very classes (almost
one-third of the hours required to graduate) that made up the program.
Each individual member of the GETF had strong departmental, college,
and administrative loyalties that they brought to the table. However, each
proved willing to set those aside in favor of listening to what our students
had said. Our commitment, first and foremost, to improving student learning, allowed us to move past some significant differences. For example, due

to our state-mandated requirements (which we ultimately had chosen not to challenge) and the constraints of highly prescribed degree programs, we reduced our required Math, Science, and Technology (MST) courses from twelve to nine credits (making this area equal with the other three disciplinary distributions). This allowed us to make space in the program for a general education capstone. Faculty members in MST did not favor a reduction in credits, but they supported the larger plan because they had been part of the discussion and, ultimately, they recognized the weight of argument in favor of a capstone as a best practice that would enhance student learning around the cross-disciplinary goals.

Where We Are Now

At the time of this writing, we are almost half-way into our first year of implementation. Already we see the pressures of the past at play: "It's such a complicated system," one faculty member moans, meaning, at least in part, "But I was used to the old way of doing things." Faculty from a traditionally general education–supplying department complain that the new goals need to be revised because their courses are not an automatic fit. GETF members push back: maybe the department needs to consider minor adjustments to the courses so that they more clearly address the new goals. And the conversation continues.

Like all general education programs, ours is a product of compromise. Compromise among individuals shaped it (yes, we will have a quantitative reasoning goal, but we will define it in such a way that it does not add a math prerequisite for vast new numbers of students, thereby adding three additional but hidden credits to general education). It is a result of compromise between competing priorities (did the new plan adequately value the math, science, and technology distribution area in comparison with other areas?). It is a product of compromise within constraints including both external factors (e.g., state board mandates) and internal considerations (e.g., fiscal realities).

Despite that, we have created many of the changes that were so clearly needed. Never has there been more discussion about general education on our campus. Never has there been greater attendance at meetings about the general education program, greater numbers of phone calls to members of the general education committees or task forces, or greater interest in general education campus-wide. Building this kind of awareness of and thoughtfulness about the program was achievable only through concerted attention to communication that engaged various constituencies; yet, it is hugely important, and a worthwhile outcome all on its own.

But that was not our only achievement. We cannot answer all of our questions about student learning until students who have completed their general education within the new program participate in our senior-level outcomes assessments. But we do know that, with the assistance of increasingly strict expectations promulgated and communicated by the GERC, faculty are paying more attention to achievement of general education goals within general education courses. We do know that students are more likely than ever before to be aware of program goals, thanks to a GERC requirement that relevant goals be identified and discussed on course syllabi and in class. And we do know that key pieces of the new program mandate more meaningful attention to recognized learning outcomes that were previously under-addressed, like social-cultural diversity and communication.

These are significant accomplishments. As the new program continues to unfold, we will learn more about the areas where progress still needs to occur. Thanks to the lessons learned about the importance of open and clear communication as new needs arise or unforeseen problems develop, we feel some confidence that the program will be able to grow with us for many years into the future.

References

Kanter, S. L., Z. F. Gamson, and H. B. London. 1997. *Revitalizing general education in a time of scarcity: A navigational chart for administrators and faculty.* Boston: Allyn and Bacon.

Kelsch, A., et al. 2004. *University of North Dakota Bush longitudinal study: What students tell us about cross-disciplinary general education goals and learning.* University of North Dakota. Retrieved January 4, 2010 from http://www.und.edu/dept/oid/getf_ assessment.htm

University of North Dakota. Office of the Registrar. 2008. *Essential studies at UND* [program goals and requirements]. Retrieved January 4, 2010 from http://www.und.edu/dept/registrar/EssentialStudies/esindex.html

CHAPTER 7

No One Should Go It Alone

ENGAGING CONSTITUENTS in GENERAL EDUCATION REFORM

by Stephanie Roach

Facing the Mountain

Larry Cuban, one of what the Association of American Colleges and Universities (AAC&U) calls "the nation's most distinguished educational historians," was once asked if he felt "optimistic or pessimistic about the prospects for curricular change in the university." Cuban's response was:

> Hmm . . . I don't like the choice. I suppose I would say that I'm a *tempered idealist*, or a *realistic optimist*. For example, say that you're climbing a mountain—you really want to know how others have experienced that mountain before, and you want to know what's at the top, and you want to know different ways of getting there, and you want to know how difficult it is going to be. And that to me is realistic. But you *do* plan on getting to the top—so that's where the optimism is. (AAC&U 2000)

Cuban's discussion raises two points critical to the idea of engaging constituents: (1) meaningful curricular reform is exceedingly difficult, and (2) no one (or no one committee) who wants to stay on this side of life or death goes it entirely alone.

There is, undoubtedly, a long history in general education research of addressing the difficulty of curricular reform, and we often use metaphors and images—mountain climbing in Cuban's example, Gothic novels (Thelin 2000), battlefields (Awbrey 2005; Newton 2000)—to describe the dangerous and deadly nature of the difficult work of reform. Gothic, epic, tragic, even morbid images of general education reform are in no short supply. For example: "The battlefield," Newton (2000) mourns, "is strewn with the skeletons of well-meaning but unsuccessful reformers" (165). Such images help conjure up the magnitude of the enterprise—and often the failure of it—but they also suggest a presence of others. Sometimes in the images of general education reform we sense the ominous presence of deadly others who have left in their wake bodies on the battlefield of reform. Sometimes we see the definite need for others as we face the mountain. Sometimes we feel the weight of others as we see reform as strange and difficult work, as in the often quoted, though not definitively attributed, bon mot "changing the curriculum is like moving a graveyard."

By looking at the "what" of these images of general education reform and thinking about the "who," we learn two things. First, in our images of reform we acknowledge the enormity of the task. Yes, it is like moving a graveyard, we think—but worse. Yet in these images of reform we also see we are not alone in the work, even if sometimes the others in the image seemingly make the task more grim. True, some of our images of general education reform suggest the danger we may face when others are involved, but the real argument in our images and the case that Cuban makes explicitly is that without others we would certainly face even more danger. No one can truly go it alone. More importantly, no one should.

It is important to remember the full maxim about moving graveyards: "Changing a college curriculum is like moving a graveyard—you never know how many friends the dead have until you try to move them." This reference to "friends" often churns up sarcastic claims about campuses trusting their problems to actuarial solutions (as in "the progress of an institution 'will be directly proportional to the death rate of the faculty'"), the kind of belittling of university work that feeds the old adage that "'academic politics are so vicious because the stakes are so low'" (Thelin 2000, 9). Yet moving a graveyard is not low stakes, and the idea of "friends" rooted in such an image is no joke. As Hardy (2001) argues, to move the graveyard and to reform general education, we must face both the "the inertia of the dead" and the "resistance of the living." Even the dead are not in it alone, and that is precisely what raises the stakes. The stakes of general education reform, then, are only low if we do not invite everyone to have a stake in reform. Ultimately, "friends" are what make or break the work. We must go into general education reform, as we would into moving graveyards, carefully, intentionally, and with a certain sense of awe. We must go into reform knowing that everyone has and everyone needs "friends."

Engaging others in the reform process is the key to reform success. Engaging others can be thought of in a variety of ways: as getting to know how many friends others have, or as building an army that can win on the battlefield, or as consulting widely to ensure you reach the summit, but engaging others must be considered. Successful general education reform requires intentionality about who is invited to be involved and how those invitations are made.

Therefore, this chapter explores the necessity of engaging others and considers what successful engagement of constituents can bring to a reform process. First, to provide more context for the importance of engaging constituents as a process variable in general education reform, this chapter reviews what we already know from the literature on general education about not going it alone. Then, the chapter focuses on how others are invited to join us in the reform effort by telling the story of how one campus focused on engaging constituents in a process oriented approach to general education reform. Finally, this chapter concludes by examining the implications for what we can accomplish when we think intentionally about the "we" in general education reform processes.

Inclusivity: The Life Line

Steele (2006) argues that curricular change "can, and usually does, modify the relationship of department curricula to institutional objectives" (Principle 1 section, par. 2). She goes on to explain: "Some courses might disappear, and others might come into existence; some departments might gain, and others lose, enrollments" (Principle 1 section, par. 2). Revising general education, then, can have very high, very negative stakes. But Steele argues that such dire outcomes are the "imponderables" that often support the status quo, stagnating a curriculum that, as a liberal education becomes admittedly more critical, cannot afford to stand still. One key, then, to meaningful general education reform, as Steele argues, is "that faculty members must get involved" and "come to have a stake." Though Steele often highlights faculty engagement, her article, on the whole, makes the case for more than just faculty involvement. The call is for engagement at all levels.

Steele (2006) is not the first nor last to make the claim that the level of campus-wide involvement can make or break general education reform. Gaff (1980) identified several "potholes" on the road to general education reform. Several of Gaff's "potholes" feature closed, exclusive, and non-consultative processes as the factors that put campuses on a collision course with failure. Twenty-one years later, Smith and colleagues (2001) are still making the case that general education reform must be open, inclusive, and truly consultative, arguing that "creating an environment for open, effective discussion is a prerequisite for any effort to reform general education, and it must be an ongoing concern" (93). In drawing from their experiences, good and bad, with general education reform, the authors insist that "an open and inclusive process needs to exist at all stages of the general education reform process": "*Promote open discussion*. This process goal is at least twice as important as any other" (92; emphasis in original).

Smith et al. (2001) suggest that the benefits of inclusion are "common sense," lest the "legitimacy and credibility" of a reform process suffer (92–93). Dubrow (2004) is one of many who echo the dangers of campus members being "taken aback" or feeling "sandbagged" and "betrayed" by processes that do not include them (124–125). Yet the obviousness of the advice to avoid undue surprise is trumped by a stronger argument for inclusion; Smith et al. affirm the fact that inclusion as an imperative of a successful, process approach has been undeniably and consistently "the conclusion of research on general education reform" (92):

> Civian et al. (1997, 659) have the same point on their list of suggestions for good practice. Kanter et al. (1997, 127) conclude "that a curriculum change process that is open and collaborative is *the only way* to insure that faculty will feel committed to the eventual outcome;" with *such a commitment being key to success* in the schools they studied (Smith et al. 100; emphasis mine).

It is worth observing the limited focus on "faculty" in earlier arguments and that Smith et al.'s argument is certainly for an "open and collaborative" process where faculty are prime but not sole stakeholders. Their bottom line: "The literature on curriculum reform is clear: openness and inclusiveness are essential" (99).

Pittendrigh (2007) further confirms that "campus-wide dialogue" is "essential to the success" of local reform efforts (43). Speaking specifically about her campus she argues: "The reform effort was successful in large part because the project leaders approached discussion of curriculum reform as a genuine dialogue and expanded a community . . . committed to improving the general education experience" (55). Similarly, Kean, Mitchell, and Wilson (2008) point to "being inclusive" as essential to the process that "paved the way" and helped them avoid Gaff's "potholes" (5).

Ultimately, the literature confirms three fundamental principles of in-clusion: first, engaging constituents is affirmed and reaffirmed as a critical process variable; second, an "open and collaborative" reform process that engages constituents is indispensable to successful reform efforts; third, the only real change in the conversation is that "faculty" are no longer the only named constituents of value. Everyone must be invited.

Furthermore, it is important to keep in mind that the desired result of an "open and collaborative" process is far more than just getting lots of peo-ple to show up at reform events. We must engage constituents so that we know who "we" are collectively, learn where we have been, and name where we hope to be going. Awbrey (2005) argues that "organization-wide change, such as the reform of general education, is not just a change in the operations of the institution. It is cultural change that is rooted in the meaning that the organization has for its members" (17). Thus, for change to be successful, reform efforts must include a serious examination of who we are as a part of the work to change what we do.

Without question, there is a long history of literature on the impor-tance of engaging constituents as a process variable in general education reform: everyone must be included. Moreover, the very identity of institu-tions and individuals inside those institutions is at stake when we engage in general education reform. Discussing engaging constituents in the context of identity underscores the foundational importance of this process vari-able. Everyone must be included as part of a reform process because, at heart, general education reform is about coming to know and renew who we are, who we believe, and who we hope ourselves to be as a campus.

Not Going It Alone This Time

In August of 2005, campus-wide general education reform was kicked off on our campus—again. Though the general education program had not changed substantially since the mid-1980s, there had been previous efforts to attempt reform on campus. Faculty believed that the general education program was an important part of how students completed degree pro-grams at our university and a critical reason why students *should* complete degree programs at our university, rather than anywhere else. Yet the in-stitution had run into difficulties getting general education reform off the ground. Previous attempts, including one underway in the 2004–2005 aca-demic year, got hung up by valued structures of faculty governance, by committees with the burden of responsibility and no authority, and by difficulties generating and sustaining momentum in times of competing concerns; and if you asked others on campus to describe what happened to previous reform efforts, each person might list three distinctly different reasons for our failure to complete the reform process.

But while previous reform efforts had failed, there was some sense in early 2005 that now might be the right time. Faculty survey data and minutes from meetings across campus were starting to reflect a surge in concerns about our general education program and an expressed need for change. Moreover, we could see more and more that we were not the only ones dissatisfied with the current general education program. Students were sending us a message loud and clear: the program was no longer working.

As part of our assessment of the general education program, we had been asking exiting seniors about their experience at the university. In bi-annual general education focus groups conducted by the College of Arts and Sciences on behalf of the university, students discussed what they valued about general education and how they experienced our general education program. Data from those groups made it clear that students saw our general education program as a scavenger hunt for credit, rather than an intellectual process of expansion and interdisciplinary application. Students perceived general education as a collection of courses to be "gotten out of the way." The question we had to ask ourselves was: looking back at the collection of courses students cobbled together to "finish off" their general education, could our students articulate what the general education *program* was all about? We would, of course, consider our disciplinary programs failures if students could not look back over their major course of study and be able to recognize and articulate some of the principles in play. Yet, we were routinely graduating students who did not see a larger value to our general education program, perceiving only a bunch of, in their words, mandatory, mundane, meaningless, and unnecessary courses, courses that students admitted taking far less seriously than the courses in their home departments.

So, what we had on our side this time as we kicked off reform was a growing and could-not-now-be-overlooked imperative for change. But more importantly, what we had on our side was process. Reform was kicked-off this time with a clear process oriented approach. If we were going to fail this time, it would not be the same old story.

The insights of process that would govern campus reform efforts in 2005 and 2006 were the direct result of our university's participation in the

AAC&U Institute on General Education in May 2005. As the then most recent general education program reform efforts were flagging in early winter semester, our chancellor became aware of the opportunity for University of Michigan–Flint to participate in the Institute on General Education. We submitted an application and were selected to participate, a singular event that would change all the ways we had ever approached reform.

When our institute team returned, they issued a public "Reflection on Participation in the AAC&U Institute on General Education" that declaimed: "Perhaps the most profound insight we developed is that a formal *process* for general education reform must be developed and approved by the faculty *before* discussions of curricular *design*" (campus-wide email, June 16, 2005; emphasis in original). Based on this insight emphasizing process, the team proposed a road map for reform guided by seven essential principles that they articulated as follows to the campus:

- *The interest of our students must be placed at the center of general education reform.* While the university consists of four distinct units, and many programs and departments within each, we need to work together to keep the students' education our central focus.

- *The process of general education reform must be transparent and all-inclusive* at every stage, from inception to implementation to assessment to revision.

- *A process of completely open communication must be built into the reform effort* from the very beginning so that everyone knows exactly what is going on at any given point. Successful communication will require responsible participation by all members of the university community.

- *The Chancellor and Provost should create and charge a committee to be responsible for guiding the PROCESS of general education reform.* This committee should not be charged with designing a new curricular model, but rather should be responsible for managing the process, as "stewards of the university as a whole" and not representatives of their respective units, departments, or programs.

- *Meaningful reform must include, as a central guiding principle, adherence to the formal faculty governance structures,* including as many opportunities as possible for discussion and debate, while progressing toward an outcome in a timely fashion.

- *Adequate resources must be provided* to ensure the short- and long-term success of general education reform, including resources in support of faculty development, staffing, communications, consulting, and community building.
- *A clear timetable for reform should be established by the General Education Reform Steering Committee* so everyone is aware of the process as it unfolds (campus-wide email, June 16, 2005; emphasis in original).

The provost named a General Education Reform Steering Committee of ten members drawn from all levels and areas of the university with the charge to create a reform process, guide the process, host events to invite people into the process, and communicate frequently, clearly, openly, and in many modes about the process and our engagement in the process. This charge, unlike any seen before on campus, clearly put process at the center and made an express commitment that the work of reform would not belong solely to the steering committee; the work of reform would be, collectively, ours. Such commitment to process and shared responsibility would radically change business as usual. Approaching the problem from a process stance meant designing new ways to work together, new ways to share that work, new ways to bring in (new) voices, and, ultimately, new ways to think about what was really the "prize" on which we were to fix our eyes.

Building on the Institute team's work with then AAC&U Institute faculty Dr. Stephen Trainor from Salve Regina University, and drawing on Trainor's (2004) *Peer Review* article "Designing a Signature General Education Program," the General Education Reform Steering Committee designed a process for the campus with four essential phases: be aware, be creative, be critical, and act. The steering committee and the Thompson Center for Learning and Teaching brought in Stephen Trainor to be the keynote speaker at our traditional fall pre-convocation workshop in 2005. Trainor was there to help define the principles of our process drawn from Vincent Ryan Ruggiero's (2003) problem-solving model, which Trainor describes in his article (2004), and to begin to build momentum behind the whole idea of process. Over one hundred faculty and staff members attended the workshop.

The steering committee then followed up by fulfilling the charge to define and guide our process and engage constituents. They began drafting and circulating drafts of key documents: the definition of the task, the timeline, the call for proposals and targeted suggestions; then later, voting procedures, and criteria for proposal selection. The steering committee began circulating process documents for votes of endorsements by the governing faculty groups of our four units. All documents, from budgets to minutes to planning drafts, were openly and widely shared, and the steering committee invited all members of the campus to participate in reform efforts. They initiated individual consultations at the request of departments and programs, sent bi-weekly updates via email to all faculty and staff, printed a monthly newsletter distributed to all faculty and staff, launched a general education reform clearinghouse discussion board open to faculty, staff, and students, and maintained a blackboard community open to faculty, staff, and students that gave access to research and reference material on general education, and handouts, materials, minutes, summaries, and/or video from all reform events, as well as ongoing announcements/updates from the steering committee. All general education reform events were advertised extensively across campus in print and electronic form, and all scheduled meetings of the General Education Reform Steering Committee were open to the public.

In the "be aware" phase, the steering committee hosted fifteen general education reform "brown bag" events from September to December 2005, each attended by roughly fifteen to thirty members of the university community, for a total of 266 individuals. Faculty, students, staff, and administration debated such issues as how we might identify the distinctiveness of our program; how general education aligns with our strategic plan; how to define common outcomes of general education and align them with requirements of program accreditation; how to best serve transfer students; how the merits of first-year experiences and capstones might meet our needs; how we might define the role of civic engagement in general education; how we could better integrate learning across the curriculum; how issues of diversity, multiculturalism, and globalization affect general education; and how our curricular goals meet the needs of business, industry, and employers.

These fall discussions were supported and furthered by major campus-wide reform events aimed at inclusion. In addition to the pre-convocation workshop, the steering committee hosted a "be aware" luncheon/workshop on "Serving Our Students Through a Revised General Education Curriculum: The Collaborative Efforts of Student Services and Academic Affairs" that was attended by eighty-three faculty and staff in November; they launched the "be creative" phase in late November with a "Call for Curricular Plans and Targeted Suggestions," and they supported creative engagement by facilitating the December return of Stephen Trainor with Andrea Leskes from AAC&U for department-specific consultations and an end-of-semester workshop on "Designing and Evaluating Curricular Models" that was attended by more than one hundred.

The "be creative" phase culminated in the campus-wide distribution in print and electronic form of the exciting and divergent curricular proposals and targeted suggestions submitted by various members of the campus faculty and staff. The 103-page book of *Proposals for a New General Education Curriculum* included eight proposals authored by twenty-four individuals with one to seven authors on each proposal and five targeted suggestions authored by twelve additional contributors with one to six contributors on each. The "be critical" phase then launched with the widely and highly attended "Presentation of Proposals for a New General Education Curriculum" in which proposal authors outlined the merits of their plans and received initial feedback from over 100 members of the campus community. That campus-wide event was followed by individual brown bag sessions with the proposers for further conversation, a large and lengthy meeting of the governing faculties to finalize and vote on selection criteria and voting procedures, the revision and circulation of the final curricular proposals, including direct responses to how the proposers saw their plan meeting the agreed selection criteria, three all campus brown bag sessions to discuss the final plans (seven final plans authored by twenty four contributors, including all the major academic units and several student services areas, with one to eight authors on each final plan) in light of the selection criteria, and a day-long general education reform event on the "study day" between classes and exams. Reform day facilitated the last of the campus-wide discussion of the *Final Proposals for a New General Education Curriculum,* as well as celebrated the campus work to date; each author of the final proposals received a plaque from the provost in formal recognition of their creative contributions. Reform day culminated the start of our final phase, "act," a series of votes leading to the selection and endorsement of a curricular model that we could then begin to refine and implement. Nearly 175 people participated in the reform day activities, and an unprecedented seventy-four percent of the governing faculty participated in the afternoon voting.

Our academic year long (eight-month) reform effort ending with definitive, initial action of selecting a curricular model would simply not have been possible without campus attention to process and commitment to engaging constituents. Our process approach was supported by the efforts of the steering committee, as well as the several hundred faculty, staff, students, and administrators who got involved directly in the no fewer than thirty major all-campus events (such as workshops and presentations) and the smaller, all campus-invited events (such as brown bag discussions) over thirty-two short weeks. Without direct, open invitation to participate and a clear sense, nurtured and made a reality by the steering committee, that one's engagement mattered, we would not have had this kind of turn out. We would not have experienced what could be called a "culture of participation" that took hold on campus.

In response to the steering committee's ongoing, multi-modal, and genuine invitations to participate, people showed up to engage in small and large group events, they spoke up through the clearinghouse discussion boards, participated in several inter- and intra-unit meetings of governing faculty, stayed informed through the bi-weekly updates and monthly newsletters and other direct email from the steering committee, kept up through the weekly flyers and mailings, read the published books of the draft and final proposals, chatted in the halls about what they saw or missed, and followed the Blackboard collection of minutes, materials, notes, supplements, video, text, and/or PowerPoint slides uploaded by the steering committee for every reform event that year. Without a process-oriented approach, we would not have had—in fact, previously we never did have—so much communication, so many events, or so much involvement. Moreover, without attention to process, without shifting our fixed focus on content, without thinking beyond what we had always done and the ways we had always done it, we would not have been as creative. We would not have paid as much careful attention to principles of general education, focused as much conversation on our students, invested as much in who we are and why we do what we do. Process was the key, and the genuinely open and collaborative approach to that process in 2005 and 2006 deserves recognition.

It is, of course, not the case that everyone was pleased with the focus on process, supported the phases of our process, or appreciated the results that came from this process. Still, of all the critiques that can be, have been, and will yet be made of our reform efforts in 2005 and 2006, there are certain attacks that are harder to wage: whatever one thinks about process, whatever fault one finds in the design or pacing of our process, whatever one might stand opposed to in the several results of the process (voting procedures, criteria, curricular models, etc.), whatever one might think of the leadership, decisions, focus, and intentions of the 2005–2006 General Education Reform Steering Committee or its successors, it is hard to make the case—as we have many times before—that this general education reform effort was not intentional, not open, not transparent, not able to generate momentum, not inviting. If there is failure to claim, it is hard to make a case for what went wrong by blaming the typical causes. The 2005–2006 reform efforts—with an intentional focus on an open, collaborative process—wrote a whole new chapter in the book of how we, the University of Michigan–Flint campus, could do business. That in and of itself is a story of success.

What "We" Can Do

Those who engage in general education reform, due to the very nature of the task, begin to see sooner or later that the work is in great part about who "we" are. In their reflections on general education reform at James Madison University, Smith et al. (2001) bemoan an unfortunate fact: "there is no evidence that anyone associated with JMU ever considered the possibility that general education reform would have an impact upon institutional identity" (95). Of course it did, and as many of us have come to see—sometimes too late—general education reform has great implications for identity. As Jeske (2002) observed, "One of the best lessons we learned about the general education reform process is the importance of re-defining the relationship of each individual faculty member to the college or university and its goals and values" (111). While Jeske is expressly focused on faculty and directly making claims for the role of individual courses in "maintaining a rich, vibrant general education program," he indirectly suggests something very important about institutional identity: an institution's identity is shaped by the dynamic between an institution's collective sense of self and the way all individuals locate themselves within the collective.

Thinking about engaging constituents in the context of how the idea of "we" shapes identity is an important implication of the stories that have been told in the general education reform literature. Engaging constituents and helping members of campus inform and be informed by identity-making components like general education requires open invitations, providing opportunities to speak, and generating trust that an individual's participation makes a difference, that both individuals and the collective can be changed by those involved.

What should be clear here is that *how* we invite participation is just as important as the fact *that* we invite participation. As Pittendrigh (2007) argues, people must "feel that there could be a real debate" and that their "input could affect the outcome of the project" (51). Pittendrigh reminds us that "a true dialogue among peers who respect and listen to each other can be a powerful force for gaining allies and expanding the community supporting core reform" (51). Her emphasis on "true" dialogue points to a key implication of inclusion, that the *way* we include people makes a difference. Drawing on the work of Ruth W. Grant, Pittendrigh reminds us that "true" dialogue requires participants to be genuinely "'open to persuasion'" (quoted in Pittendrigh 2007, 54). As Pittendrigh goes on to conclude: "If one party takes a partisan position and has no intention of yielding to the better argument, a good conversation is impossible" (54). Pittendrigh believes that such principles of "true dialogue" lead to "good conversation" and are the distinctive markers of "the kind of talk that could allow a large and complex university to find enough common ground to change its general education curriculum" (54). Indeed, complex institutions of higher learning of *every* size need such "good conversation."

The key marker of "good" conversation is participants being "willing to change their minds and revise their ideas . . . even when these changes involved giving up cherished ideals" (Pittendrigh 2007, 54). The "giving up" here should not be read as "selling out" but, instead, as coming to occupy mutually beneficial ground. As Pittendrigh, again drawing on the work of Ruth W. Grant, explains it, "'to be part of the conversation is to be part of the community'" (54). So there is a real need for an interest and willingness in thinking about, yet beyond, oneself.

This dynamic between individual and community identity and the importance of seeing oneself in the larger context of an institution is important to consider. Trainor (2004) argues, and had made the case to us on campus, that participants in general education reform need to find ways to be "free to concentrate" on what's possible, without having to worry about who is or is not going to be pleased across campus (18). The invitation, then, to submit targeted suggestions for general education as part of our reform process became one way we were inviting individuals to draw from their expertise in a given discipline, yet simultaneously distance themselves from their "territory" for the good of the conversation and community. Kean, Mitchell, and Wilson (2008) argue that "focusing on programmatic outcomes can help settle territorial disputes," (8) and those submitting targeted suggestions took the invitation to submit a suggestion as an opportunity to encourage more conversation. Specifically, authors of targeted suggestions asked the campus to think about how a general education program might value integrated science, health and well being, life experience, information literacy, and writing.

For instance, as co-authors of one of the targeted suggestions ("Toward a Coherent General Education Writing Curriculum"), our focus in drafting the suggestion was to allow our disciplinary expertise in composition and rhetoric to help shape and support the larger campus enterprise of general education reform. It is also worth observing that we were very careful to avoid declaring ours "the" only and right way. The same was also true in other target suggestions. By asking questions and not claiming or defending territory, we demonstrated a willingness to "give up" ground in the way Pittendrigh suggests by asking others to join us in standing on some mutual ground.

Taking our cue from the process approach governing reform, which was open and collaborative, and less focused on specifics of content and more focused on the principles underneath any content, my co-author and I drew on our identities as writing professionals, yet chose to extend an invitation to all to consider a program identity for writing in general education. We outlined at the start that our purpose in submitting a targeted suggestion for consideration as part of the book of *Proposals for a New General Education Curriculum* was to "provide general education proposal teams and the campus at large ways to think about writing and General Education when revising curricular proposals for submission April 3 and selecting a model April 25" (University of Michigan 2006, 89). We were clear that while we "would like to contribute some of our knowledge and experience to the conversation," our targeted suggestion would not be proposing the "best" writing plan for general education. In fact, it was our belief that a writing plan for general education should not be made independent of decisions about the principles, philosophy, and, thus, identity of what would become the new general education program.

Nevertheless, we felt that how (and how well) students learn to write at our institution would be "greatly impacted by the General Education curriculum that we choose and by the ways we choose to implement that curriculum" (89). As we explained to the campus: "The selected program will provide a context for the place writing has in General Education, for the role of the faculty in general education writing instruction, for how we articulate the goals for student writing in the General Education program, and for how writing and writing instruction will be valued and supported in the program" (89). Therefore, we opened a series of questions to encourage consideration of "the place of writing in a general education program" and provided a list of considerations for thinking about writing and the teaching of writing; though, nowhere did we defend, advocate for, or even mention current writing courses in "our" program. Ultimately, we invited discussion: "We would be glad to meet with individuals or teams to talk about the place of writing in a specific curriculum or writing and General

Education more broadly" (91). Several proposal teams (many of whom had eliminated First-Year Writing in their initial proposals or had otherwise ignored writing in their curriculums) and a few campus individuals took us up on our offer. At every single meeting, participants expressed surprise and even a little shock when they realized we truly did not come to meet with them just to beat the drum of our courses. For being genuinely inviting we earned the expressed gratitude of several colleagues, and due to the collegial and productive exchange that came from those meetings, several proposal teams significantly revised the approach to writing in their final plans.

It is not easy to commit to the process of engaging constituents when, by definition of true engagement, the outcome is not certain, yet my writing colleague and I were committed to mirroring the campus's process approach that encouraged a genuine culture of participation. As writing professionals, of course, we believe our expertise is important, yet, because of what we know about writing, we also believe in some sense of shared responsibility; no one writing course, no (set of) individual writing teachers can provide the *end* of all writing instruction for students. As we mentioned in our targeted suggestion, "A piano player must play regularly to maintain her skills and only with instruction will the player learn new playing skills. The same is true for writing" (90). In this we draw from disciplinary assumptions, expressed here by the National Council of Writing Program Administrators:

> Learning to write is a complex process, both individual and social, that takes place over time with continued practice and informed guidance. . . . As writers move beyond first-year composition, their writing abilities do not merely improve. Rather, students' abilities not only diversify along disciplinary and professional lines, but also move into whole new levels where expected outcomes expand, multiply, and diverge. (Council of Writing Program Administrators 2000)

First-Year Writing is the start of something, as the "Outcomes Statement" goes on to argue, that "faculty in all programs and departments can build on." As the director of First-Year Writing, I wholeheartedly believe in dedicated writing instruction and I believe in the value of (and acknowledge the limitations of) a first-year writing program; yet to be true to our belief in the principles of the general education reform process underway on campus, my writing colleague and I focused on the fact that "our" writing program would have little value at all if writing was not endorsed as an essential part of what we all do on campus. In encouraging open, collaborative discussion of general education program values for writing, we were inviting others to see yet another way they had something at stake in reform, and we were naming ourselves as constituents in the larger process. We recognized that our identities and the identity of "our" program and of writing in general would be affected by reform, but more importantly, we and the other authors of targeted suggestions believed our participation truly could affect the realigning and reaffirmation of institutional goals and values happening in the process of reform. We engaged constituents and became engaged constituents in the kind of good conversation necessary for understanding the dynamic possibility of "we."

Planning Our Ascent

Kean, Mitchell, and Wilson (2008) argue that campuses must now give more attention to "being revolutionary" (7). They claim that institutions are being asked by the findings of AAC&U's Liberal Education and America's Promise Initiative (LEAP) to "break out of academic silos" "and align teaching and learning practices with the realities of the new global century" (7). As campuses "attempt to meet AAC&U's challenge," they assert that institutions of higher learning must ask themselves a new question: "Who owns the truth about how courses and curriculum should be categorized?" (7). For Kean et al., neither the answers nor the approach to find the answers to this new question should be "traditional" (8). To find out who owns the truth, we have to engage in "transformational thinking," thinking that "requires reexamining" our structures, that "challenges the academic community to consider alternative ways of thinking about common theories, methods, techniques, and problems" (8). The call they are making is a call for thinking that can transform what we think we know, how we come to know what we know, and who we think we are because of what we know. The call is for us to think critically about what "we" can do and to think creatively about the processes that make our work possible, the way we define who we are, and how we invite and support successful, open collaboration in our work.

In line with the long history of work on engaging constituents and drawing on the specifics of inclusion efforts on my campus, it has been the aim of this chapter to suggest that focusing on who "we" are in general education reform is key, and that being intentional about "we"—who we are, how we know what we know, why we do what we do—is a project for many minds. For a long time researchers have been pointing out the complexity of the issues involved in general education reform, the major tensions (Newton 2000) and inherent strife in any reform process, and the fact that reformers face serious challenges of significant magnitude. The reality is, as Smith et al. (2001) remind us, that general education reform is likely to be "a major event in the history of an institution" (99). For successful reform efforts, we need a process approach that trusts and engages collective campus wisdom, drawing on what AAC&U calls "multilevel leadership" to examine the problems as we see them on campus and to find solutions that we can believe in because they are truly "ours." To achieve the kind of greater expectations that AAC&U (and others) are calling for, attention to a process that is open, collaborative, and inter-animated by the institution and its constituents is essential. Attempts to go it alone have given us the gothic, morbid images, not to mention the maddening, real-life experiences, of general education reform that ends in failure. What's before us now is to discover what we can do if we are in it together.

References

Association of American Colleges and Universities (AAC&U). 2000. Teaching and learning at the research university, an interview with Larry Cuban, professor of education, Stanford University. *Peer Review*. Retrieved January 29, 2009 from http://www.aacu.org/peerreview/pr-su00/pr-su00feature1.cfm

Awbrey, S. M. 2005. General education reform as organizational change: Integrating cultural and structural change. *Journal of General Education* 54(1): 1–21.

Council of Writing Program Administrators. 2000. Outcomes statement for first year composition. Retrieved January 29, 2009 from http://wpacouncil.org/positions/outcomes.html

Dubrow, G. 2004. Collegiality and culture: General education curriculum reform at Western Protestant University. *Journal of General Education* 53(2): 107–134.

Gaff, J. G. 1980. Avoiding the potholes: Strategies for reforming general education. *Educational Record* 61(4): 50–59.

Hardy, L. 2001. The new core curriculum: "Engaging God's world." *Calvin College Spark* [online edition]. Calvin College. Retrieved January 29, 2009 from http://www.calvin.edu/publications/spark/spring01/core.htm

Jeske, J. 2002. Nurturing rich general education courses. *Journal of General Education* 51(2): 103–114.

Kean, R. C., N. D. Mitchell, and D. E. Wilson. 2008. Toward intentionality and transparency: Analysis and reflection on the process of general education reform. *Peer Review* 10(4): 4–8.

Newton, R. R. 2000. Tensions and models in general education planning." *Journal of General Education* 49(3): 165–181.

Pittendrigh, A. 2007. Reinventing the core: Community, dialogue, and change. *Journal of General Education* 56(1): 34–56.

Ruggiero, V. R. 2003. *The art of thinking: A guide to critical and creative thought.* New York: Longman.

Smith, V. R., et al. 2001. General education reform: Thinking critically about substance and process. *Journal of General Education* 50(2): 85–101.

Steele, S. 2006. Curricular wars [electronic version]. *Journal of General Education* 55(3–4): 161–185.

Thelin, John. 2000. A legacy of lethargy? Curricular change in historical perspective. *Peer Review* 2(4): 9–14.

Trainor, Stephen L. 2004. Designing a signature general education program. *Peer Review* 7(1): 16–19.

University of Michigan. 2006. *Proposals for a new general education curriculum.* Flint: University of Michigan–Flint.

CHAPTER 8

Governance

STRATEGIZING for SUCCESS

by Nancy Mitchell, Jessica Jonson, Amy Goodburn,
Deborah Minter, David E. Wilson, *and* Rita Kean

Written in collaboration with members of the team charged with developing the proposal for a new general education program at the University of Nebraska–Lincoln (UNL), this chapter explains the importance of governance in navigating the deep, sometimes treacherous waters of reform. The role of governance in the process of any change is like an iceberg. Determining who has authority to enact change is deceptively simple on the surface, but underneath lies a whole lot of structure that needs to be accounted for to successfully maneuver around obstacles and achieve large-scale institutional change. The chapter helps demystify the complexities of change by exploring what governance means across various institutional levels —university, college and departmental. Each level lays claim to different aspects of the power of change. The institution assumes power to set the vision and organize the enterprise. The power inherent at the college level focuses on distributing curricular resources (faculty pay, approving courses proposed by college faculty, etc.) and overseeing the college's course offerings. And faculty at the departmental level develop, teach, and assess courses in conjunction with the standards of the discipline, the college, and the university. These various perspectives are not entirely discrete, and sometimes the overlap of power creates tensions that can be either constructive or destructive to the process—even when faculty and administrators share common goals. To initiate general reform, then, stakeholders in the process must heed the importance of creating a system governing the reform effort that meshes with these multi-level existing political and cultural structures. We argue that recognizing and responding to how governance is understood and enacted at these different levels is a precondition for developing the trust needed to sponsor reform. To effectively communicate and build trust, agents of change must recognize various constituencies' realities and concerns at these different levels, as well as the complex ways that governance is shaped and performed within them. In particular, this case study examines the role of governance in institutional transformation and reform at the University of Nebraska–Lincoln (UNL), a large research institution with a strong decentralized system of governance. We believe our lessons learned about governance can be effectively applied to other types of institutions.

History of UNL General Education

The strong, decentralized form of governance at UNL can both obstruct and facilitate reform. In Nebraska, as in some other states, state statute gives the colleges—and not the university—authority for setting requirements. Although our existing general education program had a set of common categories for students in all eight undergraduate colleges, each college had the right to determine which courses would count for each category. We had, then, no precedent at UNL for approving a curriculum that would cut across all eight undergraduate degree-granting colleges. The goal was to construct and propose an approval process that seemed legitimate and which could carefully navigate these governance boundaries.

Dissatisfaction with UNL's existing program of general education (Comprehensive Educational Program or CEP) ran deep in 2005. The CEP was more than ten years old and complicated. This program, like most, was founded on courses and topic areas, the typical cafeteria approach: one meat, one starch, a vegetable, a beverage, and a dessert. We had a sense that such an approach had not necessarily led to healthy students. It included more than 2,300 courses, and a small but significant percentage of them were not accepted by all eight colleges. This was a problem for students who wanted to transfer to a different college within the institution. The program was difficult to assess and courses drifted from the original program goals. Students who participated in focus groups regarding their general education experiences understood neither the relevance of courses nor how they were connected. In short, the existing program was seen as an obstacle to timely degree completion and as a barrier to new students, particularly transfer students. Furthermore, the old program was outdated and did not reflect national trends in general education.

164

Recognizing the limitations of the CEP, several institutional faculty committees attempted to tweak and revise the program; however, after numerous unsuccessful attempts it was clear that the program needed to be reformed on a larger scale. Harvey Perlman, Chancellor of the University of Nebraska–Lincoln, recognized this need and acknowledged the challenges for the reform effort in his State of the University address in 2005, saying:

> I do not underestimate the difficulty of curricular change. I would, in fact, not launch this process unless I thought it was critical to the further advancement of the university — both to enhance the quality and coherence of the education we provide for undergraduates and to enhance the recruitment and retention through graduation of a student body that matches our goals and aspirations as a university. . . . This effort will not be regarded as successful until it is adopted in every undergraduate college (Perlman 2005).

Institutional Governance

Thus, UNL's reform at the institutional level began with a comprehensive, informed, and systemic effort at re-imagining what general education could be, led by our senior vice chancellor for academic affairs (Couture 2008; Kean, Mitchell, and Wilson 2008). To initiate the reform, a small committee of faculty and administrators, the General Education Planning Team (GEPT), was formed and sent to an Association of American Colleges and Universities (AAC&U) Institute on General Education. The initial members of the planning team, those who took this trip, were selected for pragmatic reasons: two of the members had been involved in previous failed efforts at reforming general education and thus had earned some wisdom (and one of those two was a former president of our faculty senate); two of the members were added because they were widely seen as being deeply committed to undergraduate education and because they represented programs that are usually major players in a general education program; and one of the members was assigned the task of facilitating this reform process. After the trip, the planning team was expanded, this time for political reasons. Campus administrators knew that if we were to mount a successful campaign to reform general education, we needed a senior faculty member to lead the effort, rather than the administrator who had initially been tasked with that. We also knew that we needed engagement and buy-in from two key campus groups: our Undergraduate Curriculum Committee and our Academic Planning Committee. Later, as we saw what a central role our campus assessment director was playing in our attempts at articulating general education outcomes, we invited her to join the General Education Planning Team.

The goal of the initial planning team at the first summer institute was to better understand the nature and purpose of contemporary general education requirements, explore models and approaches to general education and curricular reform, and from these insights develop a plan for re-imagining general education at UNL. The AAC&U institute proved to be a successful starting point because of the team's access to international experts and colleagues from other institutions facing similar challenges. The team used the time at the conference to focus on establishing an innovative proposal that provided a vision, mission, and timeline for the reform process. This proposal identified a skeletal framework for addressing several governance-related issues:

- Forming two campus groups, a core planning group and an expanded advising group, each with distinct responsibilities for reforming general education.
- Developing a set of four sequential, accumulative proposals and approval processes for those proposals.
- Identifying rationale and key characteristics for the reform.

Ultimately, this framework led to the creation of a new 30-hour general education program we called Achievement-Centered Education (ACE).

FORMING CAMPUS REFORM GROUPS

After forming the core planning group, the GEPT, in consultation with the academic deans, identified faculty from each college's undergraduate curriculum committee who could serve as members of the General Education Advisory Committee (GEAC). We clearly needed broad representation from the University community if we were to be successful and bring about varied perspectives on the educational enterprise. In addition to the representatives from each college, we believed that GEAC needed to involve representatives from our Faculty Senate, Academic Planning Committee, and Undergraduate Curriculum Committee. It seemed wise to have staff from the Office of Admissions and the Division of General Studies (undeclared majors) program present; two students were appointed to GEAC by the student government association. GEAC membership was an attempt at being strategic. We had no governance requirements or history to look to in establishing this committee. Instead, we attempted to craft a committee that would link us to the faculty in each of our undergraduate colleges and to various campus groups that have some governance roles. This also provided a communication strategy, because not only did the committee's discussions have a voice from campus groups with governance roles, but those representatives were asked to share ideas and documents with their constituents and seek their input. The input brought back by GEAC members significantly contributed to the formation of the new program.

The discussions and communications about reform were not limited to GEPT and GEAC. Other important bodies that were consulted included various institutional committees and constituent faculty and student groups, as well as national experts and accreditation organizations. Despite forming representative campus groups and consulting various other institutional bodies, a lesson that emerged from this communication effort was that there never seemed to be enough of the "right kind" of communication—although different constituencies more than likely would have defined "the right kind" very differently. Despite efforts to communicate through the general education committees, we learned that some perceived communication efforts as inadequate. The Faculty Senate Executive Committee urged the general education committees to do a better job talking with faculty in particular. The general education committees listened—and acted, creating faculty forums and stepping up other forms of communication.

Early in the process it was difficult for the general education committees to develop a useful mechanism for keeping the campus informed. Initially, a web site (http://ace.unl.edu) included lists of university groups with which it consulted—demonstrating the number of people who had been involved in the reform process. But these lists of meetings with constituencies were not fully transparent. They did not list the types of discussions that occurred in the meetings nor provide readers with a sense of how decisions incorporated this feedback. One strategy that emerged for responding to this concern was to develop "Frequently Asked Questions" that were composed to help faculty see rationales for some of the decisions that had been made in constructing the proposals. These FAQs became increasingly important tools for helping make the decision-making process visible to those who were not on the reform committees.

Part of effective governance is listening to the perceptions of the audiences involved and addressing their concerns. We experienced some success with communication for two reasons. First, the general education committees discussed how we should communicate what we were doing almost as often as discussing the new program. Second, we continually added to and refined the communication strategies we were already using and developed several different forms of communication. Each form helped communicate to different campus audiences (e.g. college faculty, deans, students, advisers) that we were willing to be transparent and were interested in their input. The college and departmental discussions later in this chapter specifically identify different communication strategies those groups found most valuable.

DEVELOPMENT OF FOUR SEQUENTIAL, ACCUMULATIVE PROPOSALS AND APPROVAL PROCESS

AAC&U institute leaders advised the GEPT team not to prepare and present a single, comprehensive proposal to the faculty for an up or down vote. Putting all of our eggs in one basket seemed unwise. Instead, we developed four sequential, accumulative ACE governance proposals to be offered over a two-year period. The first two proposals, we hoped, would lay a foundation for the program and could be presented at the end of our first year. They detailed the "what" factor of the program, that is, its contents. Those proposals identified the specific learning objectives and outcomes that would be common for all undergraduate students at the University, and the structural criteria for students meeting the requirements of the new program. We imagined that the second set of proposals would build on the first set and be offered for approval by the end of the second year. This second set of proposals detailed the "how" factor of the program, that is, by what process the program would be created and maintained. Those two proposals would identify a framework for identifying an initial set of courses and experiences to help students achieve the institutional learning objectives and outcomes, and to establish and assign responsibilities for managing and assessing the new program.

The general education committees developed and reviewed the proposals before each set was sent to the eight colleges. Colleges held their own faculty vote on each of the two sets of proposals. When all the colleges had approved the final proposals, they were sent to the University Curriculum Committee, Academic Planning Committee, and the Senior Vice Chancellor for Academic Affairs for final approval. In addition, the Faculty Senate and student government association reviewed and endorsed the final set of four proposals that comprised the new general education program.

Apart from structuring how the four ACE governance proposals were to be approved, some unplanned issues emerged from the process. The first faculty vote by all eight colleges proved insightful. To this point, many faculty members had not been paying attention to the reform effort, had not attended any of the open forums; had not read the Chancellor's, Faculty Senate's, or our communications to the campus, nor provided input. In the press of faculty work, general education reform had slipped to the side. Some faculty had perhaps chosen to wait us out, to see whether this was something that might pass uneventfully. But being asked to vote up or down on these first two proposals brought the reform effort into focus and made it real. Some faculty had not looked at the proposed outcomes before, and now that they did, they were not certain they liked what they saw.

Politics of the reform effort began to play a significant role at this point. In two colleges, the first set of proposals was almost rejected. In one college, faculty voted the two proposals down. A small team of general education committee members visited with leaders in that college. It was negotiated that the college would have another opportunity to vote on these proposals along with the final two proposals. This would provide the general education committees a chance to respond to the college's concerns and allow the college a fuller picture of the new program once the second set of proposals was complete. The faculty of that college agreed to vote again, and they approved proposals one and two.

In a second college, the proposals were hotly debated in one of the most well attended college faculty meetings ever held, and it appeared the proposals were poised for defeat. The dean averted a negative vote by suggesting that the faculty approve the proposals, form an ad hoc committee to voice their concerns, and then communicate those concerns to GEAC.

In retrospect, that first round of voting on proposals one and two was instructive to the committee and raised the level of engagement of faculty in the colleges. Once the first set of proposals was presented to faculty, the reform seemed to become "real" to them, and more faculty became increasingly engaged in the process. Dividing the vote between the first set and second set of proposals was not originally intended as a means to engage participants, but it did become a very effective strategy. The discussions and votes within the colleges on the first set of proposals provided extensive opportunity for feedback on the content of the program (learning outcomes and structure) that once resolved allowed the committee to then focus on the second set of proposals that addressed process.

Some faculty members were resistant to approving the first set of proposals (learning outcomes and structure) when the second set of proposals (governance and assessment) had yet to be defined. It had to be clearly communicated when the first two proposals were sent that nothing would be implemented unless and until all four proposals were approved. Therefore, we asked the colleges to consider the first two proposals on their own merits and in return promised to continue to consult broadly on the development of next two proposals providing faculty additional opportunities for shaping and voting on a new general education program. In fact, there were several modifications made to the first proposal (the wording of the learning outcomes) based on feedback from the colleges' first vote. The changed first proposal was then resubmitted for a vote along with the second set of proposals. Despite our best efforts to plan for success, effective governance required a certain amount of trust that we could work out the program as it developed. Some of that trust did not get earned until after the reform effort became concrete and faculty saw proposals changed based on their input.

IDENTIFIED RATIONALE AND KEY CHARACTERISTICS FOR THE REFORM

While some faculty had come to believe that UNL needed to reform its general education program, there was no consensus among those faculty about why—and other faculty seemed content to continue with the present program. Articulating a set of reasons for this ambitious reform effort seemed wise if we were to persuade the faculty to invest in a substantive reform effort rather than a quick fix of the existing program. The GEPT team developed a set of key characteristics based on recommendations offered at the AAC&U Summer General Education Institute. The team identified one of the key characteristics, basing the program on student learning outcomes, as an important starting point for the reform effort. While this characteristic was valued by institutional leaders, it ended up being one of the most difficult characteristics to accomplish.

Starting with student learning outcomes was considered important because both faculty and students seemed to have lost a sense of purpose underpinning the courses and categories of UNL's existing general education program. We thought that outcomes would allow us to build an assessable program founded on purposes that could be shared at all levels of the institution by most stakeholders, that could be monitored and improved over time and that would encourage faculty to think differently about the role of their disciplinary courses in relation to general education.

Development of the outcomes was guided by AAC&U's Essential Learning Outcomes (2007), advice from national assessment consultants, a survey of general education programs across the country, the intent and ideals of the institution's existing program, learning outcomes for undergraduate majors at UNL, expectations of professional accreditations bodies (e.g., Accreditation Board for Engineering and Technology, Association to Advance Collegiate Schools of Business, Accrediting Council on Education in Journalism and Mass Communications), and input the GEAC sought from their represented constituencies. The process of identifying learning outcomes was difficult from the beginning because it immediately began to raise governance issues and reveal political tensions.

Like many efforts of this kind, we struggled with the issue of how broad the learning outcomes should be and who had the authority to resolve the issue. For example, should foreign language or history courses be required? Our aspirations for our students and the varied demands their post-baccalaureate lives will place on them are great. There is much that they should know. And of course our own commitments to each of our scholarly areas encourage us to require our students to study within each of them. In truth, any general education program involves compromise. Our program is no different; it sets out common expectations while anticipating that college requirements, major requirements, and students' own curiosities will lead them to exceed these. Therefore, in a consideration of governance, both in terms of what was appropriate at the institutional level and what was appropriate at the college level, the new program attempted to define general education at the institutional level in terms of tangible student outcomes and accomplishments, rather than distribution requirements. Out of respect for governance boundaries, it was made clear that colleges could prescribe distribution requirements, as appropriate for their students, in addition to ACE requirements. It was also important to communicate that this new program would not exclude any academic disciplines from consideration for satisfying the outcomes. The subject areas addressed in the learning outcomes were meant to be viewed broadly as general categories of study, not narrowly as limiting study to specific disciplines. In sum, at the institutional level we learned that the role of administrators is to create a democratic process for reform that allows and encourages input from the communities affected by it, and honors their values and traditions. Robust communication throughout the institution helps build a better program. The next section discusses the reform from the perspective of one of UNL's eight undergraduate colleges.

Governance in the College of Arts and Sciences

While the general education committees negotiated the legal labyrinth of university governance, faculty and administrators in the College of Arts and Sciences worked to understand and respond to the underlying characteristics of the reform effort in terms of the college's curricular structure and mission. The College of Arts and Sciences is the largest and most diverse college at UNL, comprising more than 380 faculty members in 17 departments and 12 programs and centers. With the liberal arts a core mission of the college, Arts and Sciences historically has been the central player in UNL's general education curriculum, teaching more than 70% of the total courses and heavily involved in the creation of the previous program. From the beginning of the reform effort, there was vigorous debate in the College of Arts and Sciences about whether a move from course content areas to student learning outcomes was a desirable direction for the general education program. This debate stemmed from two positions: philosophical and structural. While faculty generally agreed that focusing on what students should know was a good first step for evaluating the existing program, there was less consensus that framing this understanding in terms of student learning outcomes was necessary or valuable. Some faculty concerns were philosophical in that "skills" courses were forcing out "content" area courses under the guise of student learning outcomes. Some felt that the proposals emphasized skills such as writing and oral communication over the valuing of particular knowledges (particularly historical studies, an area in the CEP program that was eliminated in the new program's proposals). And faculty who had developed the existing general education program were concerned that the shift to learning outcomes would water down some of the content areas—especially several required courses focused on diversity—that had been hard won just ten years before. Oftentimes faculty couched this argument in terms of the liberal arts mission of the college, which explicitly seeks to "provide all undergraduate students with a range of knowledge and a broad intellectual experience that can form the basis for critical and imaginative thinking" (University of Nebraska–Lincoln 2008, 125). Underpinning many of these discussions of pedagogical and philosophical approaches to general education was a deep-rooted sense that the college would be giving up its curricular and structural governance if it adopted this new program.

In a college as diverse and large as Arts and Sciences, the challenge was to meet with and engage as many constituencies as possible and to figure out a mechanism for prioritizing their input. Faculty were urged to participate in the ACE process throughout. The ACE leadership team used a variety of methods to sponsor engagement: postcards, email updates, and open forums. Some faculty members were very engaged with the process, drafting sample student learning outcomes, for instance, while others wrote long manifestos on why focusing on outcomes would be detrimental to the curriculum. For the most part, however, Arts and Sciences faculty did not become engaged in the discussions until the college meeting held to vote on the first two proposals.

Once faculty were engaged, the resulting challenge was a communication issue. Arts and Sciences representatives to the general education committees had to determine how to prioritize and respond to the diverse feedback they were receiving. Whose ideas should we respond to? Whose should we discard? Were faculty speaking for themselves or for their units, and how could we know? And given the paradigm shift to focusing on student learning outcomes apart from particular courses, how could we measure the legitimacy of various constituencies' responses? For example, throughout the two-year process, several Arts and Sciences faculty argued for more required writing courses. The general education committees agreed that while writing could be "reinforced" in ACE courses, only one of the ten required ACE courses would explicitly attend to the teaching of writing. At a college meeting, a history professor who teaches large lecture courses (which do not incorporate sustained writing projects) passionately argued that students should be required to take at least five writing courses during their undergraduate career. At the same time, the English department's composition faculty had developed a proposal to require one writing course in the college's additional distribution requirements. While the composition faculty were in favour of all faculty incorporating writing into their courses, they also recognized that such a paradigm shift was not likely to occur within the existing institutional structure, and that they would probably be the ones asked to provide any additional writing courses. So how were Arts and Sciences representatives to the general education committees to process these competing perspectives about what students need? Since theoretically a course from any discipline could be proposed to satisfy the writing outcome, how could the college determine whose perspectives should hold sway? And since these discussions on outcomes were not anchored to particular courses, some faculty felt that they were being asked to trust a process not knowing specifically how these general outcomes might impact individual programs.

How the College of Arts and Sciences prioritized its constituencies' responses also was connected, in part, to how the general education committees were processing and deliberating upon feedback from across the university. While Arts and Sciences faculty passed the first two ACE proposals, at the same time they passed a resolution that an Arts and Sciences subcommittee draft a set of recommendations for the general education committees to consider regarding the proposals. The college's leadership encouraged dissenting faculty to take the initiative to express their concerns and contribute to decision-making through these recommendations. The recommendations were sent to the general education committees, but it was unclear how the recommendations would be addressed. The FAQs published by the general education committee responded to some of these concerns and contributed to the sense that their recommendations had been taken under consideration. In fact, Arts and Sciences used this model of FAQs as it developed proposals for additional college requirements to be layered on top of the ACE program. But the larger issue of trust was more difficult to address.

Throughout the process, GEAC representatives from Arts and Sciences used various forms of diplomacy as they worked via public forums and closed door conversations to identify key constituencies who might be impacted by the proposed ACE requirements. Indeed, the "behind-the-scenes" meetings with various faculty comprised much of the GEAC members' time and energy. The leadership of the new Arts and Sciences dean made passage of the ACE governance proposals a key priority. He improved communication and transparency by encouraging conversation with chairs and directors of various units and deploying associate deans to meet with other faculty groups. Other GEAC representatives worked to address faculty members' concerns about the program's assessment requirements. Most of these conversations occurred via one-on-one meetings and lengthy email exchanges. GEAC members and administrators knew that passage of the ACE proposals was only a first step in developing a successful general education program. Ultimately, the program would succeed or fail in Arts and Sciences based on faculty members' sense of ownership and trust in its promise.

Once the four proposals regarding institutional objectives and student learning outcomes were passed, the college continued to debate about the role of governance in terms of two issues. The first focused on who would be in charge of certifying courses to be included in the ACE program, since certified courses would count across the various colleges. Historically, Arts and Sciences had denied some courses from other colleges, preferring to assert local control over its curriculum. Perhaps this concern for governance stemmed from the large size of the college and the fear that Arts and Sciences perspectives were not being given a full airing. Concerns revolved around the proposed governance structure, which gave Arts and Sciences one vote on the general education curriculum committee along with the other colleges. This curriculum committee's purpose was to certify courses for the program. Since general education had historically been provided by Arts and Sciences, there was the sense that its representation on the committee should be larger than just one vote. Original proposals for ACE governance had offered a variety of options: one would have identified three Arts and Sciences faculty to represent the college's major areas — humanities, social sciences, and natural sciences. Another was to have proportional representation based on the number of faculty within each college. Still another would have created proportional representation based on the number of ACE courses offered by each college. In the end, the governance proposal allotted each college one representative, and courses required unanimous approval by all eight members. This political decision dissatisfied many in Arts and Sciences. One faculty member called it the "nuclear war" or the vote of mass destruction option, fearing that if a college voted against another college's proposal, there would be retaliations and few courses passed. This perceived concern did not turn out to be a reality. Ironically, it was this commitment to local college governance that eventually helped facilitate the passage of the ACE program.

The second issue within the College involved concerns that thirty credit hours were not enough to equip students with the background knowledge that they needed. As suggested before, Arts and Sciences faculty generally were not enthusiastic about the new focus on student learning outcomes in place of required content areas. There were concerns that thirty credit hours were not enough, that the general education curriculum was being watered down, and that students would not be equipped with the background knowledge that they needed. Some faculty felt that Arts and Sciences standards were threatened by the program's focus on accepting courses across all the colleges.

As the discussions progressed, some Arts and Sciences general education committee members began to emphasize that while the "core" ACE program would be uniform, Arts and Sciences could develop an additional overlay of requirements for its students. In open forum discussions and in

individual meetings with faculty, the persuasive value of additional requirements gained increasing traction, helping to alleviate some faculty
members' concerns with the new ACE program. Thus, what helped to facilitate the passage of the ACE proposals was the sense that Arts and Sciences faculty still would have control over their own distribution requirements, even though the university would control ACE. Having this sense
of control was important to college faculty in the face of "loss of governance" represented by the ACE program.

In the spring of 2008, a subcommittee of seven Arts and Sciences faculty created an overlay of college distribution requirements that more
closely valued what faculty wanted. In addition to the thirty credit hours
required by the new ACE program, the College of Arts and Sciences voted
to require an additional nineteen credit hours and to retain its foreign language requirement. For these additional hours, students are required to
take courses within the areas of social sciences, humanities, and natural
sciences within the college's departments. In this respect, the ACE reform
effort galvanized Arts and Sciences faculty around issues of curricular
governance and stimulated important discussions about how to meet the
institution's demands for general education reform, while also maintaining
a distinct and locally-controlled college identity. Rhetorically appealing to
the college's need for local control enabled Arts and Sciences general education committee members to facilitate the passage of the ACE proposals
with the promise that additional curricular governance would be created.

Ultimately, ACE passed in the College of Arts and Sciences and faculty are now working to populate the program with courses. The college is
continuing to negotiate faculty perceptions about the program, including
what a successful proposal for ACE course certification should look like
and how to practically and meaningfully assess student learning outcomes.
The ACE process also facilitated other curricular changes in the college
that were not initially anticipated, such as:

- The online process for submitting ACE courses has facilitated a
  transition for Arts and Sciences to have all course proposals
  submitted online.

- A committee on transfer credit is proposing a centralized system
  rather than having each college evaluate its own students' credits.

- Departments and programs are reviewing their curriculum to
  identify courses that are most appropriate for the ACE program

(a process that is leading some to "clean up" curriculum that has not been reviewed in years).

- Some units are revisiting their majors and developing new courses that will allow students to take more of the general education program within their major programs.

Governance in the Department of English

At the same time the College of Arts and Sciences was developing an "overlay" as a response to the ACE reform process, individual departments were also wrestling with what ACE might mean in terms of their curricular ownership and authority. One such example is the English department. The prospect of reforming general education had large scale implications for UNL's Department of English, where in the 2008–2009 academic year, the department ran approximately four hundred courses that fulfilled some aspect of the existing general education program at UNL. It is not surprising, then, that the English department took serious interest in engaging in the general education reform effort.

During the first year, the department devoted large portions of five different department meetings (and sometimes whole department meetings) to discussions of the revision of general education. Two of those meetings were identified as part of GEAC's communication effort—where representatives of the committee visited with the department and answered questions. For example, in November 2005, the chair of the GEAC addressed the department, sharing an initial draft of "institutional objectives" that would provide an underlying rationale for student learning outcomes. Some of the interesting work, however, transpired at meetings that were not part of GEAC's communication effort. Once the institutional objectives had been drafted and approved for campus distribution by GEAC, discussion of those objectives was the sole focus of a faculty meeting in March 2006. In these meetings, faculty wrestled with the press toward outcomes and with the challenge of being asked to endorse a reform effort that was "in process" by approving pieces of an overall program rather than a whole program. Meeting minutes suggest that faculty questioned the procedural decision to develop outcomes from philosophical principles and preferred outcomes developed out of research into student learning. Although the general education committees had national data about appropriate general education outcomes, faculty in the department were interested in local data from currently effective general education courses at

UNL. At the same time, many faculty were persuaded that despite the vitality and effectiveness of individual courses, there were serious structural and administrative problems with the current general education program. In short, efforts to convince faculty of the need to reform general education and be involved in the process were successful with this department—although faculty often preferred to engage in the process critically (rather than in a blandly supportive way).

The English department, then, took up the call for faculty participation, hopeful about the possibility of having some impact on decisions regarding the revised general education program. That response might have been less visible in the sponsored cross-campus conversations (which English department faculty attended in small numbers), but was more evident in the hours of discussion the department had both in whole-department meetings and in smaller groups. In these discussions, the faculty rearticulated commitments to some aspects of the outgoing program: an engagement with human diversity that is both disciplinarily broad and also deep; a learning environment in which students' ideas are seriously and repeatedly engaged; and, the opportunity to write across many courses. Faculty recounted stories of student learning tied to these practices and sought a process of identifying student learning outcomes that built on what was already happening in effective general education classrooms on campus. The group resolved to ensure that the department's courses retained those features, in addition to arguing for a general education curriculum that promoted those learning experiences. In this way, the general education reform prompted the department to clarify its shared commitments to particular features of general education at the department level.

Finally, across the College of Arts and Sciences and within the English department, there has been considerable nervousness about the assessment piece of the new ACE general education program. If the department remains as deeply and practically involved in general education as it has been in the past (marshaling four hundred courses, for example, with a faculty of forty-two and a cadre of graduate teaching assistants and lecturers whose workloads typically do not include units of service to the department and/or campus), assessing the department's general education offerings presents a serious challenge. How the department's responsibilities for assessment at the course level will map onto the university's efforts at ongoing assessment of the general education program is a question that is currently taken up by several initiatives. One is a cross-college effort between the department and members of the College of Journalism and Mass Communications to assess courses fulfilling the student learning outcome focused on writing. Another is a departmental effort at identifying workable processes for assessing students' capstone experiences in English, in concert with the ACE student learning outcome that addresses capstone experiences. In short, general education reform has refocused the department's attention on assessment in ways that are attracting the interest of faculty who had not previously been involved in earlier conversations about assessment.

For many in the English department, the legacy of this reform effort is that it has drawn faculty into meaningful (sometimes heated) conversations and work in support of student learning and the assessment of general education courses. Moreover, the reform effort is perceived to be ongoing. Though the initial proposals have been passed, the program has to be populated with courses; teachers at all ranks have to be prepared to do that work and collect evidence of student learning consistent with the ACE guidelines; the department has to ensure productive relationships between its major(s) and general education and build departmental structures to support both, including a viable assessment process. It is, in the perspective of this department, a work-in-progress about which there is hope mixed with concern, a sense of agency mixed with constraint and compromise. Certainly the English department is but one of seventeen departments in the College of Arts and Sciences and one of many more at the university that also seriously engaged the reform process in ways that reflected their particular disciplinary and department cultures. Across these different department and college cultures, those involved with general education reform sought to work within established governance structures (e.g., attending department and college faculty meetings when invited). Although identified as part of the communication effort, this process of working within established governance patterns had productive effects beyond communication. It reinforced a commitment to purposefully deliberative and orderly change.

Lessons Learned

We learned that governance is complex. Many stakeholders possess power to effect change. At the macro-level, the institution sets a vision and establishes the framework for the process. At the mid-level, the college has philosophical authority over how the college's curriculum plays out. At the micro-level, the department has the pedagogical authority to determine how general education is addressed in individual courses comprising the ACE curriculum. To successfully enable change, all parties must be willing to negotiate and consider compromise. Success requires communicating effectively using various means at various levels of institutions with various constituencies, and crossing boundaries to include others' perspectives. Most importantly, it demands trust. We also learned that governance does not operate in isolation. Effective leadership, communication, politics, engaging constituents, and understanding specific institutional cultures in which reform is being undertaken are interrelated and requisite components of the process.

How an institution defines success should also be carefully considered. We arrived at a more nuanced vision of success that enables those of us in higher education to talk in more complex ways about institutional change. Different kinds of success emerge at different moments in the process. Rhetorical success results when you have been able to persuade institutional constituents of a vision that is flexible and inclusive of a variety of points of view. Political success derives from harnessing the power of a place to get the underlying structure changed. Educational success occurs when you succeed in developing a curriculum that students experience as meaningful.

In large scale institutional change, this kind of nuanced experience of a reform effort is likely inevitable. Thus, the most successful initiatives must be honest about the pressures a particular curricular change exerts on different areas of the institution. Such initiatives must grow out of a process that is as respectful and responsive as possible to the widest group of players without losing sight of strategy. Not everyone in the university is at the same point of readiness to implement a new program. Some faculty and some departments do not see that general education reform is necessary and do not necessarily embrace the process of assessment that accompanies the outcomes based approach and creates extra work for them. Advisers are becoming involved in the process of learning how it impacts their work. In some ways implementing general education reform requires things to occur sequentially: policies need to be established, the program needs to be populated with courses, and then advisers can start working with students, for example. The process is one of ongoing development and it requires patience on everyone's part. As different levels of the institution come to terms with the transformation, they are able to participate in the ongoing revision of the program.

The university is in the process of certifying courses for the new general education program. The notion of governance continues to evolve. Even though different groups have taken responsibility for the program, the program's success depends on increasing involvement of faculty, students, and staff, which will result in a stronger, more stable base and more ownership of the enterprise.

Specific advice from our own reform effort:

- Know that the first tasks of a reform group are to get to know one another and build trust. Little progress will be made until individuals begin to understand there are multiple ways of seeing the university, and learn to consider the cultural and governance structures and traditions of the other colleges as well as their own. Faculty will need time before they can move outside their own disciplinary boundaries and start to see how the university and general education look to colleagues in fields unlike their own. This transformation was critical to forming effective leadership needed from the members of the committees. It allowed them to not only bring back their college's viewpoint to the committee; they also shared the viewpoints of other committee members from other colleges with colleagues in their own college.

- Every reform effort needs fire fighters on every level, people charged with constantly surveying the landscape and identifying the "brush fires" that will inevitably erupt. These people need rhetorical skills, patience, and time. UNL's reform effort was successful, in part, because we had leadership at the institutional, college, and department levels who were in tune with these arising needs and could effectively respond.

- Start with learning outcomes, not courses. We posed the following question to our faculty and students: what should all undergraduate students—irrespective of their majors or career aspirations—know or be able to do upon graduation? This was a step our institution was ready to take because locally for the last ten years we already had built a culture and some acceptance for outcomes assessment within undergraduate majors. Department and faculty involvement with major assessment in their program facilitated the decision to start development of the new program with learning outcomes.

- Reform depends on the capacity of those leading the effort to think creatively about new and existing educational structures, how different structures might help to meet constituents' legitimate concerns. In the case of our institution, it meant returning to the power of the colleges and departments to determine appropriate requirements for their majors, while insisting that general education remain a university-wide program. The respect for governing authority within the colleges was effectively balanced with desire to create a better general education program for our students.

- Employ multiple strategies for engaging people and keeping them informed. Faculty are busy and are liable to ignore these kinds of efforts until they see signals that this effort is serious. We found both the approach of dividing the vote on the ACE governance proposals and communication strategies such as faculty forums an effective means for getting constituents interested and engaged.

- Use communication strategies that help constituents who are not closely involved in the process understand how decisions are being made. Although we found different communication strategies effective for different audiences, the common emphasis in each strategy was not to persuade, but to be transparent and seek input.

A genuine reform of general education seems to produce a ripple effect. Maybe that is too gentle. It produces a tidal wave of change. Currently, a team of faculty leaders is helping faculty and staff understand the goals of the reform and develop courses focused on helping students achieve learning outcomes. The change has spawned cross-discipline discussions about teaching to achieve similar student learning processes, and even resulted in funded projects investigating the creation of meta-rubrics for outcomes. It is also forcing faculty to reclassify neat compartments of learning. The shift from a discipline-centered approach to an outcomes-based general education forces rethinking about curricular boundaries and challenges traditionally held assumptions about authority and governance. Change is a messy, slow, and iterative process requiring time and patience. We also realize change does not end with a plan for reform, but continues as that new program is implemented. Focusing on the overall goal of the students' welfare helps unify the process. Overall, we realize the importance of developing an environment of trust and dialogue. In retrospect, we realize that the process is organic; major institutional transformation like general education reform does not end when the program is approved. The process must be evolutionary, even if the thinking behind general education is revolutionary.

References

Association of American Colleges and Universities (AAC&U). 2007. Essential learning outcomes. Proposed by AAC&U's LEAP National Leadership Council in *College learning for the new global century* (12). Washington, DC: AAC&U.

Couture, B. 2008. *Balancing business and brilliance: Lessons for leading in the academy.* Unpublished manuscript, University of Nebraska–Lincoln.

Kean, R. C., N. D. Mitchell, and D.E. Wilson. 2008. Toward intentionality and transparency: Analysis and reflection on the process of general education reform. *Peer Review* 10(4): 4–8.

Perlman, H. 2005. *State of the university address.* Retrieved February 5, 2009 from University of Nebraska–Lincoln web site: http://www.unl.edu/ucomm/chancllr/sua 2005/sua 2005_4.shtml

University of Nebraska–Lincoln. 2008. *2008–2009 Undergraduate Bulletin.*

CHAPTER 9

The Politics *and* Process *of* General Education Reform

KEY POLITICAL PRINCIPLES

by Blase S. Scarnati

Initiatives that bring about change that impact important aspects of the university are often pursued either through the regular means of campus governance (university curriculum committee and faculty senate), or by a dedicated task force or ad hoc committee appointed by the president or provost. Irrespective of the means, the most successful initiatives are achieved through a process that results in a consensus among constituencies. This process is inherently political, in that the process itself lives amid the shifting coalitions of various constituencies and their respective interests. The concept of politics as it is used here refers to that aggregate of interest groups and their interests on campus. Political discourse will capture the actual demands, the perceived needs, expendable issues, posturing, and the symbolic vestment of any constituency concerning curriculum. To the degree that curriculum embodies the values of the various communities that are a university, it is one of the most powerful statements of identity for groups within the university, as well as the outward reflection of the internal culture, fundamental values, intellectual richness, and self-image of the institution.

Ultimately, reform of general education can succeed only to the degree that constituencies in the university can find a common position (or set of positions) among themselves. Most importantly, through negotiation, constituencies must reach consensus in areas of disagreement. In other words, for the most contentious issues on campus (such as reforming general education), constituencies in a university must intentionally negotiate a common position so that all may benefit.

This chapter explores the process where various constituencies at Northern Arizona University (NAU), a research-intensive public university with enrollment of approximately 23,000 students, intentionally negotiated a common position in general education reform so that all could benefit. These key political principles may serve as a checklist as others begin to consider general education reform.

Key Political Principles to Facilitate Reform of General Education

The following key political principles proved to be critical strategies, attitudes, and tactics that facilitated a political negotiation among constituencies that resulted in the reform of NAU's general education program, called liberal studies. Some of the principles focus more broadly, while others are quite specific:

- Initiate campus-wide curricular reform only through bodies that have standing with faculty.

- Populate a reform committee with members who have influence and credibility with key constituencies.

- When a reform proposal has been worked out, sell it.

These three principles focus on concrete situations and are very strategic in nature. The following three principles may appear more abstract, yet they address issues that are fundamental (curricular change as political process) and that also deal with the institution and its constituencies (institutional culture, values, and the conditions for change):

- All politics is local: know before one begins what the conditions are for change (know the institutional culture and conditions).

- Curricular change is foremost a political process, nearly to the exclusion of the substance of the reforms themselves.

- Keep the discussion on student learning outcomes (institutional values).

Each of these six key political principles are discussed herein and illuminated through recent liberal studies reform efforts at NAU.

Liberal Studies Reform
at Northern Arizona University

In 1997, NAU began a process that resulted in a major restructuring of its liberal studies (general education) program, with implementation beginning in the fall of 1999. The goal of the 1999 liberal studies program was to develop the necessary skills of citizenship in our students through a combination of foundation requirements (English and mathematics), distribution courses, and courses embedded within the academic major. To meet the demands of living in an increasingly complex society, courses emphasized one of three thematic foci: the environment, technology, and the diversity of human experience—each grounded in the university's mission and strategic plan. In addition, courses identified one of five distribution blocks: aesthetic and humanistic inquiry, cultural understanding, lab science, science/applied science, and social and political worlds. Students took one, or as many as three, courses in each distribution block according to sets of sliding scales (for example, taking a minimum of one course in a block would necessitate taking up to three courses in another). Finally, each liberal studies course focused on addressing several of the nine essential skills (critical thinking, creative thinking, critical reading, effective oral communication, effective writing, ethical reasoning, quantitative/spatial analysis, scientific inquiry, and use of technology).

In a progressive move for the time, the program also established university-wide requirements for courses embedded within the academic major, such as junior level writing and senior capstone courses. A new liberal studies council was established (later becoming the liberal studies committee, a faculty senate committee functioning as part of the self-governance structure) to oversee policy and review courses for inclusion in the program. However, the scope of the authority of the committee remained an ongoing area of dispute with the university curriculum committee. Additionally, a culture developed within the liberal studies committee where it came to believe that it had no independent authority to transform either the program or itself.

Nevertheless, the 1999 liberal studies program had many successes, including being a finalist in the Association of American Colleges and Universities' *Greater Expectations: The Commitment to Quality as a Nation Goes to College* (AAC&U 2002) initiative. By 2004, though, the faculty senate concluded that the required university freshman colloquium had fallen short of achieving its learning outcomes, and the course was withdrawn. Additionally, the cultural understanding distribution block had lost focus and coherence, and a new university-wide diversity requirement was established and implemented in the fall of 2005.

It also became increasingly clear to faculty and students that the liberal studies program was too complex, with some 450 courses parsed among three themes, five distribution blocks, and nine skills. In January 2004, the liberal studies committee recommended to the faculty senate that a review committee be instituted to make recommendations on restructuring the liberal studies program. A set of recommendations that reformed liberal studies was adopted by the faculty senate in April 2006 and has since been implemented in successive stages by the liberal studies committee.

Rather than discuss the process of reform at NAU as a case study, this chapter casts that story through the lens of the six key political principles enumerated above. Examples are drawn from the NAU experience in such a way that the process variable of politics is the immediate focus, yet several of the other process variables used throughout this book are referenced.

ALL POLITICS IS LOCAL:
KNOW THE CULTURE AND THE CONDITIONS FOR CHANGE

It is essential that key constituents know what is going on, has gone on, and what might be possible before attempting any reform of general education. First, ask whether the campus has experienced continual change, reorganization, or severe budget cuts. Know your campus culture and conditions well. If your campus has experienced continual change, then perhaps some time needs to pass before starting to consider further change. On the other hand, when times are good there is often little impetus to change. Times that see continual flux might be (almost counterintuitively) the best time to try to bring about change. When the balls are moving on the table, it is easier to begin to set others in motion. People often are more willing to make dramatic change when they are already in motion.

That said, if the campus has experienced a great deal of change or stress, one must be sensitive as to whether the faculty still has enough emotional space and energy to even consider further change. While faculty cannot control the economy, the state legislatures, the university's governing board, or even their own upper administration, faculty can control the curriculum and what it believes a graduate from their institution should learn and experience. While turbulent conditions might initially indicate that further reform or change is sure to fail, curricular change can empower faculty in a time when they believe that they have little control or influence over their institution or situation. Nevertheless, one must be able to cast a cold eye over the campus landscape, culture, and conditions to both see what is possible and with whom one can use common cause to bring about change.

Widespread dissatisfaction among students and faculty at NAU fueled the desire to reform the liberal studies program. The desire for reform of general education at NAU was grassroots, not top down. While the state's economic conditions at the time and the university's budget were both good, this broad dissatisfaction with liberal studies created a space at NAU for change — *all politics is local.*

INITIATE CAMPUS-WIDE CURRICULAR REFORM ONLY THROUGH BODIES WITH FACULTY STANDING

The issue of what body may have standing with the faculty is a political issue in itself, in that faculty perception of the legitimacy of any reform group varies greatly from university to university. At NAU (like at many universities), the task force or ad hoc committee that is appointed by upper administration to reform general education is often viewed as the least legitimate body to address curricular reform. The faculty is often quite protective of its ownership of the curriculum, irrespective of the practical impact that administration has on the day to day shaping and oversight of the curriculum. Who initiates curricular reform — either faculty governance structures such as the faculty senate, committees to which the senate delegates authority such as the university curriculum committee, or the president, or provost — is critical. In particular, attempting to reform the *details* of curriculum through an ad hoc committee or task force appointed by the president or provost is least likely to succeed. Perhaps counterintuitively, the presidential ad hoc committee or task force can be quite successful in recommending larger structural recommendations such as the reorganizations of academic units, mission, strategic planning, and university-level learning outcomes, especially if there is perceived to be real and meaningful faculty participation. At NAU, the most successful reforms are generated through the regular means of faculty governance, such as the faculty senate or appropriate senate university committee.

The impetus for reform of the liberal studies program at NAU began in the liberal studies committee itself, which responded to faculty and student discontent with the existing program. Gaining endorsement of the university curriculum committee on the way to the faculty senate, the liberal studies committee's request to begin a review and generate a set of reform recommendations lined up key constituencies: relevant faculty committees and the senate responding to general faculty discontent.

In the spring of 2004, the faculty senate liberal studies review committee (hereafter, review committee) was charged by the faculty senate to consider various models for liberal studies reform and also to make recommendations to reestablish a first-year academic program. The review committee was asked to develop a set of recommendations to the senate and/or keep the senate informed of its progress. The review committee would ultimately vet the recommended reforms with the liberal studies and university curriculum committees on the way to the faculty senate. Recognizing the importance of the existing governance processes by vetting the recommendations through these existing committees allowed the review committee to proceed with limited resistance.

During the political process followed at NAU to establish a review committee all of the important faculty constituencies, committees, and oversight bodies were consulted. Since the review committee was a creature of the faculty through the senate and its committees, it was widely viewed as legitimate and as having standing with the faculty.

POPULATE A REFORM COMMITTEE
WITH INFLUENTIAL AND CREDIBLE MEMBERS

When forming a committee to consider general education reform, the membership of the committee must appear to the faculty as "balanced," in that key constituencies either see themselves or honest brokers as members. This does not imply that one should appoint a representative from every constituency to the committee, but rather members should be appointed who have broad credibility and who, when faculty know they are involved or are advocating on its behalf, would tend to give the project the benefit of the doubt.

So, should the committee be representational, or not? The realities of one's campus culture will ultimately dictate the answer. If there is mutual distrust among key constituencies, then a representative membership may be best (although if there is great distrust the whole enterprise might well be doomed from the start). If honest brokers or key constituencies will suffice, then the membership can be less strictly representative.

Whether to include representatives from co-curriculum on a committee to reform general education also is largely a matter of the campus culture. If it is widely acknowledged that a great deal of learning occurs outside of the classroom, then key co-curricular representatives should have a place at the table. If the (faculty) campus culture sees learning as occurring primarily in the classroom, then only those who teach in a classroom should participate. Likewise, the value of including key administrators or staff from academic affairs will largely be dictated by the internal culture.

Ultimately, one will need to connect with key constituencies to gain the support needed for any reform initiative. "You have to find that common ground with each person you meet. . . . There's a line to everybody and you have to find it," wrote former majority leader of the United States House of Representatives Tip O'Neill (O'Neill 1994, 175). The review committee at NAU consisted of elected representatives from the six colleges and academic units, the chair of the liberal studies committee, and a member from the faculty senate (who also chaired the review committee). Through this structure, key constituencies were able to place representatives into the committee. The chair of the review committee was a senior faculty from the Department of Psychology who was widely respected in both the faculty senate and by the faculty at large. She possessed wonderful organizational and people skills.

In addition, the review committee included respected faculty members from the sciences and humanities as part of the membership, as well as a former president of the faculty senate. The representative membership of the review committee was also the first step taken in selling the proposal (a key political principle, discussed more fully below).

CURRICULAR CHANGE IS FOREMOST A POLITICAL PROCESS

Not to dismiss the substance of any reform, but often the values captured by any reform (or embodied in any existing program) are more powerful than any argument that can be mustered based on the details of the reform. Powerful or meaningful change must capture the values of the group, constituencies, or the institution (preferably the latter, which should embody all of the former), so that the reform is foremost a statement of values and not a collection of proposals or fixes.

To mediate a discussion among constituencies in a reform committee that remains focused on shared institutional values, the quintessential political art of compromise is paramount. Only compromise can successfully drive a political process. Members of any reform committee must be both prepared and readily willing to compromise. If constituencies within a reform committee cannot compromise so that all may benefit as the main focus of its work, then it is unlikely that compromise will occur once the recommendations begin to be worked over by the campus.

Many faculty, however, seem eager to go over the cliff with all flags flying—remaining inflexible and refusing to compromise is somehow interpreted as exhibiting standards. If posturing is the goal, then there are many paths available. If, however, something is to be accomplished—"you can't win without the votes . . . the essential ingredient of politics is compromise," wrote Tip O'Neill. "People often think when you compromise, you are compromising your morals or your principles. That is not what political compromise is. Political compromise is deferring your idea so a majority can be reached" (O'Neill 1994, 87, 92).

In May 2005, NAU sent members of the review committee to the Association of American Colleges and Universities' Institute on General Education, where they worked with resident faculty and other institutional attendees. The institute experience was critical to the success of reform efforts, since members of the committee were able to focus on negotiation, avoiding pitfalls, and developing compromises that benefitted each constituencies' interests. Additionally, members of the committee analyzed the constituency structure on campus, looking for cracks and gulfs between constituent groups and interests. In particular, discussion with institute faculty focused quite closely on the politics, strategies, and mechanisms for achieving institutional change. Many of the strategies employed by the reform committee on campus were ultimately worked out, at least tentatively, in day-long meetings with committee members and with institute faculty.

When a Reform Proposal
Has Been Worked Out, Sell It

"People like to be asked," said Tip O'Neill. "Asking is the most important part of a campaign" (O'Neill 1994, 8). The general education reform committee must be absolutely intentional in the fact that it is engaged in a campaign that is asking for people's support or, in other words, selling a proposal to the campus. This process of selling is not based exclusively on the merits of the proposal, since the proposal will move in an explicitly political arena, so the committee must ask for the support of key constituencies and the faculty at large. The merits of the argument for any set of reform proposals will take things only so far, and it is ultimately political arguments that will carry things to the close.

Beginning in the fall of 2005, the NAU review committee met bi-weekly to work out a set of reform recommendations. Soon thereafter, the committee sponsored four open faculty forums and another with the student legislature to begin to gather input on reforming the current general education program and what aspects of the program it might be possible to change. These public forums were the first step in selling a final set of reforms, through engaging the most motivated faculty and constituencies in conversation. Additionally, involving key faculty and constituent groups in these forums began to invest them in the outcome of the process.

In these public forums, a wide range of faculty, staff, administrators, and community college representatives participated (the three state universities and the community college system have a high degree of course articulation dictated by state law). An initial forum failed, whose homogeneous participants were largely made up of same department and college faculty, when the discussion degenerated into quibbles about self and group identity, student credit hour generation, and impact on budgets and funding, rather than what learning experiences students should engage in through the liberal studies program. Thereafter, the committee organized each forum to be open to all who were interested, yet engineered a mixed group of invited faculty from a variety of disciplines, departments, and colleges, as well as others, to discuss potential reform proposals.

Through forums and by email, the review committee communicated with its constituencies. Political speech was used, in that even when seeking input and further recommendations, the committee was pushing solutions by framing the conversation largely (if not exclusively) around those solutions. To a degree, this can be construed as using "strong arm tactics." However, the review committee was not a group of outsiders imposing its vision on insiders. Rather, the committee consisted of members of "insider" constituencies, and the forums and other means of communication were used to push a solution negotiated in the committee to its constituencies. While the reform recommendations were always open to modification, the reality was that suggested modifications gathered in forums, by email, or in faculty senate discussions were often changes at the margins or in specific detail. Suggested changes did not address the basic positions negotiated by the constituencies within the reform committee and actualized in the set of reform recommendations.

A preliminary set of recommendations was emailed to the campus community (all faculty, staff, student government, and administrators) for comment in late spring of 2005, and by November the reform committee was ready to email a draft report of recommendations to the campus for additional feedback and discussion. Further campus forums and discussions resulted in a revised draft report of recommendations in February 2006.

Members of the reform committee also spent a great deal of time meeting individually with key members of campus constituencies. Much like the process that assembled constituencies of influential faculty within the reform committee itself, this larger process helped bring along key campus voices in advance of a discussion of the recommendations in the faculty senate. The faculty senate leadership was also specifically targeted for individual meetings. In the end, the process of meetings was very political, in that people were consulted for their opinions on the recommendations and were also explicitly asked to support them. In individual meetings and in faculty senate debate, the point was repeatedly made that while not every constituency saw everything that they wanted in the final recommendations, each had significant points placed in the recommendations, and that for the process to succeed, everyone needed to acknowledge that there had to be compromise for the benefit of all. A final draft set of recommendations was submitted to faculty senate by the reform committee for consideration in March 2006, and the recommendations were subsequently approved in early May.

Keep the Discussion on Student Learning Outcomes (Institutional Values)

So often when it comes to curriculum, faculty immediately want to discuss additions and changes to courses and programs. In general education reform, one must keep the discussion focused on student learning outcomes for the program, because it is at that level that meaningful curricular change can occur, be assessed, and have its value demonstrated. This also focuses the discussion on areas of broad agreement (the institutional values that are captured by student learning outcomes) and keeps faculty from arguing about personal, disciplinary, or departmental turf.

At NAU, when it came time to take the draft report and share its reform recommendations with the campus, it was imperative that the discussion be kept focused on institutional values, a strategy that proved to be critical to the success of the process. Because curriculum is the most direct and profound means by which a university can embody its values, it was imperative that the mission and goals of the liberal studies program surface institutional values as embodied in the university's Mission and Strategic

Plan, which in turn reflected the values of constituent groups at NAU. As long as the conversation was kept "at thirty thousand feet," then most individuals could find that they aligned with the institutional values surfaced in the reforms. If nothing else, the review committee attempted to line up support with key faculty, so that even if an individual could not support the complete set of reform recommendations, they would not *actively* oppose the recommendations.

The review committee proposed a new mission for the liberal studies program, focused around the idea that citizenship be viewed as a dynamic concept that must be constantly investigated by the students. This twist on citizenship connected with long-standing ideas in the NAU Mission and Strategic Plan. It was also believed to be consistent with higher education at a broad level as reflected in a recent statement from the board of directors of the Association of American Colleges and Universities (2004, 3–4). The review committee cited *Greater Expectations: A New Vision for Learning as a Nation Goes to College* (AAC&U 2002), a panel report of the Association of American Colleges and Universities. Issues of social engagement were also emphasized in the reforms, so that "the understanding gained in examining a life itself comes to permeate that life and direct its course" (Nozick 1989, 12). The committee argued that an examined or self-reflective life that embraces the "capacity for critical examination of oneself and one's traditions" and the ability to see oneself as not simply a member of a local group, but "above all as human beings bound to all other human beings by ties of recognition and concern" (Nussbaum 1997, 8, 9–10) embodied critical institutional values as outlined in the NAU Mission and Strategic Plan.

NAU has long been a participant in various AAC&U initiatives and has used the *Greater Expectations* framework and its successor initiatives as key resources. Our use of national data and our involvement in the national conversation regarding liberal learning, outside of our own institution, has been important and long standing. NAU President John Haeger had earlier sponsored an AAC&U dialogue on February 3, 2003 that brought together over one hundred university and community members with AAC&U President Carol Geary Schneider to discuss the need to enhance student engagement, inclusion, and achievement in higher education.

The liberal studies reform recommendations at NAU sought to sharpen the focus of institutional values in the program. For example, the review committee reported that, for many faculty, the thematic foci of the 1999 liberal studies program were considered to be too restrictive. Students considered the foci as having little meaning. The review committee, though, believed that institutional values that were embodied in the foci connected with the NAU Mission and Strategic Plan, especially environmental consciousness and valuing the diversity of human experience, should be retained both within the revised liberal studies mission statement and explicitly in the recommended principles to guide the development of student learning outcomes for the program. The statement of principles was intended to guide the liberal studies committee as it developed and evaluated student learning outcomes for the program. Institutional values, captured as student learning outcomes, ground any set of initiatives in the common space that is easiest for various constituencies to embrace. If the conversation can be kept at the level of shared values, then it is unlikely to fracture along lines of disciplinary self interest and departmental turf.

Conclusion

Reform of the general education program at Northern Arizona University, its liberal studies program, was possible largely because those involved were attuned to the political, cultural, and constituent issues on campus. Leadership of the campus constituencies who were also members of the review committee understood the necessity to compromise, build coalitions within the committee and on campus, communicate repeatedly and in an effective manner, and understand that if all constituents at the table did not leave with something in hand, then it would be unlikely that any reform would succeed.

NAU's review committee and key members of the campus's constituencies understood that "all politics is local," and that they needed to know the institutional culture and conditions for change before they began. Reforms were initiated only through bodies that had standing with faculty, and the review committee was constituted with members who had influence and credibility with key constituencies. The committee and key constituencies within it understood that change is foremost a political process, nearly to the exclusion of the substance of the reforms themselves and that when the reform recommendations had been worked out, they needed to sell it. Ultimately, reform efforts were focused on student learning outcomes and the institutional values that were embodied in them.

An institution such as a university is by nature a political body, in that it is a community assembled from the shifting coalitions of various constituencies and their respective interests. In the interstices between the interests of constituencies, the conjunction of what is possible can appear and coalitions can be formed to support reform. Understanding the varied political dimension(s) of campus culture must be one of the key objectives of any reform effort, and it is hoped that the use of the key political principles outlined in this chapter will be of use to those contemplating general education reform.

References

Association of American Colleges and Universities (AAC&U). 2002. *Greater expectations: A new vision for learning as a nation goes to college.* National panel report. Washington, DC: AAC&U.

Association of American Colleges and Universities (AAC&U). 2004. *Our students' best work: A framework for accountability worthy of our mission.* A statement from the Board of Directors. Washington, DC: AAC&U.

Nozick, R. 1989. The examined life: Philosophical meditations. New York: Simon & Schuster.

Nussbaum, M. C. 1997. *Cultivating humanity: A classical defense of reform in liberal education.* Cambridge, MA and London: Harvard University Press.

O'Neill, T. T. 1994. *All politics is local and other rules of the game.* Avon, MA: Adams Media Corp.

CHAPTER 10

Hand *in* Hand

THE ROLE of CULTURE, FACULTY IDENTITY, and MISSION in SUSTAINING GENERAL EDUCATION REFORM

by Tim Riordan *and* Stephen Sharkey

Consider for a moment the number of organizations, conferences, grant programs, consortial projects, and other entities that have come into being in the last twenty years to advance general education reform. Literally hundreds of campuses have been involved in reform efforts. And, as was pointed out in the introduction to this collection, many simply never get anywhere because of the devitalizing politics of organizational life and/or a failure of those involved to focus on both campus culture and the processes of change. Some may begin well but fade away or be revised to death.

Yet some do actually get off the ground, survive, and even succeed—at least by what we would consider *three central measures of success*: sustained faculty engagement, demonstrably effective student learning, and ongoing renewal. In this chapter, we hope to explain how Alverno College has been one of those: a program that for over thirty years has intensely involved virtually all of the faculty; employs assessment methods that readily demonstrate to ourselves, students, and other publics what learning has occurred; and finally, has both maintained enduring disciplinary and pedagogical themes, and adapted over time to the needs of the contemporary world. Speaking in terms of the model of effective reform proposed in this book, we argue that our effort was indeed nourished by careful ongoing reflection on academic organizational culture. We have used that reflection to shape our program design to intentionally foster decision-making and other processes that enhance shared responsibility and mediate conflicts over student learning outcomes. At the same time, our experience has taught us that, although having some general sense of direction at the outset of a reform initiative is helpful, it is not always a clear path. "Where we are going" evolves over time and comes into clearer focus as ideas are tested and judged. The journey shapes the destination, and this implies for leadership the capacity to sustain and champion not only one particular goal, but the capacity of colleagues to keep working to improve their program within a general, adaptable framework.

On our campus that adaptable framework may be called a *culture of teaching and learning*. Within that culture co-exist many norms and values, practices and habits of mind, related to deciding what general education consists of, how student learning will be assessed, what faculty ought to spend a lot of time doing, and how they will be resourced and rewarded.

The specific initial reform involved instituting a curriculum that required all students to demonstrate a set of learning outcomes in order to graduate from the college — what is known as an ability-based curriculum. But the bigger story is the culture of teaching and learning that has emerged from that initial reform, and this is as much about the nature and role of the faculty and the way they think about and judge student performance as it is about curriculum itself. Alverno College took up the challenge of forging a new set of student requirements, but also a new working definition of faculty roles and rewards that made teaching for those requirements feasible and desirable. We understand that the particular practices we have found most effective for us may not always be directly transferrable to other institutional contexts, but we are confident that the principles are, and that the practices suggest ways of acting on them. We begin with an overview of the discussions that led to the initial curricular reform.

Out of Crisis, Opportunity

In the introduction to this book, Gano-Phillips and Barnett talk about the tendency of many campuses to exhibit cultural stagnation and inertia, an often unwritten way of campus life that undermines change efforts by emphasizing nostalgia for some (dubious) past era, fostering fear and competition over turf among siloed academic units, and sending paradoxical signals about the relative weight of teaching and research in faculty career advancement. The upshot is organizational paralysis or, more positively, preservation of the known evils of the status quo. But what if a campus actually takes perceived and real threats to its very existence and functioning seriously, so that the status quo becomes a luxury no one can afford? This was the situation of Alverno at the origins of its reform movement: we had to change — we needed to change — or there would be no reason for us to continue what we were about. Thus, specific historical circumstances of the college interacted with a broader sense of exploration and innovation already part of its educational tradition as a women's college, to create an *assumption of cultural change and dynamism* that has never left us.

This expressed itself in some core questions about college education we determined to ask of the entire faculty and educational staff, who would assemble together each week for a long time to debate. The most important and thought-provoking one was perhaps this, set out initially by then-president S. Joel Read in 1970: "What is it that students cannot afford to miss in your field of study?" Alverno was at an important crossroads in its mission and purpose. For many years previously, it was responsible for educating the School Sisters of Saint Francis, the religious order that founded the college. When the order decided that they would admit members to the order only after they had graduated from college, one of the primary missions of the college disappeared, and enrollment declined precipitously. But this practical crisis was not the only factor. Since the late 1960s, faculty had already been talking about what a college curriculum would look like if they were to critically examine previous practices and start with a fairly fresh slate. If the college were to survive and thrive, it needed a new reason for being — and a basis of inspiration for reform drawn from both within the institution and from the best developments in contemporary higher education. In this context, Read thought it important that faculty seriously consider the educational purposes of the institution and the latest thinking in their disciplines.

Faculty met regularly in departments during that year to explore the question posed by the president. From a process point of view, why did they do this? It was clear to the faculty that these meetings were their responsibility, and it was important that new faculty were given explicit roles in managing the debates and discussions. This invited them to try to learn sooner rather than later what effective leadership would look like in our sort of collaborative culture. Furthermore, transparency was central: conversations and white papers were frank, and doubts were important to share. In meetings about how to manage the ongoing reform, agendas usually included how to maintain collegiality and help faculty stay focused on student learning issues, rather than their disciplinary territories. As the discussions ensued, the faculty increasingly focused on what students should be able to do and how they should be able to think as a result of study in their respective disciplines. This emphasis is important to note because it reflects a turn away from focusing just on what students should study, to capabilities and ways of thinking they should develop. This kind of emphasis is at the heart of what the faculty would eventually agree to as an ability-based curriculum, and what enabled them to transcend some of the mental divisions and structural barriers that so often impede reform.

During the following year, the faculty engaged in biweekly cross-disciplinary meetings to share the results of their departmental discussions. They discovered, in these discussions with one another across disciplines, that their ideas about what students should learn in their disciplines were often more similar than different. In other words, the expectations for student learning that they were beginning to articulate in their departments may have had unique qualities based on disciplinary differences, but there were also ways of thinking and doing that seemed to be important across disciplines. This led to faculty discussion of whether there were ways of thinking and doing that should be expected of all students, no matter what their majors or course of study. In May of 1971, the faculty held a series of workshops for one another in which they explored together the outcomes of a liberal education based on their previous discussions.

For two years following the workshops, faculty worked within a structure of committees and a four-person task force charged with designing a curricular framework that reflected the kinds of abilities emerging as critical across disciplines. As a result of this extensive and intensive process, and after considerable debate and revision, the faculty agreed to establish an ability-based curriculum with eight institutional learning outcomes at its core. Those eight abilities in their most current form are:

1. Communication

2. Analysis

3. Problem solving

4. Valuing in decision-making

5. Social interaction

6. Developing a global perspective

7. Effective citizenship

8. Aesthetic engagement (Alverno College Faculty 1973/2005)

How did such a decision come about? It emerged gradually by consensus of the faculty, rather than by some segment of the faculty in a committee. To make this possible, faculty had to commit to the basic principles of an ability-based program, and know that the real work was shaping their courses and assignments to bring it to life. Faculty in a discipline would know best about how to do this, so in that sense no one was being told what courses to teach or how to teach them. The abilities framework was therefore a process strategy *sui generis*, as it shifted faculty discourse toward a common goal of defining learning. The abilities became the currency of discourse across fields of study. On the other hand, although there was a strong consensus about these abilities, there was some disagreement about how soon to actually implement the curriculum. Some thought that taking more time to fine-tune the curriculum would be a good idea, but, after discussions with faculty, the president decided that they should move ahead with the implementation in 1973, rather than delay any longer.

The eight abilities are still at the heart of the general education curriculum at Alverno and are taught across disciplinary and interdisciplinary courses that all students experience. We have what might be called a modified distribution system, with course requirements across the liberal arts developed by faculty teams in disciplinary areas, with a number of interdisciplinary courses as well. They also strongly inform the learning expectations of the majors. The definitions of abilities have been refined and revised often by faculty over the years, but faculty have remained committed to these institutional learning outcomes as graduation requirements. This means, for example, that the general education program is better seen less as a distribution system of content arranged as a compromise among competing academic interests, and more as a way to arrange the teaching and assessment of student learning outcomes that we think are crucial. It also means that study in majors and minors across the curriculum share a focus on integrating content and abilities: we teach the disciplines as frameworks that engage students in the practice of the abilities at the heart of those disciplines and that cut across disciplines.

And what was it about the process of initial reform that led to such significant and enduring results? Several things stand out. As the editors of this volume suggest, reforms that emerge from a wide range of constituents, rather than from a top-down fiat, are more likely to take root. In this instance, the president did ask the initial question for departments to consider, but the actual development of the curriculum was grounded in what faculty thought was important in their own fields of study. In this sense, the process appealed to the disciplinary interests of faculty, involved them in the actual articulation of what students should learn, and included discussions within and across departments so that all felt some stake in what was being considered.

At the same time, the process invited faculty into intense conversations across disciplines about how each field was reinforcing what everyone thought was important for students to learn how to do. At a certain point, the president did step in and say it was time to act on what the faculty had developed, and this decision suggests another key to the process, we think. In curriculum reform, perhaps especially in reform of general education, there will always be unanswered questions and perceived obstacles that lead us to hesitate before moving forward. At some point, however, the only way to determine the quality of a reform is to try it and learn from our practice. This is what the president understood and compelled her to push the faculty to move ahead. Then, as the president stepped back and more departmental and institutional leaders stepped forward, this sense of practical experimentation and evaluation was a hallmark of their practice. How did this work?

Our Ultimate Goal? "Learning that Lasts"

In taking up, amplifying, and broadening President Read's original question over the last three decades, Alverno faculty and staff learned that they needed to regularly step back from their daily work to reflectively examine the dynamics of our culture, with the ultimate goal of improving our teaching practice in the service of fostering what is often called "lifelong learning." This has occurred in three ways or venues: (1) the more local study and evaluation of teaching and learning, particularly at the course and department level; (2) the periodic program and institutional evaluations that are part of both formal accreditation and special larger evaluative projects; and (3) perhaps most significantly, a more comprehensive scholarship of teaching and learning in relationship to institutional culture in general, where we learn from our own studies and those of colleagues at other institutions.

In our most recent comprehensive published synthesis of this culture of self-evaluation, *Learning that Lasts* (Mentkowski and Associates 2000), we called these three standpoints or postures *standing in*, *standing beside*, and *standing aside* our educational practice. We developed an empirical analysis of how and when our campus and others successfully transform themselves in an ongoing way to foster high levels of students learning, and effectively document quite specifically how and when students' learning is most strongly a product of their curricula. We based this on our own experience plus that of the many other institutions with whom we have collaborated over the years in project teams and as consultants. We repeatedly found that successful campuses—those that teach well and produce student learning connected explicitly to the curriculum offered—have reflected on their educational practices from these three sorts of standpoints, regardless of what they called them, and used what they learned to improve their overall campus performance.

Here are some more specific definitions of these standpoints:

Standing In: Developing an integrated understanding of what kinds of learning frameworks, strategies, and structures work at one's own campus, arrived at through analyses of practice and campus documentation.

Standing Beside: A continuing analysis of practice in partnership with other institutions that can shape one's own transformational acts and guidelines of institutional transformation.

Standing Aside: Tailoring literature and practice review to specific campus issues (Mentkowski and Associates 2000, 366).

Some of the main features of Alverno's culture that have emerged since the implementation of the curriculum in 1973—features that have enabled us to sustain a transformative project over time—are described below. We utilize these three standpoints, shifting back and forth between what we learned locally, to what we learned from others, to what we learned from the scholarship of higher education, in order to make decisions about how to be more effective at what we do.

Principles Informing Ongoing Reform

Important principles emerged and guided the work of the faculty following the initial implementation of the curriculum and have remained constant. We want to highlight two here. The first was that *faculty recognized the need to think developmentally about student learning.* More specifically, after committing to the eight abilities as learning outcomes in the curriculum, the Alverno faculty asked themselves what each of the abilities would look like at different stages of a student's program of study. What would be the difference, for example, between what a student could do in her first year as opposed to her fourth year? How would an ability "look" in a student as she moves along? Based on this principle, the faculty articulated six levels of learning for each of the eight abilities. Following is an example of one of the abilities, analysis, and each of the levels articulated by the faculty (Alverno College Faculty 1973/2005):

Analysis:

Level 1. Observes accurately.

Level 2. Draws reasonable inferences from observations.

Level 3. Perceives and makes relationships.

Level 4. Analyzes structure and organization.

Level 5. Refines understanding of frameworks and identifies criteria for determining frameworks suitable for exploring a phenomenon.

Level 6. Independently applies frameworks from major and minor discipline to analyze complex issues.

In order to graduate from the college, students are required to demonstrate through level four of all eight abilities, and this constitutes much of the general education curriculum. Students also specialize in some of the abilities at levels five and six depending on their majors and what the departments have determined are most germane to their fields. For example, nursing students might specialize in problem solving and social interaction, while political science majors might specialize in effective citizenship and developing a global perspective. Faculty in discipline areas articulate student learning outcomes for majors and minors drawing on the basic ability framework, adapted to their particular area of study.

Another conclusion faculty quickly reached was that requiring students to learn the abilities articulated in the curriculum would necessarily mean a *significant change in the ways they determined whether students were learning or not.* They recognized that determining whether students were learning the abilities and specific content required in the curriculum meant faculty needed to design forms of evaluation that involved student performance of the abilities using the content they had studied. Many of the traditional approaches to testing simply were not appropriate for authentically determining how students were able to think and what they were able to do as a result of their studies. Understanding this was one thing; designing assessment of student learning with this in mind was quite another. Faculty looked to other institutions and to the literature on learning, but they actually found more help in contexts outside higher education, sometimes in companies that were developing forms of assessment to determine the abilities and performance of their employees. Even these examples were of limited help due to the very different contexts involved. In short, faculty themselves have learned how to create situations in which students use what they are learning to show what they understand. Student success in their courses depends on demonstration of learning outcomes in *performance-based assessments*. Alverno College has acquired a significant reputation in higher education circles for its work on assessment, but the faculty did not set out to create a culture of assessment; nor were they responding to calls for accountability. They have come to see design of assessment as an integral part of teaching, not an addition to it.

Structures and Processes

But how has Alverno managed to create the impetus and opportunity for the discourse and decision-making that lead to the articulation of these kinds of principles, the shared commitment to them, and the actions that make them a reality? First, the faculty and administration looked at the academic structure. Given the significance of the eight abilities at the heart of the curriculum, the faculty decided early on to create interdisciplinary departments for each ability area, and set forth the expectation that each faculty member serves in both a discipline and ability department. In addition to membership in discipline departments, faculty—and some academic staff—join ability departments depending on their interest and expertise. Each department has a chairperson, appointed by the vice president for academic affairs, and faculty apply to the department they are interested in joining. Faculty usually join an ability department after one or two years at the college. These departments do ongoing research on each ability, refine and revise its meaning, provide workshops for the faculty, and regularly publish materials about how to better teach and assess for it. These departments provide a powerful context for cross-disciplinary discourse and are just as significant as the discipline departments in taking responsibility for the quality and coherence of the curriculum. For example, the developmental levels of the curriculum referenced earlier are articulated by the ability departments, and they have been continually revised and refined over the years. These departments are critical to the ongoing inquiry of the faculty and the improvement of the curriculum.

How, in turn, has this kind of collaboration among faculty been supported? On many college campuses, faculty complain that they simply do not have time or cannot find common meeting times. The Alverno faculty knew and the administration agreed that having time was just as important as having a structure. To create time for faculty to meet and work on issues of teaching, learning, and assessment, no classes are scheduled on Friday afternoons, and the faculty also hold three "institutes" each year, in August, January, and May, devoted to that work. These institutes and Friday afternoon sessions are organized and designed by faculty for one another and it is the expectation that all faculty participate. We consider it our responsibility to participate in order to develop as educators by learning from one another about ways to improve student learning.

It was at one of these college institutes in the early 1980s, while faculty were discussing the qualities of effective teaching, that someone pointed out how vague our criteria were for faculty performance at the different academic ranks. For example, for teaching, the sole criterion for each rank was "teaches effectively." As a result of that discussion, a committee of representatives from the faculty senate and the discipline division chairpersons was formed and worked for the next year on more explicit criteria for the academic ranks. The committee developed criteria that spelled out more explicitly and more developmentally (as we had for our curriculum) the expectations for each academic rank, and they were approved by the faculty in 1986. These criteria include close attention not only to the qualities of good teachers as they develop from novice to experts, but also to the quality and significance of contributions faculty make to the ongoing discourse on teaching, learning, and assessment across the college. This means that faculty are evaluated as scholars of teaching who are making public their ideas to one another in order to take collective responsibility for student learning. We take this kind of "publication" as seriously as other more traditional forms of publication. It means that the faculty role is compellingly defined and rewarded in terms of helping students learn, and seeing their disciplines as frameworks for learning (See the appendix at the end of this chapter for a brief summary of Alverno's criteria for faculty rank; Alverno Faculty and Staff 1986/2005).

In what follows, we describe one example of how we have studied the ongoing culture of learning at the college, what we have learned, and how we have used the results to inform our ongoing practice.

The Making of Educators

Alverno experienced significant enrollment growth during the early 1980s, especially because of its successful Weekend College, leading to a rapid growth of new faculty for most of the decade. As the faculty expanded, the natural questions were, how do we define who we are looking for in new colleagues, and how should they both contribute to and carry on the learning culture that had been established? We knew we needed to sustain and deepen our culture of teaching and collaborative inquiry about teaching and learning. Thus, for example, applicants for faculty positions have always been interviewed by a broad group of both faculty and staff from across the college with whom they are likely to work, and are also required to submit a teaching philosophy and evidence of teaching effectiveness for consideration. But beyond committing to that sort of process, what else did we need to do? We already had an ongoing and resource-intensive faculty development program, described earlier in this chapter. How should it be shaped to meet the needs of second- and then third-generation faculty?

In the early 1990s, two faculty members organized focus groups of faculty from the full range of cohorts over a two-year period, asking them to explore their concerns and needs and to reflect on their process of personal and professional evolution (Cromwell and Sharkey 1993). Well over half the total faculty was involved directly. Respondents commented on key qualitative transitions in their performance, in terms of both what might be called professional "maturity factors" related to acquired experience with courses and curricular development, but also factors directly connected to the learning offered through our particular system of institutes, our ability-based teaching and assessment model, and opportunities to take active responsibility for parts of the curriculum comparatively early in their careers.

This resulted in some important insights about how academics became *educators* more fully over time and could structure their teaching as intellectually and professionally rewarding scholarship. These results, which were reported back out to the full faculty, helped set our ongoing development and training agendas for a considerable period thereafter. What struck us was how excited our colleagues were about their own growth, and the consistent nature of the transitions they described.

So, what did they say? Faculty reported significant shifts in *five* important aspects of their professional identity and practice. Several things stand out about these shifts—especially at well over a decade of distance from this project. At the risk of being somewhat artificially dichotomous, here are capsule summaries of what we learned about the difference between more novice faculty and those who were more expert:

1. *Their view of what teaching is and how to use the substantive material they assign.* As novices they were highly focused on the details of their presentation's content. They experienced perpetual "coverage guilt." When asked, "How was your class?" they tended

to respond with "I talked about x and then I talked about y." Their goals for student learning were almost entirely implicit.

Experienced faculty focused much more on the relationship between what they were doing as instructors and what they could observe students doing with that, cognitively and affectively. They used active/experiential learning strategies much more. When asked, "How was your class?" they responded, "The students worked on . . ." And their student learning goals were much more explicit, used as a framework for class session design.

2. *Their emotional priorities and values.* Beginning teachers were quite concerned about controlling the class and students, and valued their security as experts. They tended to get apprehensive about student questions, had short wait times when posing a question themselves, and were prone to seeing students as having to be managed in order to avoid their interfering with course progress.

   More experienced faculty learned to encourage more student responsibility and tended to teach classes by improvising off a general outline, even in dense subjects. They certainly encouraged more questions in general, and created intentional space for students who might be particularly apprehensive about saying something. They would often take risks by shifting a class to follow a signal raised by a question, and they strongly valued the "teachable moment."

3. *Their ability to analyze and reflect on the teaching/learning process.* Novices tended to look for "teaching tips" and rules of practice to handle teaching situations, even after they had been teaching a particular course for some time. They were not aware of links between their disciplinary content or frameworks and the pedagogy of that material. They sometimes saw a concern for pedagogy as a weakness, or a distraction from their true calling as a transmitter of expert knowledge.

   Experienced faculty had learned the value of theorizing about teaching, and tended to draw on fields like educational psychology, moral development, small group dynamics, and others to inform their practice. Very crucially, they said, they began to search for ways to integrate theories and research on student development with particular constructs from their home disciplines, even in the natural sciences.

4. *Their approach to assessment of student learning.* Faculty seeking positions at Alverno tended to know at least something about our model of assessment. Even so, as beginning colleagues they tended to be most concerned with how students recapitulated and organized information they had provided. Their feedback to students was very general ("good point" in the margins), and mostly negative, emphasizing what the student had done wrong. New faculty also tended to struggle with unpacking their grading sensibilities and shifting to the use of more explicit and developmental criteria for judging student work.

More experienced faculty had strongly shifted to seeing student work as "performance," and analyzing that performance's quality in terms of explicit criteria, even if they were not satisfied with the criteria they were currently using. They also tended to design assessments in developmentally-appropriate ways—for example, not asking freshmen to do things they were not ready to handle—while at the same time allowing room for performances beyond expectations.

5. *Finally, their relationship to their discipline of origin.* Some new faculty indicated they were slightly aware of initiatives within their academic discipline around teaching and learning, but despite their interest few had actually been involved in them. Even if they wanted to focus more on teaching, they tended to express their discipline's traditional view of educating as transmission, as "passing on the discipline to the next generation of best and brightest." They often viewed their courses as gates and their role as gatekeepers—their dominant professional reference group was their academic discipline.

More experienced colleagues broke through to a new professional understanding, seeing their "field" as the teaching of that field. They also were more concerned about the full range of ways their discipline might be used by students after graduation, including post-graduate education, but also including other venues, thus framing their discipline as a way of knowing that could be employed in many settings. The primary reference group of these faculty tended to be the segment within the discipline engaged with teaching issues, and also higher education groups that sought to bridge disciplines, undergraduate education, and professional development.

And to what did faculty tend to attribute all these changes? Four main features of Alverno's institutional culture, features that we have articulated earlier in this chapter, came up again and again:

1. The extensive time set aside for collaboration on teaching and learning;

2. The extensive commitment to the support of teaching, through financial resources, technology, and other means;

3. The pervasive norm of publicly discussing teaching activities and designs, the requirement to inquire systematically into teaching and learning processes, and the permission to make mistakes; and finally

4. The ability-based curriculum, which serves as a common foundation and language.

These were our findings from the early- to mid-1990s about what was working, and why, to help develop faculty as collegial educators, in terms of their professional identity and practice. These sorts of transitions are *still* how faculty discuss their own professional development over time here, in the context of our explicit teaching mission. And all faculty are continually asked to do this, both formally and informally, as part of their regular annual review—even tenured faculty who have been here for forty years.

Our approach to sustaining reform emphasizes the place of faculty values, norms, and identity in anchoring a culture of learning that can endure the natural ups and downs of both personal and institutional life. If the faculty and educational staff see themselves in the terms we portray here, they have a deep source of energy and commitment to teaching that can weather the "routine of continuous improvement," put the organizational difficulties over resources and student enrollments in a longer term perspective, and provide the enjoyment of involvement in a constantly changing creative process.

Furthermore, as the editors of this book argue, it is crucial for an institution to "identify, embrace, and address" any cultural shortcomings that can undermine or detract from successful general education work (9). Our studies, such as the one just outlined, were also meant to help discern these—and they did. For example, in a highly collaborative environment like ours, with many groups and stakeholders weighing in on any given issue, it is easy for responsibility and initiative for some needed change to become too diffused, slowing down needed action. Cognizant of this tendency in our culture, we have worked more to foster groups setting forth new ideas and proposals more assertively, and seeing what happens. Others need to learn that not everyone has to be involved in every decision. An idea with shortcomings may simply need to be tried out. One case in point: We have sought to loosen up the range of disciplinary courses that meet general education learning outcome requirements, so students have a bit more choice of classes upon entering the college. Instead of having a large general education committee figure out what the course list could include, discipline divisions do that in cooperation with a group of advisors from ability departments and other offices.

We hope we have provided some picture of how close attention to organizational process and campus culture play out, *and play out hand in hand*, in sustaining our particular general education reform. We also hope that our story might serve as data to bring to life what it means to carry forward a reform effort. It does not mean so much having a set curricular plan and destination at the start, so much as working with an adaptable framework that points toward a clear vision of student learning that can be realized in various ways.

In the mid-1980s, Alverno was invited to contribute an article to a collection called *Opportunity in Adversity: How Colleges Can Succeed in Hard Times* (Green and Levine 1985). As the title implies, this collection addressed key principles of higher-education effectiveness through case studies about colleges that seemed to be succeeding against the odds. We agreed to contribute our case study at that time not only to make more public something of our educational model so that others might learn, but also to take the chance to systematically review Alverno's evolution over the first decade of our reform to see what we could learn about our own organizational culture. Both President Read (a historian by training and inclination) and the college archives had preserved considerable documentation about the emergence of the new ability-based curriculum. Read partnered with a sociologist of organizations to review not only the formal record of memos, minutes, reports, and student information, but also the more off-the-record recollections of faculty who had been around in the first generation of reform. It is interesting to see how well the now 20-plus year old article, *Alverno College: Toward a Community of Learning* (Read and Sharkey 1985), holds up even today, and how it reflects some of the same themes we have discussed here. We conclude here by reviewing some of those themes.

Clearly, developing a *strong and widespread consensus* around the direction of any reform is crucial. The initial curriculum reform at Alverno grew out of discussions among the entire faculty, and proceeded based on insights from the faculty themselves. Perhaps what was somewhat unique about Alverno was the breadth and depth of the commitment to teaching and learning at the outset and how congruently working toward it was rewarded. This has meant that from the start *responsibility and authority for curricular reform and management have been widely and quite democratically distributed*. Many opportunities have been developed to bring newer faculty and educational staff into the circles of decision-making. This slowed us down at times, but also ensured the depth of buy-in regarding any important decision. It was true that the initial impulse for organizational change came from a core group, and that President Read led by agenda-setting. But the reform quickly spread out horizontally and vertically through the institution, and remained that way. Taking collective responsibility for student learning has been a hallmark of the learning culture at Alverno and has allowed us to sustain and enhance the general education reform of nearly forty years ago.

The structures and processes of the college that have been developed over the years have clearly reinforced this shared responsibility and have supported the principles of the curriculum. The *organizational design of faculty responsibilities into a matrix structure of crosscutting disciplinary and ability departments* has encouraged both interdisciplinary teamwork among the faculty and cohesion in the curriculum. Put as simply as possible, everyone is involved with the overall curriculum in one way or another; and the curriculum, with its ability focus and constant exploration of how abilities are expressed in the study of different fields, has supported a common educational terrain with a common language.

Our reward structure and processes for evaluation of faculty for faculty retention, tenure, and promotion have ensured that there is *not a dichotomy between the expressed values of the institution and the actual practice within it. If student learning is to be at the heart of an institution's mission, we have learned, recognition of that work and allocation of resources in support of it must be of the highest priority.* In effect, we have expected the same sort of focus on learning among faculty and staff that we expect of students. At the heart of this organizational commitment has been *using our assessment model on ourselves.* Thus, for example, we articulated sets of criteria for successful performance as a teacher and colleague that operated the same way for us as they did for students. Our peer review process, annual self-evaluations, and more comprehensive reviews for promotion were all structured around a general process of self assessment using a set of explicit criteria and incorporation of feedback from those in a position to know our work best. We also are students.

As we suggested at the beginning of this chapter, some of the particulars of our practice over the years may be unique to our institutional context. For example, what works for a liberal arts college for women may differ from what makes a difference at a large comprehensive university. We have found in our collaboration with colleagues across higher education, however, that the themes and principles discussed here and throughout this book surface consistently in discussions of curricular and institutional reform. We hope that the processes we have explored here will provide some help in the challenging effort that still lies ahead for all of us in higher education in fostering the kind of student learning we envision.

APPENDIX: Criteria for Academic Ranks

Excerpted from Alverno Faculty and Staff (1986/2005). *The Alverno educator's handbook.* Milwaukee, WI: Alverno College Institute. [Original work published 1986, revised 1989, 1990, 1996, 1998, and 2005.]

BEGINNING ASSISTANT PROFESSOR

Teaches Effectively:
- develops understanding of ability-based curriculum and assessment
- teaches for appropriate abilities in disciplinary context
- provides direction, clarity, and structure for students
- provides timely and helpful feedback
- is available for and respectful of students
- communicates enthusiasm for one's discipline

Works Responsibly in the College Community:
- participates in required meetings and workshops
- collaborates effectively with other faculty and staff
- uses formal and informal feedback to improve performance
- implements departmental, divisional, school, and institutional goals
- explores opportunities for individual contributions
- identifies, refines, and acts on individual faculty development goals

Develops Scholarship:
- formalizes plans for continuing education or degree completion
- identifies scholarly activities/research areas in discipline in relation to teaching
- develops connections with professional community

Serves the Wider Community:
- identifies possible areas of service
- participates in outreach activities

EXPERIENCED ASSISTANT PROFESSOR

Teaches Effectively:

- creates learning experiences and assessments that reflect integration of discipline and generic abilities
- organizes learning experiences that assist students to achieve outcomes
- provides feedback directed toward specific abilities and individual need
- responds to students in a variety of settings with sensitivity to background and learning style
- generates student enthusiasm for learning
- refines teaching practice based on self-assessment and feedback

Works Responsibly in the College Community:

- makes significant conceptual contributions to meetings and workshops
- initiates collaboration with other faculty and staff
- enacts individual faculty development plan
- makes workable relationship between individual goals and goals of department, division, school, or institution
- makes contributions that influence the institution in the department, division, school, and beyond

Develops Scholarship:

- makes progress in continuing education or degree completion
- pursues scholarly activity that integrates disciplinary area and teaching
- participates in broader professional community

Serves the Wider Community:

- contributes actively to the wider community

ASSOCIATE PROFESSOR

Teaches Effectively:

- integrates disciplinary/professional learning with teaching experience to shape teaching practice

- applies developmental frameworks and learning theory to teaching practice
- organizes learning experience to allow for flexibility in responding to students
- creates alternative forms of feedback and assessment
- creates a variety of opportunities for students to pursue specialized interests
- engages in dialogue about teaching in the higher education community

Works Responsibly in the College Community:
- provides leadership in developing curriculum and teaching effectiveness
- develops institutional role through significant contributions
- creates strategies to enhance effective collaboration in the institution
- pursues opportunities to improve the quality of teaching and learning across the institution

Develops Scholarship:
- holds terminal degree
- pursues specialized scholarly research that integrates disciplinary area and teaching
- applies specialized scholarly research to improvement of teaching and curriculum development in the institution
- makes contributions to broader professional community

Serves the Wider Community:
- renders distinctive service to the wider community

PROFESSOR

Teaches Effectively:
- expands scope of scholarship to include new areas/other disciplines to inform student-centered teaching practice
- takes leadership in developing materials, presentations, etc., that address significant curriculum concerns

- influences professional dialogue about teaching scholarship in the higher education community

Works Responsibly in the College Community:
- provides distinctive leadership in the institution
- assists others to develop in leadership roles

Develops Scholarship:
- holds terminal degree
- engages in substantive scholarly/research activity that contributes to higher education
- takes leadership in encouraging research that improves the quality of learning in the institution

Serves the Wider Community:
- provides substantive service and leadership to the wider community

References

Alverno College Faculty. 1973/2005. *Ability-based learning program* [brochure]. Milwaukee, WI: Alverno College Institute. [Original work published 1973; revised 1980, 1983, 1985, 1988, 1991, 1992, 1993, 1994, 1996, 2000, 2002, and 2005.]

Alverno Faculty and Staff. 1986/2005. *The Alverno educator's handbook.* Milwaukee, WI: Alverno College Institute. (Original work published 1986; revised 1989, 1990, 1996, 1998, and 2005).

Cromwell, L., and S. Sharkey. 1993. *The making of educators.* Unpublished manuscript. Milwaukee, WI: Alverno College Institute.

Green, J. S., and A. Levine. (Eds.). 1985. *Opportunity in adversity: How colleges can succeed in hard times.* San Francisco: Jossey-Bass.

Mentkowski, M., and Associates. 2000. *Learning that lasts. Integrating learning, development and performance in college and beyond.* San Francisco: Jossey-Bass.

Read, S.J., and S. Sharkey. 1985. Alverno College: Toward a community of learning. In J. S. Green and A. Levine (Eds.), *Opportunity in adversity: How colleges can succeed in hard times.* (195–214). San Francisco: Jossey-Bass.

CHAPTER 11

Utilizing Change Theory *to* Promote General Education

PRACTICAL APPLICATIONS

by Stephen C. Zerwas *and* J. Worth Pickering

As higher education confronts the challenges of the twenty-first century such as access, accountability, assessment, and accreditation, we are forced to change—and change more quickly than we are accustomed. As institutional leaders propose changes to meet those demands, someone typically replies "you are changing the culture for faculty" (and administrators as well). The inference is that changing the culture is a negative thing, but in fact it may be quite positive. Nevertheless, changing the culture in higher education is a challenge. And it raises questions about how one changes the culture, and who are the leaders capable of doing so. As Rountree, Tolbert, and Zerwas noted in Chapter 1, meaningful cultural change demands the voices of all constituents; thus leadership can come from administrators, staff, or students, as well as faculty. In the introduction to this book, Gano-Phillips and Barnett identified institutional culture as one of two issues that could defeat any change effort, and challenged us to think about changing that culture as part of our process to reform general education. The goal of this chapter is to explore some ideas for changing the culture to promote general education reform.

Managing a reform or change initiative in higher education is a highly complex and difficult task. The reform of general education is made even more difficult because it results in the convergence of many different cultural and institutional elements that may strongly disagree about the purposes and priorities of education, academic freedom, faculty autonomy, and shared governance. It is not simply an issue of actions and reactions. Any reform effort can take highly unpredictable and unexpected paths and be influenced by many unknown forces. The application of change theories does not guarantee the success of a reform effort, but it does increase the likelihood of success. Change theories provide a structure through which the reform process can be better understood. The application of change theories enables users to identify significant elements within the institutional culture and their impact on the reform process, and provides a compass to guide action and implementation. Change theories highlight the need to analyze the shared attitudes, values, goals, practices, and histories described in Chapter 1. Please note that in the process of discussing change we have referred to theories rather than one individual theory. No single theory or model can account for all of the complexity and variability found within higher education. It is only through the use of multiple change theories and models that reform efforts can be better understood and implemented. There are a wide variety of theories and models to choose from, including Lewin's change model, systems approaches, and constant adaptation models, to name but a few (Van de Ven & Poole 1995).

Kurt Lewin's (1952) classical change model described behavior as a dynamic balance between driving and restraining forces. His model has been influential, and elements of it are common in many other, more recent change models. In Lewin's model, through the analysis of driving and restraining forces it is possible to create an environment in which change can more readily occur. Lewin's change model describes three distinct stages: unfreezing, moving, and refreezing. Each stage is described as part of a sequence in which specific tasks must be accomplished.

In the first stage, *unfreezing*, it is necessary to analyze the existing status quo to better understand the interplay of driving and restraining forces. As discussed in Chapter 1, although there are many voices demanding change and reform, there may also be many constituencies who are highly invested in maintaining the existing system and the culture that supports it. The status quo is seen as a balanced equilibrium of these driving and restraining forces. For change to occur it is necessary to upset the balance inherent in the status quo. Imbalance can be accomplished through decreasing restraining forces, increasing driving forces, or a combination of both approaches. Edgar Schein (1995), elaborating on Lewin's change model, identified three elements in the unfreezing process: dissatisfaction with the status quo, the ability to recognize that dissatisfaction, and the creation of the requisite sense of security to enable action. Promoting dissatisfaction with the status quo requires encouraging the university community to grapple with the deficiencies of the existing system. Promoting the requisite sense of security necessary for movement requires communication, transparency, and involvement as has been discussed in previous chapters by Burney and Perkins (Chapter 2), Brailow and Whitney (Chapter 4), and Mitchell, Jonson, Goodburn, Minter, Wilson, and Kean (Chapter 8). The creation of the feeling that "if change does not occur, it will not be possible to meet existing needs" is a prerequisite to a change-ready state.

The second stage, *moving*, consists of an implementation stage in which previous behaviors are exchanged for new behaviors. Three activities can facilitate movement: identifying inherent weaknesses in the status quo, viewing status quo from alternative perspectives, and collaboration to explore new behaviors to resolve the problem and adapt to the changing environment. During this stage, resistance will occur and must be addressed. Identifying the sources of resistance and implementing appropriate antidotes to that resistance is a function of the change leadership, one of the key variables addressed in this book. Change strategies must be applied to ensure cooperation and involvement with the change effort. Developing strategies to promote engagement were shown by Dennis, Halbert, and Phillips in Chapter 3, Beal and Trigger in Chapter 5, and Roach in Chapter 7 to be critically important in promoting a culture in support of change.

The third stage, *refreezing*, deals with ensuring that the change which has occurred will continue over time. Implementing timelines, another of the key process variables addressed in this book, is not only necessary to effect the desired changes, but it is also necessary for monitoring and assessing the impact of the change process. In order to achieve lasting reform, it will be necessary to institutionalize new behaviors and develop new processes that will ensure their continued implementation. Institutionalizing a reform effort involves rebalancing driving and restraining forces so that the reform effort remains a new status quo.

Lewin's (1952) model has been criticized for suggesting that refreezing and reestablishment of the status quo is a permanent position. However, Lewin argued that refreezing is a necessity, even if it is only achieved for a short period of time. Without refreezing, old habits, practices, and modes of behavior will reassert themselves, and although the institution may continue to maintain the *image* of change, it is more likely that some form of the previous status quo will reassert itself. As shown by the Alverno College experience (Riordan and Sharkey, Chapter 10) the price of maintaining a reform is ongoing vigilance. Through incorporating support of the change process in criteria for faculty rank, ongoing support of the reform effort was institutionalized in their culture of learning.

The application of Lewin's (1952) change model to higher education has been questioned also because of the uniquely complex nature of higher education. Change efforts in higher education must cope with shared governance, goal ambiguity, faculty independence, academic values, and tenure and promotion. In higher education it is not simply a matter of focusing on the behaviors of the leaders who make decisions and then eliciting support from the troops. Although there is a hierarchical administrative structure in higher education institutions, they are also complex social organizations in which a multitude of cultures are in play: departmental, political, collegial, social, and collegiate, to name but a few. As Gano-Phillips and Barnett described in the introduction to this book, successful change results in a convergence of processes and cultural factors in which no one process will work with all cultural elements. Decision-making may be a function of personal relationships, traditions, and the participation of many people. This makes it difficult to apply a rational, linear, top-down approach to higher educational reform (Birnbaum 1991).

Despite its limitations, Lewin's (1952) change model provides insights and explanations that make understanding change more manageable and accessible. Other change models describe change from a variety of different perspectives, including looking at change from the perspective of the changee, or from different institutional cultures, or looking at the complexity of the change. Each of these models provides additional insights that can be applied, depending on who will be promoting change and the importance of interactions among the different cultures.

This chapter focuses on the moving and refreezing elements of change and examines how these stages apply to general education reform. Before looking at the moving and refreezing of general education reform, it is assumed that the elements of unfreezing have occurred. The culture has recognized the need for reform and has established the security necessary to enable new behavioral adaptations. A significant weakness of many reform efforts is that they have established themselves in opposition to current structures, rather than building upon existing elements and institutional priorities (Ewell 2002). While it is necessary to develop a distinct identity for the reform effort and articulate the weaknesses in the current status quo, it is also necessary to honor the contributions of the many who created and supported the current general education program. The limitations of the current system reflect the best attempts of our colleagues to address student and institutional needs, and these limitations may simply reflect the changing needs of our students and institutions.

The reform of general education represents a transformational change for an entire institution. It challenges many of the things we do and the way we think about them. It challenges beliefs and understandings and requires changes in cultural norms and in behavior. It may involve reforming an existing program or creating something totally new, but it fundamentally changes the way we function, and therefore, it is the most difficult type of change to achieve, and will require the greatest diversity of change strategies.

Moving

It is presumed that when implementing a reform the preliminary work of clearly defining the reform and confirming that the reform is necessary have been performed. As is shown in previous chapters, the use of national (Beal and Trigger, Chapter 5) and local (Kelsch, Hawthorne, and Steen, Chapter 6) assessment data were found to be highly effective in promoting the change agenda, despite substantial differences in institution size and type. It is also assumed that the forces promoting and hindering reform have been identified. In addition, while we are focused on changing the culture, we cannot lose sight of the fact that the culture is composed of a variety of individuals who may require different strategies for change to be effective. The selection and application of a change strategy (or change strategies) is heavily dependent upon both the individuals involved and the institutional culture. In order to achieve meaningful reform, it is necessary to honor the existing cultural norms even when we may be attempting to change them (Mitchell et al., Chapter 8). An inappropriate change strategy may actually inhibit reform, rather than promote it.

Lewin's (1952) change model described change as movement, rather than a series of distinct steps. It is a process of trial and error where the changee attempts to adapt to new conditions and circumstances. The focus of the changing or moving stage is on the behaviors of the changee. It is recognized that individuals, departments, and units may find themselves at different stages simultaneously. If the unfreezing was insufficiently achieved, it may be necessary to re-address these issues even after tentative movement has begun. Some individuals, departments, and units may still be at the unfreezing stage while others may have successfully transitioned into the movement stage. Any change approach must account for differences in the ways that individuals, departments, and units respond to change and adjust strategies to meet them where they are, rather than where we would like them to be.

Individuals, departments, and units will adopt change only if they can envision the benefits outweighing the costs. They will change their behaviors if they feel they need to, if it is beneficial to them, and if they have the capacity to do so. This requires focusing on the needs, wants, perceptions, and abilities of those who will be changing their behaviors. It should be recognized that change requires the acquisition of new information, the adoption of new behaviors, and potentially an alteration of values and beliefs. Important elements in motivating the change, whether it be in an individual or a program, are to support the reform and monitor the degree to which the reform is occurring. Commitment to change is difficult, because it involves giving up the security of a known state for an unknown future, as recognized by Brailow and Whitney in Chapter 4.

One of the "seven habits of highly successful people" is "seek first to understand and then to be understood" (Covey 2004, 235). Understanding the reform process from the perspective of the changee provides understandings that can direct actions. Harvey (2001) identified three elements that assist in understanding change from the perspective of the changee: *potential, payoff,* and *pressure*. Potential is the capacity of a person to achieve the change or the reform. Payoff is the answer to the question, "What's in it for me?" Pressure addresses the appropriate level of stress that is needed to affect the desired reform. When implementing reform, attention to these three issues from the perspective of the changee cannot be underestimated.

Increasing the *potential* for change is the first element, and involves ensuring that faculty members have the information, skills, and resources they need in order to participate in the reform. This includes fostering an understanding of the intents and purposes of general education, describing the needs for reform, clarifying deficiencies in the current general education program, and promoting faculty development activities that will enable faculty to effect the reforms sought. People implementing change must have the necessary resources: the personal, emotional, and intellectual capital required to accomplish the desired behaviors. If a person does not understand the general education reform and their role in it, they do not have the potential to change their behaviors. If a person does not know how to revise their course to achieve general education outcomes, general education reform will not be achieved. The need to develop potential may vary greatly from individual to individual, but it cannot be assumed to be the same for all people. The ability to change behaviors is a prerequisite for any reform movement.

The second element described by Harvey (2001) is *payoff*. In order to address payoff, it is necessary to answer the question: how are faculty recognized and rewarded for their contributions to the reform process? There may be benefits for students, parents, legislators, and administrators, but how do the people who will actually be implementing the change benefit? The reality is that reform may result in more work, less time, less recognition, and fewer rewards. People will only implement change if they can see some benefit that will make their efforts worthwhile. Faculty may see personal benefit and rewards in the accomplishments of their students. If it is believed that students will truly benefit, faculty are more likely to derive intrinsic benefit. Without this intrinsic benefit, will participation in the reform effort result in decreased work, increased recognition, better pay, better working conditions, or is it simply another unfunded mandate thrust on their plate that is already perceived as too full? To ignore the fact that real change comes at a cost is unrealistic. As described in several other chapters, there must be an institutional commitment to provide necessary resources to effect change. Perhaps the flip side of the payoff dilemma is the answer to the question, "What will happen to me if I do not support the reform effort? Will I lose rewards if I do not support the desired reform, or will I be rewarded for my lack of support?"

The third element described by Harvey (2001) is *pressure*. Pressure involves the motivation to effect change. Pressure can be generated at any level, by peers, by students, and by administrators. The pressure may be intrinsic in terms of an individual's need to see students succeed and to be part of the contribution to that learning. Normative pressures can be created through comparisons between where the institution is and where we want it to be. Pressure can also be applied by the supervisors, legislators, students, and parents. Sources of pressure can include the institution's leadership, accrediting agencies, local and national data, and institutional entities whose needs are not being met. The application of pressure can be as important in motivating the changee to support the reform as providing them with payoff through rewards and recognition.

CHANGE STRATEGIES

The selection of a change strategy requires an understanding of the people who are responsible for its implementation. The implementation of a reform strategy requires the answer to three questions: Do the faculty have the resources they need in order to deliver the reform? Is there any personal benefit to the implementation of reform? Finally, do the faculty feel any need to implement the reform? Harvey (2001) identified three strategies for promoting movement and change. These included *power-coercive, rational-educational*, and *normative–re-educative* strategies. In reviewing the three approaches it is apparent that they can be used in combination with one another for a more effective approach.

A *power-coercive* strategy is mandated from the top down. Examples of this type of change strategy include a decision by a university system that reform is necessary and that the reform can be achieved through a directive demanding that institutions adopt the reform. Another illustration of a power-coercive strategy could include mandating the adoption of requirements from regional accrediting agencies. The primary advantage of the power-coercive approach rests with the ability to implement change rapidly. A significant disadvantage of the power-coercive approach rests with the fact that it may have been only superficially adopted without any significant commitment to maintain the reform. Ownership of reform is not something that can easily be commanded from the top. It can only be built through a culture of mutual respect.

The power-coercive strategy can take two forms. One form would be the directive approach, in which the people delivering the reform are expected to adjust their behaviors because they are told to do so. As noted above, the advantage of this approach is that change can occur very quickly, although those who are expected to implement the reform are left out of the decision-making process—even though they may have had potentially valuable information to share. A significant risk of this strategy is that the reform will occur without any commitment to its implementation, and thus the reform may be superficial and short lived.

Another approach to reform within the power-coercive model that is more inclusive is a negotiated approach. This approach still involves a power-coercive element; however, it allows for greater involvement based on increased discussion of the reform and a negotiation of its application. It has the advantage that involving the faculty in the decision-making and application process can result in a greater likelihood of their support of the change.

The *rational-educational* strategy is based on the premise that if people are aware of the need for reform, they will be more likely to act based upon that knowledge. Educational activities for this strategy may include persuasion, conference participation, professional development activities, and hiring outside consultants. In comparison to the power-coercive approach, this approach will require a significantly greater amount of time. Utilizing this strategy promotes a shared set of institutional values and common understanding, but may not result in the actual desired behavior change. This approach can result in the "knowing–doing gap," in which the need for reform is recognized, but there is no personal commitment to making reform happen. This was best illustrated by the early experiences at the University of North Dakota (Chapter 6), where faculties were aware of the need to change, but did not feel the need to translate that awareness into action.

In some ways, all the chapters and contributing institutions describe having used the rational-educational approach. As educators, we naturally gravitate towards this approach. Unfortunately, of all the change strategies, this approach has been shown to be one of the *least* effective. Simple awareness and understanding does not guarantee a willingness to act upon that understanding. However, the rational-educational approach does provide a context through which a reform effort can be understood and evaluated.

The final approach articulated by Harvey (2001) was the *normative re-educative* strategy. This strategy requires the participation of those who are most directly affected by change in determining the content and the direction of that change. This type of change is slow, and its final outcome is more difficult to predict. A major advantage of this change strategy is that more people are likely to support the reform, because they were directly involved in crafting it.

While the normative–re educative strategy seems the most appealing and potentially the most successful approach, a comprehensive change strategy might involve elements of all three change strategies. Typically, early in the process the president and/or provost, perhaps with the support and involvement of their immediate staff, decides that it is time to reform general education. They appoint a committee or task force and set a deadline for completion and implementation. This is the power-coercive strategy. As the committee meets, hopefully they will decide to share their process and findings with the faculty through a series of open forums. This is the rational-educative strategy. If the committee is well informed and knowledgeable about the process of changing the culture, they will also develop some normative–re-educative strategies to be more inclusive of all faculty who will be involved in implementing the reformed general education curriculum. How does the committee pull all of this together and apply theory to practice?

APPLYING THEORY TO PRACTICE

The first question in applying theory to practice is: who is responsible for changing the culture? The obvious answer is the president, provost, vice president for academic affairs, or similar official who has decided that the change is necessary. Rarely do those responsible for general education reform recognize themselves as empowered change agents first. However, the power to effect change frequently relies on the vision and commitment of a few people dedicated to promoting an agenda of reform. Presidents and provosts must support the work and speak about it whenever possible to motivate others to participate, but they have too many other issues that they are supporting to offer their full, daily support. They have tasked others to perform this work and will hold them accountable for achieving it. After accepting the responsibility, it is helpful to recognize that, in addition to planning the general education reform, we also have to plan how to implement it and assess its effectiveness, and now we realize that we must also plan our change strategy. How are we going to change the culture to support general education reform?

In the introduction to this book, Gano-Phillips and Barnett provided a good definition of institutional culture as "the set of shared attitudes, values, goals, and practices that characterizes an institution—the unwritten rules of business that determine who contributes to what decisions, when, where, why, and how" (see page 8). They went on to suggest that "an institution's culture is typically viewed as extremely stable and apparently immoveable." Gano-Phillips and Barnett challenge us to think about how we plan to change the culture of the institution as part of the process of reforming general education.

Several skills are required, including leadership, empathy, communication, collaboration, and assessment. Actually, empathy, communication, collaboration, and perhaps even assessment, are embodied in good leadership. In addition, leadership, communication, and assessment (using data to inform processes) are several of the key process variables discussed in this book. Servant leadership seems uniquely suited to work within the culture of higher education, with its decentralized decision-making structure:

> The servant-leader is servant first. . . . It begins with the natural feeling that one wants to serve, to serve first. Then conscious choice brings one to aspire to lead. He is sharply different from the person who is leader first, perhaps because of the need to as-

suage an unusual power drive or to acquire material possessions. The difference manifests itself in the care taken by the servant-first to make sure that other people's highest priority needs are served. The best test, and difficult to administer, is: do those served grow as persons; do they, while being served, become healthier, wiser, freer, more autonomous, more likely themselves to become servants? And, what is the effect on the least privileged in society; will he benefit or, at least, will he not be further deprived? (Greenleaf 1991/2008, 15)

The key question is, do those served grow as persons? How do we help the faculty and administrators responsible for implementing the change grow as a result of this process? According to Keith (2008), servant leadership involves self-awareness, good listening skills, the ability to develop colleagues, coaching rather than controlling, and the ability to energize colleagues and engage their knowledge and skills in the task. Compared to the more power-based forms of leadership, servant leadership involves sharing power rather than accumulating power, and helping people to accomplish tasks rather than making them accomplish tasks. Servant leaders welcome others, including subordinates, as leaders as well. All members of a team can engage in leadership of different tasks or parts of the general education reform project, which helps them in their own personal and professional development.

Many of us are able to identify servant leaders who have been very effective and have, through their leadership style, had positive impacts on our lives. According to Keith (2008), servant leadership is also endorsed by a variety of management experts, including Ken Blanchard (*Leading at a Higher Level* 2006), Jim Collins (*Good to Great* 2001), Stephen Covey (*The 7 Habits of Highly Effective People* 2004), and Peter Drucker (*The Effective Executive* 2006). Who are the servant leaders at your institution? Who are the people who seem to get a lot accomplished by building good relationships with colleagues across campus? Are those skills that you possess or can learn? What can we do to identify potential leaders at our institution and marshal their abilities in support of change?

In *The Tipping Point*, Gladwell (2000) discussed the importance of contagiousness, the occasionally large effect of little causes, and the way that an epidemic happens in one dramatic moment—the tipping point. While epidemics typically carry negative connotations, there are also positive epidemics. How does one begin an epidemic in support of general education reform? Gladwell stressed the important contributions of three types of people—mavens, connectors, and salesmen. Each of these types are potential leaders who can be empowered to support change. In a social epidemic, mavens are data banks. They provide the message. Connectors are social glue—they spread it. But there is also a select group of people—salesmen—"with the skills to persuade us when we are unconvinced of what we are hearing" (Gladwell 2000, 70). Mavens, connectors, and salespeople can help us to make reforming general education contagious. As we lead the general education reform on our campus, can we identify mavens, connectors, and salespeople who will help us to tip the reform movement?

After writing *The Tipping Point*, Gladwell (2000) heard from a variety of people who helped him to refine and extend his ideas. Two ideas in particular are helpful to creating an epidemic in support of general education reform. Gladwell warned "beware the rise of immunity" (271). Just as many of us have become immune to telemarketers, we have also become immune to "marketing" etc. via email. Gladwell suggests a resurgence in the importance of word-of-mouth for communicating important ideas. Are we going to be able to sell the reform of general education via email, or will we be better served with word-of-mouth communication using mavens, connectors, and salespeople? And, if the latter, how do we find these people? While Gladwell suggests that connectors may well find us, he suggests that we may need "maven traps" to identify mavens. We need to find faculty and staff among us who can see the importance of reforming general education and have the respect of many of their colleagues. Mavens are the people that their colleagues will seek out for information about many topics and will generally follow their advice. In Chapter 9, Scarnati offered good advice about the political nature of the process of reforming general education and a variety of key issues to consider as we select our general education committee.

Becoming servant leaders, building a team of servant leaders among our colleagues and subordinates, and identifying mavens, connectors, and salespeople all seem to be part of the normative–re-educative approach to change described by Harvey (2001). Recognizing that few have power in higher education to make things like sustainable general education reform happen, the servant leadership style is well suited to engage colleagues in completing the task of reforming general education.

The importance of leadership is highlighted by many of the authors in this book. It is evident that leadership is perhaps the key variable among all seven addressed in this book. Leadership of a reform effort can take place at a multitude of levels. It can include the institutional leadership of the chancellor/president, provost, or university system. Leadership can also be provided at a group level such as faculty senate, general education council, general educational review committee, or assessment committee. Leaders can also be found among influential campus individuals whose influence is based on personal characteristics rather than position or affiliation. There is no single pattern of leadership. Top-down and bottom-up leadership are both required. It is critical to the success of the general education reform effort for the general education committee to take a leadership role and develop leaders at many levels.

RESISTANCE

Resistance is an inevitable part of any change process. Outram (2004a) recommends that resistance should be "understood, anticipated, accepted, and used." Resistance to change and reform can take two forms, active and passive. Each presents its own unique challenge. The absence of resistance indicates that either the reform is not necessary, or that there is so little investment in the reform or belief in its impact that it is unnecessary to resist. This would reflect a passive form of resistance because it is not immediately observable. Apathy, denial, and avoidance all represent potentially passive forms of resistance. Active resistance is much easier to address, simply because it is overt and visible, and as such is more amenable to resolution. It should be assumed that both active and passive forms of resistance are present and require action to minimize their impact on the reform process.

Active and passive types of resistance can take many forms. Forms of resistance can include boredom, superiority, apathy, hostility, fear, procrastination, need for recognition, scapegoating, and disengagement to name but a few. Through developing resistance strategies that match the unique forms of resistance presented it is possible to address resistance and not allow it to derail the reform process (Harvey 1995; Outram 2004b).

A variety of resistance strategies can be employed depending upon the form resistance takes. Making the reform meaningful, relevant, and feasible can diminish resistance through creating manageable win–win situations. Through involvement in decision-making, collaboration, providing support, and recognizing contributions it is possible to build trust and promote reform. Responses to apathy, fear of the unknown, loss of control, and needs for security can include clear communication, authenticity, transparency, reassurance, and involvement. Procrastination can be addressed through the application of reasonable timelines. Although these strategies may appear self-evident, it will require the ongoing monitoring of the campus environment to identify resistance as it occurs so that it can be dealt with productively (Harvey 1995; Outram 2004a).

Institutionalizing the Reform Effort: Refreezing

The process of unchanging is identical to the process of changing. Without attention to the same elements that were responsible for the reform, the institution can quietly return to its unreformed state. Refreezing in the new location does not simply happen. It is the result of a reduction of driving and restraining forces and monitoring the delivery systems of reform and their outcomes. If driving forces are reduced without a reduction of the restraining forces, then unchanging and unreform will occur. If the reform process goes unmonitored, then the reform effort may be lost without anyone becoming aware of the loss. Riordan and Sharkey (Chapter 10) discussed the process of sustaining their culture of learning once change had occurred.

Refreezing may be made more difficult by the strategy employed to effect change. The use of the power-coercive strategy requires that change occurs, because people are forced to participate. This creates the problem of what will occur when the power and coercion are withdrawn. Have the restraining forces been permanently reduced, or are they only held in check by the actions of a person or group with power? There are three conditions under which the power-coercive approach to reform will continue to be effective: (1) if it continues to be applied, (2) if the restraining forces for reform are diminished, or (3) if another change strategy such as a normative–re-educative or rational-educational strategy takes its place. Naturally, the application of the alternative strategies may be made more difficult because of the conflict generated by the method of reform. The rational-educational strategy only works if three conditions are met: adequate resources, clear and unambiguous goals, and no conflict over priorities. When any of these elements is not present, the reform may no longer be supported.

In order to ensure that the reform effort is fully implemented and continues to be implemented, it is necessary to create some form of oversight. Several chapters in this book have addressed the need for and creation of new faculty structures to provide the oversight and accountability necessary for maintaining a reform effort. As transitions occur through faculty movement, reassignment, and attrition, it is necessary to ensure new faculty continue to deliver the reform as it was intended. This requires using data to monitor performance and attention to governance, which are two of the process variables addressed in this book. Although individual differences in the delivery of the general education reform can be encouraged, the fundamental elements of reform should not be compromised. Continued faculty engagement will only be possible with the continued application of the principles of payoff, pressure, and potential. Ongoing efforts to provide training and professional development for instructors will be required. The Alverno College experience described by Riordan and Sharkey (Chapter 10) provides numerous exemplary approaches used by that institution to sustain and enhance desired change.

General education courses themselves will continue to evolve over time. Simply because a course at one time delivered the desired elements of general education does not guarantee that it will continue to do so. Course evolutions may be either supportive or detrimental to the intent of reform. A process of accountability must be established to ensure goal delivery continues. A system of ongoing review must be established. This will require the creation of a process to certify and recertify courses providing general education and a process of quality assurance for those unable to do so. Several chapters have discussed the perils of the unmonitored delivery of general education and the need to refocus courses that have drifted from the intent of the general education program. The re-certification process ensures an atmosphere of ongoing collaboration and discussion of the general education program. Faculty are required to take responsibility for the delivery of general education goals and document their role in achieving them. Likewise, it is necessary to verify the consistent quality in the delivery of general education goals in multiple sections of the same course. The process of recertification and approval requires the active involvement of faculty both in understanding general education and the recertification process. Faculty involvement in establishing criteria for course approval and recertification across the institution emphasizes the purposes of general education and encourages its ongoing delivery.

Assessing student learning provides a second element in the movement and refreezing process. Without the ability to provide convincing evidence that desired levels of student learning are being achieved, it is difficult to make the case for maintaining the status quo or for change. As was illustrated by Scarnati (Chapter 9), when faced with a growing body of evidence disconfirming institutional expectations, movement became inevitable. Since the purpose of general education reform is to promote student learning, it is reasonable to assess the extent to which students have achieved these outcomes. Monitoring student learning provides an indicator of the impact of the change process and the extent to which faculty behaviors have changed. Engaging faculty in ongoing discussion and analysis of student learning outcomes can act as a powerful incentive to participate in reform activities and as a force for institutionalizing a reform. In the Alverno College experience, Riordan and Sharkey (Chapter 10) described the development of interdisciplinary departments that provided a powerful incentive to maintain faculty engagement in the process.

It is apparent that assessment is an important element of all stages of the reform process. It was assessment activities that were instrumental in identifying the need for reform; it was assessment activities that helped to move the process of behavior change forward; and it is assessment that both ensures reform delivery and plants the seeds for future reform and innovation.

Conclusion

In this book, the editors identified seven key variables in the general education reform process (leadership, time frames, using data to inform process, communication, engaging constituents, governance, politics), but it is clear that these systems-level processes interact in complex ways with individuals' own motivations and abilities to engage not only in reforming general education, but also in changing the culture within which they and their institution operate. It is at the juxtaposition of the individual members' own skills and abilities and the systemic institutional processes that the real work and opportunities for true general education reform occur.

When is the general education reform process complete? Reform should be viewed as an "emergent, iterative, complex, contested inherently political, continuous, and discontinuous process of responses to internal and external contexts" (Blackwell and Preece 2001, 6). The reform process is complete when all of the goals of reform are achieved, but that is inherently impossible. Completion implies that the work of reform has reached stasis, and that no further change can and will occur. It is unrealistic and counterproductive to view general education reform as solely a product. In a rapidly changing world it would be inappropriate to view the needs of students as permanent, unchanging, and unchanged. Therefore, the process of reform can be revised, reconsidered, and renewed, but never completely abandoned.

The reform of general education is process, but it is also a product. While the processes may be more important in promoting reform, it is also necessary to achieve outcomes that are a result of those processes. Even small achievements can be used to demonstrate feasibility and further promote the reform agenda. Some would prefer to change general education frequently, because it enables them to be in a constant state of transition in which accountability is not possible. Thus they resist change and reform through promoting it. Change for change's sake should be discouraged and resisted unless there is evident potential benefit.

An error in any reform process is an unwillingness to evaluate the process itself. While we are asking others to change we need to examine our need to change as well. Through examining the process it will be possible to enhance the reform effort itself to make it better. Problems and failures provide valuable insights into how to improve our processes and promote the outcomes we desire. Through honest analysis of the process it is possible to promote a flexible change-adaptable institution that is responsive to a changing world. Just as we expect the culture to change and evolve to meet changing needs and demands, our reform efforts must also evolve to meet changing circumstances.

In *The Tipping Point*, Malcolm Gladwell (2000) demonstrated that very minor changes can have major impacts. Every person in the institution has the potential to effect institutional change and promote general educational reform. It requires only empowerment, vision, commitment, and perseverance. Through focusing on the process, reform can be viewed as an ongoing activity in which small wins, incremental steps, pilots, and significant successes all have their place. Through an ongoing process of self-discovery, institutions can continue to evolve and improve their general education programs in ways which will more effectively meet the needs of the twenty-first century and beyond.

References

Birnbaum, R. 1991. *How colleges work: The cybernetics of academic organization and leadership*. San Francisco: Jossey-Bass.

Blackwell, R., and D. Preece. 2001.Changing higher education. *International Journal of Management Education* 1(3): 4–14.

Blanchard, K. 2006. *Leading at a higher level: Blanchard on leadership and creating high performance organizations*. New York: Prentice Hall.

Collins, J. 2001. *Good to great: Why some companies make the leap . . . and others don't*. New York: HarperCollins.

Covey, S. 2004. *The 7 habits of highly effective people*. New York: Fireside.

Drucker, P. F. 2006. *The effective executive: The definitive guide to getting the right things done* (rev. ed.). New York: Collins.

Ewell, P. T. 2002. *Across the grain: Learning from reform initiatives in undergraduate education.* This monograph is publically available on the Teagle Foundation web site at http://www.teaglefoundation.org/learning/pdf/2002_AAHE_Monograph_Ewell.pdf

Gladwell, M. 2000. *The tipping point: How little things can make a big difference*. New York: Little, Brown/Warner Book Group.

Greenleaf, R. K. 1991/2008. *The servant as leader*. Westfield, IN: The Robert K. Greenleaf Center.

Harvey, T. R. 1995. *Checklist for change: A pragmatic approach to creating and controlling change*. Lancaster, PA: Technomic Publishing Co.

Harvey, T. R. 2001. *Checklist for change: A pragmatic approach to creating and controlling change* (2nd ed.). Lanham, MD: Scarecrow Press.

Keith, K. M. 2008. *The case for servant leadership*. Westfield, IN: The Robert K. Greenleaf Center.

Lewin, K. 1952. Group decision and social change. In T. M. Newcomb and E. L. Hartley (Eds.), *Readings in social psychology* (2nd ed., 459–473). New York: Holt.

Outram S. 2004a. *55 Interesting ways in which colleagues resist change*. Educational Developments 5(2): 1-4

Outram, S. 2004b. *55 Ways of managing resistance to change*. Educational Developments 5(4): 22-24

Schein E. 1995. *Kurt Lewin's change theory in the field and in the classroom: Notes toward a model of managed learning* (revised). Accessible on http://dspace.mit. Edu/bitstream/handle/1721.1/2576/SWP-3821-32871445.pdf?sequence=1

Van de Ven, A.H., and M. S. Poole. 1995. Explaining development and change in organizations. *Academy of Management Review* 20(3): 510–540.

CHAPTER 12

General Education Reform Processes

A NATIONAL and INTERNATIONAL
PERSPECTIVE

by Terrel L. Rhodes

In 1980, Jerry Gaff published an article, "Avoiding the Potholes: Strategies for Reforming General Education," which summarized the lessons learned about the process of curricular change by fourteen diverse colleges and universities participating in the Project on General Education Models, sponsored by the Society for Values in Higher Education. In 2009, the Association of American Colleges and Universities (AAC&U) asked Paul Gaston to join Gaff in producing an update of the "potholes paper" (Gaston and Gaff 2009). In the intervening twenty-nine years much research on student learning, curricular revision, and theories of change had occurred; however, as the authors of the revised article noted, "change in general education remains as difficult as ever. Three decades after the launch of this 'movement,' one might think that much has been learned about the process of curricular change. Yet the professional literature on the topic is remarkably thin" (Gaston and Gaff 2009, 6).

This paucity in both the literature and essential curricular change in general education has prompted the current volume. As documented in the preceding chapters, general education remains a recurring focus on campuses across the country. For some, the fact that a campus periodically revisits its general education program often invokes amusement or trepidation akin to double-digit budget reductions. Yet, the mandate emerging from new research on the evolving needs of baccalaureate graduates compels modification and change in general education like any other part of the collegiate curriculum and co-curriculum. Even in the prevailing budgetary climate, general education continues to need modification in response to new research, emerging knowledge, and evolving environments on and off campus. Indeed, higher education in this country is experiencing a resurgence of interest both within and beyond our borders.

In recent years, the call for accountability in learning emanating from federal sources, coupled with the needs denoted by employers and business leaders for broadly educated graduates competent in applying their learning to real world problems, has sharpened interest in organization and delivery of general education. For decades, accreditation organizations have been challenging campuses to articulate their expectations for their students' learning and to provide assessment evidence that students actually learn what has been expected. Higher education associations have been identifying the learning outcomes for student success as perceived by faculty; from workforce studies about the skills required for current and emerging jobs; and from civic organizations, global observers, and scholars about the abilities associated with democratic health and vibrancy in the twenty-first century (AAC&U 2002; AAC&U 2008; *Partnership for 21st Century Skills* 2008).

The accountability clamor is also heard abroad. The Organization for Economic Cooperation and Development (OECD) is engaged in the development and piloting of an international examination that can be used at the post-secondary level, based to a modest degree on their widely used Programme for International Student Assessment (PISA) exam for fifteen-year-old students' knowledge preparation (2009) that can be used at the post-secondary or tertiary level to provide similar evidence of student preparation within and across national boundaries. OECD is developing a CLA-type test, *Collegiate Learning Assessment*, (Council for Aid to Education 2009) that will rely upon scenarios and short essay responses to demonstrate student learning on written communication, critical thinking, and problem solving. The test is being developed in a select set of disciplines and is being piloted in a limited number of higher education institutions in a handful of countries. This pilot is encountering the same types of challenges that the CLA and other standardized tests in the United States encounter, surrounding the administration of the test to samples of non-randomly selected students, divorced from the typical classroom settings, and focused on a very limited set of outcomes. The fact that the test is focused on cross-cutting learning outcomes, though, is a recognition of the importance that employers and policy makers are placing on the skills and abilities that students need in addition to content knowledge; that is, students need to be able to use their knowledge to address increasingly complex and often unscripted problems to be successful in their careers and their lives.

Similarly, Europe has been engaged in what is commonly referred to as the Bologna Process. In an effort to provide student transfer and mobility across national boundaries in the European Union, the Education Ministries and campus faculties have been working on both framing exercises for defining what constitutes a degree and tuning processes that define what disciplines (e.g., political science, economics) expect from students studying in their respective departments. Although the Bologna Process, because of the absence of general education in their baccalaureate degrees, is focused on the major, there also is a recognition of the broader range of student learning outcomes that students need, referred to in Europe as cross-cutting outcomes, and in the United States as liberal education outcomes. In the United States, many of the disciplinary associations also have been at work over the past decades on articulating the liberal learning outcomes in the major and in general education courses offered by departments. In both settings, faculty have been actively engaged in defining content and cross-cutting student outcomes.

At the same time as these European initiatives are underway, delegations of higher education and political leaders from abroad continue to visit the United States to better understand how our post-secondary education produces individuals with the creativity and innovation that they often find lacking in their own students, and that they associate with the United States in some sectors of the economic, social, and political arenas. In most of the world, baccalaureate education does not include general education, but rather focuses almost exclusively on the major and preparation for the career or profession. Internationally, general education is assumed to have occurred prior to undertaking the baccalaureate degree. Also, visiting educators are interested in how general education may be a distinguishing feature, especially when done well, which provides an integrative and expanded perspective-taking for the major, and which they seem to suspect is important for developing the creativity and innovation they seek in their own students.

Yet, it is apparent to many faculty and administrators that too often what we have created in the name of general education suffers from two inherent implementation problems alluded to in the introductory chapter — a lack of deep engagement in the actual content or materials contained in general education programs, and the lack of intentional integration of ideas and curriculum. We have too often settled for a menu of courses that have merit in and of themselves, but have no or little integrative connection beyond broad titles or groupings of historical traditions, with little coherence or effort to integrate learning across disciplines or with the major. Exposure has become the rationale for general education, or what a colleague calls the inoculation approach to educational health — one shot and you'll be fine for life.

However, the nature of the conversation around general education renewal is rapidly changing in this country. Increasingly, faculty and students are realizing that we have settled for too little; that the one-quarter to one-third of an undergraduate degree that is devoted to general education often is wasted if we cannot communicate clearly to ourselves and to our students what the purposes of general education are and should be.

Assessment information has provided the catalyst for many conversations, as several of the examples in this volume illustrate. Moving from a catalyst and a desire for change to implementation of an intentional program of study with articulated learning outcomes remains a challenging endeavor on every campus. In particular, this volume focuses our attention on important factors that can facilitate successful change processes that lead to programs for student learning that include significant intellectual substance and coherence.

Importance of Culture on Process

In the introduction, Gano-Phillips and Barnett point out the importance of institutional culture in the success of general education change and redesign. The diversity of higher education institutions and their missions is cited as a strength of higher education in this country. Out of the missions of our institutions arise varied cultures, within which the operations of a campus occur, faculty, staff, and students live, and decisions are made. As the introductory chapter punctuates, ignoring the culture of an institution can be a distinct impediment to accomplishing even noble goals. As the preceding chapters amply illustrate, campus culture is really shorthand for multiple cultures on a campus. An institution constructs an overarching culture that helps define the institution, yet faculty governance often has its own version of that culture for how to do business. Furthermore, a college or school within a university may establish its own culture (e.g., a school of business may operate quite differently than a school of fine and performing arts). Even departments within a school or college may invent their own culture around teaching and research, curriculum review, or interactions with each other or students.

Understanding culture remains essential to success in any endeavor. Culture is something that faculty typically understand quite quickly as they attend to their own success in achieving promotion and tenure, professional standing within their discipline, or doing what is necessary to renew a contract for adjunct colleagues. The importance of culture often slips off the radar screen as issues recede from personal relevance, and therefore are more likely to become a potential obstacle or barrier to achieving desired outcomes, especially when the topic is general education, which typically is not central to day-to-day life for most faculty. On many campuses, general education still does not reside at the center of individual faculty members' lives.

How Did We Get to Where We Are?

If we trace the university as a degree granting institution at baccalaureate, masters, and doctoral levels to its origins, we find ourselves in the medieval era. The medieval Madrasahs, or *Jami'ah* in Arabic, are the earliest degree-granting universities identified, beginning with The University of Karaouine in Morocco in 859 AD (Makdisi 1989). Many of the *Jami'ah* had separate faculties for theology, law, astronomy, grammar, philosophy, logic and medicine (Alatas 2006). In the eighteenth century the precursor of the research university arose with journals to formally record the work of faculty and students. The nineteenth-century German and French models became the prototypes for universities today in the United States and Europe. The modern university, therefore, is deeply rooted with a reputation for not embracing change, yet it has evolved over the intervening centuries by adapting to changing environments—more perhaps with respect to curriculum than basic structures.

The university curriculum has also changed over time. The earliest book on the curriculum was published in 1918 by John Franklin Bobbitt and aptly titled, *The Curriculum*. Bobbitt writes that the concept of a constructed curriculum can be traced to the Latin word for *race course*, suggesting a course of experiences and actions that by moving progressively through them, students would transform into the adults they needed to be for success in society. The course of study included a whole set of deeds and experiences, in and out of the university, experiences that were planned and unplanned, directed and not directed (Bobbitt 1918). Although the words have changed, Bobbitt's conception of the curriculum embodied many of the conceptions that characterize a traditional liberal education.

Most curricula today will hearken back to Bobbitt's notion of a developmental change process, but the contemporary curriculum that general education committees encounter on many campuses exhibits more restrictive definitions, omitting much of the earlier intent to form character and judgment in students through an intentional intellectual and social development process grounded in experiences requiring practical application of knowledge. Some significance arises from the fact that many of the curricular components espoused by Bobbitt at the beginning of the twentieth century have reemerged at the beginning of the twenty-first century through renewed emphasis on applied learning, community or civic engagement, and creativity and critical thinking in unscripted situations. In fact, the absence of such experiential learning in current general education curricula stirs faculty and administrators to embrace curricular change. Therefore, the focus of this book on the processes that can facilitate curricular and cultural change on a campus does not ignore the importance of the actual structure and content of curricular change as a significant factor in any general education reform process. To illustrate, Frederick Community College (Chapter 5), guided by its open enrollment mission, adapted both their curriculum and the co-curricular academic support resources to facilitate the learning needs of their changing student body with an increased population of adult learners, students less prepared for academic success than their former student body of traditionally-aged students. In fact, those faculty and administrators succeeded in realigning their curriculum and support programs in the presence of state laws and regulations that were simply not attuned to the needs of the adult students. The typical or traditional conceptions of what was needed and what would work no longer meshed with the reality on the ground. Like Frederick Community College, institutions across the country are encountering a sea change in the composition of their student bodies. For instance, at LaGuardia Community College in New York City a huge immigrant and first generation student body has enrolled that has little idea of what higher education means and what types of support are necessary for student success. LaGuardia recognized this disconnect between their students and the college and responded with curricular and pedagogical changes by forming learning communities (academies) and engaging their students and faculty in creating e-portfolios so students could literally capture their work to show to their families and friends around the world, as well as to help their students understand in a tangible manner what it meant to go to college.

The changing student body is evidenced throughout United States higher education communities. Like many major public universities, the University of Nebraska at Lincoln (Chapter 8) made reaching out to the community colleges from which they received their transfer students an important priority in their general education reorganization to ensure that their new expectations and curricular structures were known and aligned with those of the two year campuses. Nebraska identifies another aspect of the changing collegiate environment—the swirl of students that is occurring when local options are available for students to attend various institutions. In rural areas, and particularly in urban areas, some students elect to attend more than one institution at the same time; to alternate between two and four-year institutions from term to term; to start and stop attending; and to transfer from four-year to two-year institutions. Aligning curriculum and learning expectations among institutions is increasingly critical for student success in an environment of constrained resources, and in turn, requires the proponents of process-centered reform on our campuses to understand that the lessons of communication, culture, governance, and engagement, for instance, contained in the preceding chapters, include acknowledging and encompassing cross institutional issues and differences as well.

Even when change is concentrated within the context of a single institution, one of the potential barriers to changing general education remains the absence of faculty engagement. On some campuses, general education may have its own faculty and administrative unit, but this is rare. However, what now constitutes general education was, in earlier incarnations, the core curriculum. Yet, the reality persists on most campuses that faculty members are hired into and owe their primary allegiance and identity to the department in which they are hired to teach. The major or concentrations arrived on campus only in 1910 when President A. Lawrence Lowell of Harvard introduced them. As is still the case, Harvard's actions had broad impact on higher education in the United States, and the idea of the major as the primary focus of a student's development of intellectual and academic abilities within a narrowly defined content or knowledge base quickly became ensconced as a key component of modern higher education. As the major ascended as the focus for hiring and promoting faculty, general education transformed into an activity of lesser importance and value for faculty identity and professional success, a mere equivalent of a service obligation.

More recently, there has been a recognition that many of the skills and abilities that faculty seeks to develop and instill in its majors also are the very skills and abilities that general education is expected to provide. This awareness has rekindled conversations on campuses that are reconnecting the work of faculty in the departments and in general education. Just as the faculty in the disciplines relies on general education to lay the groundwork for writing, speaking, critical thinking, and analytic reasoning, the realization that these same expectations rest within the majors, is creating an awareness of shared responsibility, that had not been well articulated in past years.

External Catalysts for Change

A frequent catalyst prompting general education revision that runs through so many of the campuses featured here is accreditation—the need to do a better job of demonstrating student learning based on assessment information. Accreditation organizations—regional and professional—have been pushing campuses to adopt more intentional and comprehensive approaches to learning assessment. In fact, legislative bodies and educational administrative offices in states and federal government compound the demand for increased accountability from higher education to document the improved learning among current students. Even as administrative and political changes occur through elections, the call for greater accountability persists.

The efforts in the European Union to facilitate transfer among the universities of member nations, has provided a model for articulating the outcomes of a baccalaureate degree. Since baccalaureate education in Europe is primarily focused on the major, much of this work—the tunings—have taken place within the disciplinary faculties. Also, as part of the framing for the degree, various levels of expectation have been developed for the award of variable credit based on types of effort required from students for different assignment categories. Coupled with the penchant for testing in Europe and the success of European students on the tests compared to their counterparts in the United States, calls for looking more closely at the European processes and adopting similar ones on this side of the Atlantic have increased in the past year (Gaston 2010).

However, there are also important differences that prompt the United States to pursue alternative approaches to outcomes and processes. Most European higher education is nationally unitary with standard policies and procedures promulgated through national Ministries of Education that have created a landscape that is much more aligned across institutions than in the United States. Tertiary education in Europe, as mentioned earlier, is the major and does not include general education, and therefore ignores many essential outcomes (e.g., personal and social responsibility and civic engagement). Even though these important differences exist, the processes and results of the Bologna process in articulating shared expectations for learning that are the products of obtaining a degree are the very things that are emerging in the public debate in the United States, and it behooves us to pay attention to these driving forces from abroad.

Where Do We Go from Here?

Given the coordinated assessment process in Europe and its growing impact on the discussions in the United States, how will higher education in this country respond to the demands for accountability and assessment without ceding the strengths of diversity and faculty-driven leadership on our campuses? Whether the terminology we use reflects the United States usage (accreditation), or that used internationally (quality assurance), there is demand for information on student success. Because so much attention is being focused on student success outcomes, and so little on what is actually being learned and how well, it is critical that faculty and staff on our campuses seize the opportunities we have to articulate our expectations for learning, to demonstrate what quality learning looks like, and to keep the conversation focused on the importance of actual student work, not on simplistic proxies that are of limited usefulness to students and faculty, or that do not address learning at all.

Accountability became the main driver in the United States in 2006 with the release of the Spellings Commission report (U.S. Department of Education 2006) on the future of higher education. The report prompted substantial activity among campuses and higher education associations in response to the commission's recommendations. Even with administrative changes in 2008 at the federal level in the U.S. Department of Education and Congress, the momentum and direction of the national conversation on student success and learning continues to be focused on outcome measures. What are the national responses emerging to refocus the accountability and assessment conversation?

One of the responses to the commission's call for greater transparency and accountability was a major grant by the U.S. Department of Education to three national higher education associations to support projects to inform the accountability and assessment dialog (AASCV 2010). Two higher education associations, the Association of Public Land-Grant Universities (APLU, formerly NASULGC, the National Association of State

Universities and Land Grant Colleges) and the American Association of State Colleges and Universities (AASCU), created the Voluntary System of Accountability (VSA) for public universities. The VSA is a web-based template for reporting an array of indicators in three broad categories: student and family information, student experience and perceptions, and student learning outcomes. The nation's private college higher education associations have developed a similar web-based reporting template without a section on student learning. Much of the information is already collected and reported by campuses, but through the VSA *College Portrait* web template the information is presented and extended in a visually more accessible and clear manner.

The student learning outcomes section of the VSA relies on one of three standardized tests of general knowledge focused on three abilities — written communication, critical thinking, and problem solving/analysis. As part of a larger, three component U.S. Department of Education Fund for Improvement in Post Secondary Education (FIPSE) grant award, APLU led a validity study of the three VSA recommended tests — the Measure of Academic Proficiency and Progress (MAPP), the Collegiate Assessment of Academic Proficiency (CAAP), and the Collegiate Learning Assessment (CLA) (ACT 2009; CAE 2009; ETS 2009) — to determine the extent to which these three tests measure the same learning outcomes, as well as whether the mode of administration for the test makes a difference in student scores. The results of the validity study found that the three tests do measure distinctly different skills and abilities, i.e. written communication, critical thinking, and problem solving/analysis; that at the institutional level, the three tests are comparable measures of these outcomes; the mode and form of administration does not make significant differences in results; and that seniors do better than freshmen on all but one measure. The study could not point to specific actions or factors associated with the individual institutions that accounted for the improvements, nor were the scores useful for individual student analysis (AASCU 2010). VSA continues to consider alternative ways for campuses to report on student learning that would expand the learning outcomes to a fuller array of essential outcomes, including personal and social responsibility, intercultural knowledge and competence, and civic engagement and integrative learning, for example.

AASCU, spearheading the second component of the FIPSE grant, developed and piloted a new survey focused on some of the outcomes that are not addressed in existing tests. The *Degrees of Preparation* student survey focuses on preparation for success in the workplace, preparation for civic engagement, and acquisition of global marketplace skills. The AASCU survey was piloted on a sample of campuses and continues to be refined for public release. In a separate project, AAC&U developed a campus audit for faculty, staff, and students focused on the personal and social responsibility outcomes through its Core Commitments project, involving twenty-three campuses across the country that have tested the instrument and engaged in exploring changes in policies and practices to address identified gaps between commitment to the outcomes and the reported experience in practice on the campuses. Both instruments were made available in the summer of 2009 (see Dey and Associates 2009 and AASCU 2010).

In a third component of the FIPSE grant, AAC&U led a major initiative entitled, Valid Assessment of Learning in Undergraduate Education (VALUE) that worked with teams of faculty and other campus professionals to develop rubrics for fifteen of the Essential Learning Outcomes (AAC&U 2007). The rubrics build from collections of rubrics that had been written by campus faculty and from the expertise of the individual team members for each rubric. The teams identified common or shared criteria or dimensions of learning for each of the outcomes to synthesize the most common characteristics of learning into a foundational set of criteria with four levels of progressively more sophisticated demonstration of specified learning. Over one hundred campuses participated in the rubric development and testing to assess student work through examination of student e-portfolios or hard copy examples of work produced through the regular campus curriculum and co-curriculum. The rubrics are available at www.aacu.org/VALUE and in print (Rhodes 2010).

VALUE is designed to move the national conversation on assessing student learning from snapshot tests of a limited set of outcomes at one or two points in time (e.g., the CAAP, MAPP, and CLA) to a robust representation of student learning on all of the essential outcomes based on the actual work of students as they move through their respective educational pathways. These cumulative collections of student work are being captured and communicated effectively through electronic portfolios (Chen and Penny-Light 2010). The initial findings from the project indicate that there is a broadly shared understanding on our campuses of what student learning in all the outcome areas is, what it looks like when students demonstrate the learning, and that learning both occurs and can be presented in a variety of forms (e.g., text, graphical, visual, oral, and performance), on and off the traditional campus. The use of rubrics also provides faculty with useful feedback to improve instruction, and provides students with clearer statements of expectations for quality performance by which to increase their own abilities to judge their progress toward mastering learning outcomes.

The three components of the U.S. Department of Education FIPSE grant and the emerging efforts to bring the European Bologna "tuning" process to the United States are examples of the directions higher education is moving as it formulates evidence and indicators for national policy makers. The next few years will substantially advance our knowledge of how to engage in assessment of student learning and expand our abilities to capture and represent the multiple ways in which our students learn and can demonstrate their learning.

As this volume argues, the processes involved in each of these efforts are an important component for successful results that benefit student learning on our campuses. The standardized tests that were a first response to the call for outcomes are of limited use to faculty and students. The emerging surveys of student development outcomes and the faculty-derived and tested rubrics for multiple outcomes grow out of the grassroots campus cultures, and therefore may hold more promise for usefulness and sustainability on campuses. The incipient Bologna "tuning" processes focused on outcomes through the major may also reflect a grassroots process within national disciplinary frameworks that will engender high levels of faculty ownership. As the preceding campus stories illustrate, if we ignore the processes by which our assessments of learning and what our students learn, are derived, we heighten the risk of failure in our efforts to create more coherent and intentional educational programs. So, how can renewing general education inform and be informed by these trends and circumstances?

Change Factors in General Education Take Many Forms

What we have been learning over the last decade is that the process of changing curriculum and culture on our campuses involves a whole set of factors to ensure success. Change sometimes happens despite a lack of attention to one or more of these factors; however, success is enhanced by paying attention to how all of these factors interact together to create a complete process for change.

On virtually every campus that has engaged in general education reform, there is a catalyst; some definition or recognition of a problem. The examples in this volume are representative of the types of catalysts underlying the start of a process. Most often, as was the case at the University of North Carolina at Greensboro (Chapter 1), the University of North Dakota (Chapter 6), and Franklin College (Chapter 4), the immediate catalyst is regional accreditation reports recounting the need to do a better job of assessing student learning. In others, it is low retention and graduation rates, state laws or regulations (Frederick Community College [Chapter 5]), the recognition by faculty and others that the existing program did not work for the espoused outcomes it was meant to achieve (University of Nebraska–Lincoln [Chapter 8], University of North Dakota [Chapter 6], University of Michigan–Flint [Chapter 7], and Alverno College [Chapter 10]), or administrative leadership changes. Frequently, a combination of these factors converges at the same time.

LEADERSHIP

Regardless of the catalyst, nothing is likely to happen unless there is leadership that articulates the need to act. This leadership can come from outside the institution, from the top of an institution, from faculty governance, or from administrative units charged directly with monitoring general education or the curriculum. Someone or some group has to take the initiative to push for and to articulate the problem and the need for action to try to address the problem in a positive manner. Whether campus leaders recognize the need to act or not, the trends suggest external pressures may rush to fill the void. One of the embedded threads in the preceding cases is the need to sustain leadership for change. Too often, the champion for change arises and begins a process of general education renewal only to be distracted or to move on to another institution. As a result, the process may stall or expire. Developing a succession plan for leadership is critical to sustaining change. As the authors point out, the successful process enlists faculty governance, multiple committees and units, and the engagement of individuals across the campus.

TIMELINES

As academics, we are accustomed to organizing our lives by the calendar—academic year beginning and end, semesters and quarters, courses and sequences, grade reporting and exam schedules. The recognition that the academic year is really only six or seven months long is typically missing. Thinking through how much can be accomplished and when and how becomes especially important prior to major reforms of curriculum. Every campus has a schedule for curriculum consideration; exceptions can be made, but exceptions open the door for additional criticism around circumventing approved procedures. Having a timeline with periodic decision points for moving the process forward, though, is essential for actually accomplishing change, rather than exhausting everyone through endless conversation. An ambitious timeline is desirable, especially if tempered with the reality of the academic year schedule. Demonstrating early in the process that the reform process is taken seriously, including honoring the timeline, sets a tone that the work is important, valued and necessary.

DATA

The power of the anecdote and the lore of a campus are powerful influences; however, being able to document through the collection and dissemination of data about what has actually been happening in a general education program (e.g., course-taking patterns, grading patterns, information on measures of learning, student voices) can have an immense impact, both on convincing the campus that change is necessary and in establishing some of the baselines for determining whether alternative "solutions" to the perceived problems improve the accomplishment of intended goals. The types of data available may not be sufficient. Knowing what you are trying to "fix" needs to be clearly stated before data become the focus, or a campus runs the risk of having the data drive the change discussion, rather than the goals or objectives desired by the faculty driving the reform outcomes. Franklin College (Chapter 4), North Dakota (Chapter 6), and Nebraska–Lincoln (Chapter 8) all demonstrate the important role that data can play in advancing serious discussion of general education changes. Building in assessment data from the beginning, helps to demonstrate the important learning that is occurring for both internal and external audiences.

In addition, campus reform efforts are often strengthened by engaging the campus in learning how it fits within the national picture. Frederick Community College (Chapter 5) turned to the *Greater Expectations* report (AAC&U 2002) to focus and bolster their campus processes. More recently, analyses of national data from the National Survey of Student Engagement (Indiana University Center for Postsecondary Research 2009) have allowed campuses to use their local data within a national context (Kuh 2008). Being able to ground general education renewal in local data and culture while positioning it within national data and trends provides powerful confirmation of faculty thinking and confidence that local action is supported on a broader scale.

EFFECTIVE COMMUNICATION

Communication has become a mantra for every campus, whether it means communicating to external constituencies, or to the internal community. As with all aspects of our lives these days, information overload is pervasive. Having a planned process for communicating the work of changing general education is essential, but again, elegant plans can easily fail to achieve desired results. We all receive more communication each day than we can adequately process, respond to in a meaningful manner, or want to receive. Having multiple ways or modes to communicate, especially to the campus community, is important, but modulating what is communicated in degree and depth and to whom and when is equally important. No matter how well thought out and planned, campuses will always have individuals who "never heard about this before." Acknowledging this reality is a step in keeping the focus on making sure that very honest and multiple modes of keeping people informed have been undertaken, and the process will continue as planned.

ENGAGING CONSTITUENTS

Closed processes that involve a small number of "true believers" or "experts" is an unlikely success strategy for any campus — even on a large campus where general education is clearly on the periphery of faculty work (see University of Nebraska–Lincoln, Chapter 8). It is wise to have a smaller group to coordinate activities, to ensure that the process is moving, to steer the process toward successful completion, and to prepare the formal proposal; however, the process of discussion of purposes, goals, outcomes, design, and assessment strategies and results must invite broad participation (see University of Michigan–Flint, Chapter 7). Do not draft the language of a proposal in the faculty senate meeting called to approve the proposed plan. Not every one will, or can, participate. Being invited to participate and being presented with opportunities to participate are critical; listening to the dissenting voices and engaging the "nay-sayers" is important. Not letting the discordant voices stop the process is also important.

GOVERNANCE STRUCTURES

Ultimately, general education change involves the curriculum. The curriculum is still a key faculty prerogative. For any general education reform to be successful, faculty governance must be a part of the process, although the creation of special entities or the expansion of existing structures (e.g., of committees) may be necessary. If we think about the existing faculty governance structures, they typically have more than enough business each year to keep them busy. Alternatively, they may have so little to do that they are perceived in practice to have little standing as campus influencers of major changes in the curriculum. If general education reform is a priority, then serious consideration of what the capacity of existing governance structures is for accomplishing the work is essential.

NEGOTIATING POLITICS

Ultimately, everything is probably negotiable. History on our campuses reveals that general education reform is never fixed, even when it takes fifteen or twenty years to revisit general education requirements. General education designs typically evolve from the original and eventually become the focus, or catalyst for a renewed process. Improving on the current program, including a process for measuring the impact of the changes on student learning, is the goal.

Change is ultimately a political process. Successful and sustainable general education renewal engages the barriers to change, whether these are the self-interests of departments, colleges, or programs; or traditions that are defended by venerable individuals or practices. Self-interest and perceived high-stakes risks (e.g., loss of credit hours or faculty positions) will mobilize otherwise disinterested individuals and units on campus. Listening to those opposed to change, sorting through the bases for the opposition, and finding areas of common ground are the beginnings of compromise and pathways for moving the process of renewal forward. A combination of personal and individual negotiation with administrative or structural pressure and engagement are needed to bring multiple sets of actors and interests into a positive movement toward successfully revising general education. Perfection is not attainable, so be ready to accept what promises to be an improvement (with evidence to inform judgments about success for learning) as the outcome of the process of reform. Of course, setting high expectations for the outcomes is desirable.

Conclusions

The one factor that remains constant in our lives is that nothing remains constant—change is always occurring. As academics we understand the importance of theory, practice, and evidence; yet we often are willing to ignore these factors in favor of the status quo because change requires us to spend precious time and energy to accomplish change, and this time and energy we would rather spend on other activities or priorities. Academics, like everyone else, prefer continuity to change if we can do so with minimal dissonance between our preferences and our reality.

The current volume takes several change theories and extracts the key components, listed above, that have been associated with success in moving from one set of policies, practices, and structures to another. Further, it has enlisted a broad range of institutions in telling their stories of how they were able to achieve change in general education programs by successfully adhering to the components of change associated with positive outcomes. No story is the same. Building on institutional culture is essential, but not sufficient. In a very real sense, general education renewal requires us to engage in the practices advocated in this volume; that is, we must assess or analyze how campus culture supports and/or stands in the way of reforming general education by gathering evidence that illustrates the disconnect between existing practices and beliefs and need for new directions, and that links aspects of current culture to newer trends, practices and outcomes in higher education nationally, internationally, or among peer institutions. Different paths can lead to successful outcomes. However, it is also clear that attention to key aspects of the process for change improves the probability of desirable results for general education renewal. The preceding examples illustrate that, by starting with the processes that will be used on campus and planning for key components of the process prior to beginning a general education change, the chances of a successful result that can be "owned" by most of the campus community are enhanced.

The elements of the change process addressed by these campus examples illustrate how campus culture can be honored, challenged, and changed in ways that result in advancing general education renewal that benefits faculty and students and provides information on learning that is needed for continual improvement in curriculum and pedagogy. By simultaneously emphasizing the processes of reform and the need to assess, challenge, and possibly change aspects of institutional culture through new processes, institutions maximize their chances for substantive and sustainable general education reform.

Too often the response to a catalyst for change in general education is to begin by formulating a solution, a new curriculum. By minimizing the importance of process in change, the outcomes are much less likely to be accepted broadly or to meet the perceived needs that prompted the calls for change in the first place (i.e., bringing about changes in institutional culture required for sustainable improvement). Of course, allowing the process to become more important than the outcome is also a way to derail meaningful progress. Both process and cultural change are important for genuine curricular reform that can be embraced by the campus and that can improve student learning and understanding of the importance and role of general education in undergraduate education. Focusing on structure or curricular content at the outset and ignoring the processes of change and the culture of a campus clearly reduces the probability for success in revamping general education to prepare our students for a global society, a fulfilling life, and a civically engaged contribution to democratic society.

References

ACT, Inc. 2009. *Collegiate assessment of academic proficiency.* Retrieved March 19, 2009 from http://www.act.org/caap

Alatas, S. F. 2006. From jami`ah to university: Multiculturalism and Christian–Muslim dialogue. *Current Sociology* 54(1): 112–132.

American Association of State Colleges and Universities. 2010. *Rising to the challenge: Meaningful assessment of student learning.* Washington, DC: AASCU.

Association of American Colleges and Universities. 2002. *Greater expectations: A new vision for learning as a nation goes to college.* Washington, DC: AAC&U.

Association of American Colleges and Universities. 2008. *College learning for the new global century.* Washington, DC: AAC&U.

Bobbitt, J. F. 1918. *The curriculum.* Boston: Houghton Mifflin.

Chen, H. and T. Penny-Light. 2010. *Electronic portfolios and student success: Effectiveness, efficiency, and learning.* Washington, DC: Association of American Colleges and Universities.

Council for Aid to Education. 2009. *Collegiate learning assessment.* Retrieved March 19, 2009 from http://www.cae.org/content/pro_collegiate.htm

Dey, E. and Associates. 2009. *Civic responsibility: What is the campus climate for learning?* Washington, DC: Association of American Colleges and Universities.

Educational Testing Service. 2009. *Measure of academic proficiency and progress* (MAPP). Retrieved March 19, 2009 from http://www.ets.org/portal/site/ets/menuitem

Gaff, J. G. 1980. Avoiding the potholes: Strategies for reforming general education. *Educational Record* 61 (4): 50–59.

Gaston, P. 2010. *The challenge of Bologna: What United States higher education has to learn from Europe, and why it matters that we learn it.* Sterling, VA: Stylus Publishing.

Gaston, P., and J. Gaff. 2009. *Revising general education — And avoiding the potholes.* Washington, DC: Association of American Colleges and Universities.

Indiana University Center for Postsecondary Research. 2009. *National survey of student engagement*. Retrieved March 19, 2009 from http://nsse.iub.edu/index.cfm

Kuh, G. 2008. *High impact educational practices: What they are, who has access to them, and why they matter*. Washington, DC: Association of American Colleges and Universities.

Makdisi, G. 1989. Scholasticism and humanism in classical Islam and the Christian West. *Journal of the American Oriental Society* 109(2): 175–182.

Partnership for 21st century skills: A resource and policy guide. 2008. Washington, DC: Partnership for 21st Century Skills.

Programme for International Student Assessment (PISA). 2009. Retrieved March 19, 2009 from http://www.oecd.org/department/0,3355,en_2649_35845621_1_1_ 1_1_ 1,00.html

Rhodes, T. L. 2010. *Assessing outcomes and improving achievement: Tips and tools for using rubrics*. Washington, DC: Association of American Colleges and Universities.

United States Department of Education. 2006. *A test of leadership: Charting the future of U.S. higher education*. Washington, DC: U.S. Department of Education.

Index

The Editors

SUSAN GANO-PHILLIPS is an Associate Professor of Psychology and former director of the Center for Learning and Teaching at the University of Michigan–Flint. She co-chaired (with Robert Barnett) the 2005–2006 General Education Reform Steering Committee and served on UM–Flint's General Education Design Team from 2006 to 2008. She completed a Fulbright Fellowship in General Education at City University of Hong Kong during the 2008–2009 academic year.

ROBERT W. BARNETT is Associate Dean of Arts and Sciences and Professor of Rhetoric and Composition at the University of Michigan–Flint. Before that he served as UM–Flint's Writing Center Director, Writing Program Director, and Writing Across the Curriculum Director. With Susan Gano-Phillips, he co-chaired the University's General Education Steering Committee during the 2005–2006 academic year; during that year, the campus created, voted on, and approved the framework for a new General Education Curriculum.

The Contributors

SUZANNE BEAL is Vice President of Learning and Professor of English at Frederick Community College. Prior to FCC, she served as the Dean of Instruction and Chair of Humanities and Arts at Dundalk Community College in Baltimore, Maryland.

DAVID BRAILOW has served as Vice President for Academic Affairs at Franklin College since 2001. Earlier he chaired a general education reform process at McKendree College, where he was Professor of English and Associate Dean. Recent publications have been on contemporary Shakespearean performance and on faculty scholarship.

NONA M. BURNEY is an Associate Professor of Secondary Education at Roosevelt University. She is also the Academic Director of the University's Center for Teaching and Learning, which was created by and for faculty to promote effective, innovative instruction. Through this position, and as a member of the General Education Task Force, she continues to facilitate processes that institutionalize general education reform at Roosevelt.

CHRISTOPHER DENNIS is Associate Vice Provost for Undergraduate Studies and has taught in the English department and the Intellectual Heritage and Honors programs at Temple University. He led Temple's initial planning team to the AAC&U Institute on General Education and worked as administrative liaison to the General Education Executive Committee. He has also written and presented on a variety of topics on undergraduate education, including campus-wide reading programs, learning communities, and teaching assessment.

AMY GOODBURN is Dean for Faculty, College of Arts and Sciences and Professor of English at the University of Nebraska–Lincoln. She is co-coordinator of the Peer Review of Teaching Project and co-author of *Inquiry into the College Classroom: A Journey Toward Scholarly Teaching* and *Making Teaching and Learning Visible: Course Portfolios and the Peer Review of Teaching*.

TERRY HALBERT is the Director of General Education and Professor of Legal Studies in Business in the Fox School of Management at Temple University. She has been recognized as one of Temple University's Great Teachers and has long practiced interdisciplinary teaching which is evidenced in her approach to general education reform and also in her co-authored textbooks, *Law & Ethics in the Business Environment* and *CyberEthics*.

JOAN HAWTHORNE currently serves as Assistant Provost at the University of North Dakota, with responsibilities that include assessment and initiatives related to teaching and learning. She served on the General Education Task Force during development of the new program, and continues to serve on the Essential Studies Committee (formerly named the General Education Requirements Committee).

JESSICA JONSON is Director of Institutional Assessment in the Office of Undergraduate Studies at the University of Nebraska–Lincoln (UNL). She has led and coordinated outcomes assessment efforts at UNL since 1999 and was a member of the general education reform planning team. Currently, she is involved in the implementation of the new Achievement-Centered Education (ACE) general education program.

RITA KEAN is the Dean of Undergraduate Studies and Professor of Textiles, Clothing, and Design at the University of Nebraska–Lincoln. She has worked on the development and implementation of the ACE program and has administrative oversight of the ACE program.

ANNE KELSCH is the Director of Instructional Development and an Associate Professor of History at the University of North Dakota. She served as the co-leader of the Bush Longitudinal Study on General Education and co-chaired the General Education Task Force. She continues to work with faculty development around the new Essential Studies Program.

DEBORAH MINTER is an Associate Professor of English at the University of Nebraska–Lincoln where she coordinated the Composition program and is currently serving as Vice Chair with responsibilities for course scheduling and instructional support. Her research interests include English education, writing instruction, and faculty development.

NANCY MITCHELL is Director of General Education and Professor of Advertising at the University of Nebraska–Lincoln. She has taught at the university since 1990 and participated in the general education reform process at UNL. She now leads efforts to implement the new program.

PRISCILLA PERKINS is an Associate Professor of English and Associate Dean, College of Arts and Sciences at Roosevelt University. She also chairs the General Education Committee of the College. As Associate Dean and one of the original members of the General Education Task Force, she is guiding her college's departments through the process of curriculum mapping, the second stage of general education reform at Roosevelt.

JULIE PHILLIPS, Associate Director of General Education at Temple University, is a former Assistant Professor of Teaching & Instruction in the department of Strategic and Organizational Communication in the School of Communications and Theater. In addition to serving as the Associate Director, she currently heads the General Education Assessment Team, and is responsible for implementing programmatic assessment of the new curriculum.

J. WORTH PICKERING is Assistant Vice President for Institutional Research and Assessment at Old Dominion University. He frequently conducts workshops at regional and national conferences on building the assessment toolbox and changing the institutional culture for assessment or for first year students. His other research interests are in the area of promoting student success among first year students.

TERREL L. RHODES is Vice President for Quality, Curriculum, and Assessment at the Association of American Colleges and Universities (AAC&U). He is Director of the VALUE project (Valid Assessment of Learning in Undergraduate Education), a major component of the Liberal Education and America's Promise, or LEAP initiative at AAC&U, focused on enhancing the quality of student learning and assessment. Prior to joining AAC&U, he spent thirty years as a professor and academic administrator at St. John's University, the University of North Carolina at Charlotte, and Portland State University. He is the author or editor of three books and numerous articles on politics, public administration, and assessment.

TIM RIORDAN is Professor of Philosophy and Associate Vice President for Academic Affairs at Alverno College. He has written extensively on the scholarship of teaching and learning, and has worked with institutions nationally and internationally on issues of teaching, assessment, and curriculum design.

STEPHANIE ROACH is the Writing Program Director at the University of Michigan–Flint. A team participant in the 2006 AAC&U Institute on General Education, she served on UM–Flint's General Education Design Team from 2006 to 2008. Recently she has focused on contributing to the university's Higher Learning Commission Self Study on the topics of general education and assessment.

KATHLEEN ROUNTREE is Provost and VPAA at Ithaca College in New York after serving for three years as Associate Provost at The University of North Carolina Greensboro. She has written and presented on undergraduate education and assessment at the conferences of AAC&U, SACS, AASHE, CIC, and at meetings in her academic field, music.

BLASE S. SCARNATI is an Associate Professor of Musicology, founding director of the University First-Year Seminar Program, and current and former chair of the University Liberal Studies Committee at Northern Arizona University. He has been involved with general education and university curricular reform at NAU, including serving as President of the Faculty Senate, and was closely involved with the University Liberal Studies Program's most recent reform efforts.

STEPHEN SHARKEY is a Professor of Sociology and Dean of the School of Arts and Sciences at Alverno College. He has consulted on general education reform, student assessment, and faculty development with colleges around the country, and co-chaired Alverno's General Education Committee.

THOMAS STEEN is the Director of Essential Studies at the University of North Dakota, where he is also Associate Professor of Physical Education, Exercise Science, and Wellness. He's been involved in UND's recent revision of general education since the project's beginning and was appointed as the new program's first administrator in August, 2008.

LISA C. TOLBERT is an Associate Professor of History at the University of North Carolina at Greensboro and chair of the General Education Council. She led a campus team to the AAC&U Institute on General Education and has spoken on general education reform processes at SACS.

KELLY TRIGGER is Associate Professor of English and current Chair of General Education at Frederick Community College. She assisted with establishing FCC's General Education Institute and is a former FCC General Education Fellow. Her scholarship focuses on interdisciplinary studies, cultural competence, and cyberculture.

Associate Professor DEDAIMIA S. WHITNEY has a bachelor's degree from Shimer College (1971) and an MFA in fiction from Indiana University (1992). She joined the faculty of Franklin College in 1995. In addition to courses in the English department, she has also taught regularly in both the general education program and the liberal arts program. Professor Whitney represented Franklin College at two of the AAC&U's Institute for General Education and was the chair of the task force that facilitated its curriculum reform.

DAVID E. WILSON is Associate Vice Chancellor for Academic Affairs and Professor of Teaching, Learning, and Teacher Education at the University of Nebraska–Lincoln. His present responsibilities include curriculum development, support for teaching, and international programs. Wilson's scholarship has focused on teacher development and institutional change.

STEPHEN C. ZERWAS is the Director of Academic Assessment at the University of North Carolina at Greensboro. He is a frequent presenter of workshops and sessions at national and regional conferences on the topics of change, assessment, and general education reform. He is the author of several computer applications for assessment activities, including an objective builder wizard and content analysis programs.